THIRD TEXT

Print ISSN 0952-8822, Online ISSN 1475-5297

Disclaimer

Subscription information

For information and subscription rates please see www.tandfonline.com/pricing/journal/ctte

Informa UK Limited, trading as Taylor & Francis Group, has a flexible approach to subscriptions enabling us to match individual libraries' requirements. This journal is available via a traditional institutional subscription (either print with online access, or online only at a discount) or as part of our libraries, subject collections or archives. For more information on our sales packages please visit www.tandfonline.com/page/librarians

All current institutional subscriptions include online access for any number of concurrent users across a local area network to the currently available backfile and articles posted online ahead of publication. Subscriptions purchased at the personal rate are strictly for personal, non-commercial use only. The reselling of personal subscriptions is prohibited. Personal subscriptions must be purchased with a personal check or credit card. Proof of personal status may be requested.

Back issues: Taylor & Francis Group retains a two-year back issue stock of journals. Older volumes are held by our official stockists to whom all orders and enquiries should be addressed: Periodicals Service Company, 351 Fairview Ave., Suite 300, Hudson, New York 12534, USA. Tel: +1 518 537 4700; fax: +1 518 537 5899; email: psc@periodicals.com.

Ordering information: Please contact your local Customer Service Department to take out a subscription to the Journal: USA, Canada: Taylor & Francis, Inc., 530 Walnut Street, Suite 850, Philadelphia, PA 19106, USA. Tel: +1 800 354 1420; Fax: +1 215 207 0050. UK/Europe/Rest of World: T&F Customer Services, Informa UK Ltd, Sheepen Place, Colchester, Essex, CO3 3LP, United Kingdom. Tel: +44 (0) 20 7017 5544; Fax: +44 (0) 20 7017 5198; Email: subscriptions@tandf.co.uk.

Dollar rates apply to all subscribers outside Europe. Euro rates apply to all subscribers in Europe, except the UK where the pound sterling price applies. If you are unsure which rate applies to you please contact Customer Services in the UK. All subscriptions are payable in advance and all rates include postage. Journals are sent by air to the USA, Canada, Mexico, India, Japan and Australasia. Subscriptions are entered on an annual basis, i.e. January to December. Payment may be made by sterling check, dollar check, euro check, international money order, National Giro or credit cards (Amex, Visa and Mastercard).

US Postmaster: Airfreight and mailing in the USA by agent named Air Business Ltd, c/o Worldnet Shipping Inc., 156-15 146th Avenue, 2nd Floor, Jamaica, NY 11434, USA. Periodicals postage paid at Jamaica NY 11431. Please send address changes to CTTE, Air Business Ltd, c/o Worldnet Shipping Inc., 156-15 146th Avenue, 2nd Floor, Jamaica, NY 11434, USA.

Subscription records are maintained at Taylor & Francis Group, 4 Park Square, Milton Park, Abingdon, OX14 4RN, United Kingdom.

All Taylor and Francis Group journals are printed on paper from renewable sources by accredited partners.

THIRD TEXT

CRITICAL PERSPECTIVES ON CONTEMPORARY ART & CULTURE

144 VOLUME 31 ISSUE 1 JANUARY 2017

Special Issue: Social Reproduction and Art
Guest Editors: Angela Dimitrakaki and Kirsten Lloyd

Third Text Ltd is a registered charity, no 11108974, governed by the board of trustees. *Third Text* is published by Routledge on behalf of Third Text Ltd.

Third Text has established itself as the leading international journal dedicated to the critical analysis of contemporary art in the global field. It has brought with that analysis a particular focus on both the impact of globalisation on cultural practices and the lessons of postcolonial theory.

Open Systems, Vienna, is a project and research partner of *Third Text*.

The body is a factory.
This room is a factory.

Third Text, 2017
Vol. 31, No. 1, 1–14, https://doi.org/10.1080/09528822.2017.1358963

Social Reproduction Struggles and Art History

An Introduction

Angela Dimitrakaki and Kirsten Lloyd

The Present, the Crisis, the Struggle

Jean-Luc Godard and Anne-Marie Miéville, *Numéro deux* (Number Two), (detail), 35mm and video, © 1975 Gaumont/ Société Nouvelle de Cinématographie.

1 See Kate Bezanson and Meg Luxton, eds, *Social Reproduction: Feminist Political Economy Challenges Neo-Liberalism*, McGill-Queen's University Press, Montreal and Kingston, London and Ithaca, 2006; and Cinzia Arruzza, 'Functionalist, Determinist, Reductionist: Social Reproduction Feminism and its Critics', *Science & Society*, vol 80, no 1, January 2016, pp 9–30. Marina Vishmidt offers a careful and illuminating account of the histories of the debates on social reproduction in her article included here. Beth Capper then expands on Vishmidt's account, attending to the racialised division of labour specifically in relation to the perspective of Black Women for Wages for Housework.

2 Indicatively, see Robyn R Warhol, Diane Price Herndl,

This special issue explores approaches to social reproduction in art history. These approaches are relevant to debates that engage feminist critique and that cross into art practice and theory. While 'social reproduction' has historically referred to processes concerning the replenishment of labour power as well as the maintenance of human life traditionally performed by women for free in the home, recent theorisations have offered a more expansive account to stress the concept's value in elaborating non-reductionist accounts of capitalist production more broadly.[1] Here, we seek to explicitly connect the concept of social reproduction with that of struggle; the ongoing struggle of feminism. We use feminism in the singular, challenging the fragmenting plural 'feminisms' that surfaced at a particular moment to address and 'tidy up' the multiple perspectives circulating around the object and subjects of this struggle.[2] This splintering was not a random outcome arising from theoretical debates. Rather, as the feminist struggle's complexity grew, so did socioeconomic divides that cut so deep as to invite some sort of compromise, some sort of accommodation of the diversity of positions in order to forge inclusivity. But, to us, the pluralisation of feminism into feminisms has not signalled, or achieved, inclusivity, but rather an opting for parallel (as in never meeting) discourses and trajectories that threaten to hold feminism hostage to a divided field of micropolitics and relativist perspectives inherited from postmodernism. In opposing this trend – which gained strength in the early 1990s, at the moment when 'post-feminism' was about to be dropped as an extinguishing blanket on the intellectual and political fire that feminism had lit – social reproduction is deployed here as a complex framework of potential references and directions in which the diverse concerns of the feminist struggle can hopefully enter into dialogue.

eds, *Feminisms: An Anthology of Literary Theory and Criticism*, Rutgers University Press, New Brunswick, New Jersey, 1991, and its updated edition in 2010; Jenny Coleman, 'An Introduction to Feminisms in a Post-feminist Age', *Women's Studies Journal*, vol 23, no 2, November 2009, pp 3–13; Malin Hedlin Hayden and Jessica Sjöholm Skrubbe, eds, *Feminisms Is Still Our Name: Seven Essays on Historiography and Curatorial Practices*, Cambridge Scholars Publishers, Newcastle, 2010.

3 George Caffentzis, 'On the Notion of a Crisis of Social Reproduction: A Theoretical Review', *The Commoner 5*, Autumn 2002, http://www. commoner.org.uk/ caffentzis05.pdf, accessed 10 March 2017

4 Here we do not invoke arguments about capitalism stalling or the alleged advent of post-capitalism. Rather, we allude to liberal arguments such as that pursued in Hernando de Soto, *The Mystery of Capital: Why Capitalism Triumphs in the West and Fails Everywhere Else*, Basic Books, New York, 2003, which appear far less plausible after the austerity turn. On the ambivalence and 'formerisation' of the term 'the West', see Maria Hlavajova and Simon Sheikh, eds, *Former West: Art and the Contemporary after 1989*, BAK, Utrecht and Cambridge, Massachusetts, The MIT Press, 2016.

5 Heather Stewart, 'Women Bearing 86% of Austerity Burden, Commons Figures Reveal', *The Guardian*, 9 March 2017, https://www. theguardian.com/world/ 2017/mar/09/women-bearing-86-of-austerity-burden-labour-research-reveals, accessed 10 March 2017

6 See Norbert Trenkle, 'The Rise and Fall of the Working Man: Towards a Critique of Modern Masculinity'

We see this dialogue as central to feminism's intersections with art history in the twenty-first century – that is, central to how feminism can move forward at a time that has been defined in terms of a 'crisis'. Some have identified the crisis society is faced with as a social reproduction crisis. As George Caffentzis notes, the perception that capitalism was evolving into a social reproduction crisis goes back at least to the early 1990s, when his own understanding developed in proximate relation to the 'Zapatista revolution' in Mexico.[3] We consider this association between social reproduction and revolution important, and see in social reproduction feminism an essential question: if feminism can be revolutionary, what is its revolution about? If this apprehension of a social reproduction crisis was gaining traction at the time among a relatively small circle of intellectuals and activists connected with Autonomist Marxism, the exacerbated conditions of misery, anger, disillusionment and division defining global capitalism – plain for all to see in 2017 – have contributed to the increased popularity of this idea today. Indeed, the recent revival of social reproduction debates suggests that a crisis needs to be addressed, or at least discussed. The urgency of this task cannot be underestimated, as capitalism has stopped working even where it used to – that is, in the 'advanced' economies or what used to be 'the West'.[4]

There are many ways in which we can proceed from here in describing the nature of the disaster – by which we mean both that something is being destroyed and that this process constitutes a disaster for the societies that experience it. What is being destroyed is the 'welfare state', the very thing that kept together Western, liberal democracies and for which an earlier workforce exchanged its prospect of rebellion. It is being destroyed at a time when two processes are underway: first, as globalisation, expressed both as arms trade and as extension and reconfiguration of colonialism (note the move of China to Africa, note the Syrian civil war and its origins), generates millions of dispossessed; secondly, as capital is undoing the workforce into a 'precariat', generating unemployment, underemployment and greater poverty, as well as debt-bondage extending from students to sovereign states. Combined, these two processes institute an updated regime of scarcity, regulated and managed by the political decision to up the antagonism. European states frantically closing their borders not just to 'economic immigrants', but also to refugees, is principally driven by right-wing populism inveighing against the perceived grab of welfare services by the 'new arrivals'. But when we read that in the UK those hit by 'austerity' are expected to be mainly women – who shoulder a devastating 86% of the burden – we understand that gender inequality is at the heart of capital's unsocial work; its commitment to dissolving anything that stands in the way of its own reproduction.[5] While the social reproduction crisis is disproportionately lived through by women, it is interesting to note that, at the same time, the *crisis of labour*, reported to accompany capitalist globalisation, has been identified with a crisis of masculinity, thanks to the humiliation and redundancy of the so-called white male industrial proletariat.[6]

These two differently named 'crises' seem then to have a specifically gendered subject at their core – an observation that we find alarming since they implicitly accede to the over-familiar division: labour is publicly performed and belongs to men while something-other-than-labour is privately performed and belongs to women. In some social and intellec-

[2008], in Neil Larsen et al, eds, *Marxism and the Critique of Value*, MCM', Chicago, 2014.

7 Perry Anderson, 'Why the System Will Still Win', *Le Monde diplomatique*, March 2017, https://mondediplo.com/2017/03/02brexit, accessed 25 March 2017

8 In relation to art, see Pascal Gielen, *The Murmuring of the Artistic Multitude: Global Art, Memory and Post-Fordism*, Valiz, Amsterdam, 2010 and Julieta Aranda, Brian Kuan Wood and Anton Vidokle, eds, *Are You Working Too Much? Post-Fordism, Precarity, and the Labor of Art*, Sternberg Press, Berlin, 2011.

9 Indicatively, see Damien Gayle, 'Robots "Could Replace 250,000 Public Sector Workers"', *The Guardian*, 6 February 2017, https://www.theguardian.com/technology/2017/feb/06/robots-could-replace-250000-uk-public-sector-workers, accessed 29 March 2017.

10 On the gendering of post-Fordism see Angela McRobbie, *Be Creative: Making a Living in the New Culture Industries*, Cambridge, Polity Press 2015.

11 G Frederick Thompson, 'Fordism, Post-Fordism, and the Flexible System of Production', undated, Atkinson Graduate School of Management, Willamette University, Salem, Oregon, http://www.willamette.edu/~fthompson/MgmtCon/Fordism_&_Postfordism.html, accessed 10 March 2017

12 Nancy Fraser, 'Feminism, Capitalism and the Cunning of History', *New Left Review* 56, 2009; Hester Eisenstein, *Feminism Seduced: How Global Elites Use Women's Labor and Ideas to Exploit the World*, Paradigm, Boulder, Colorado, 2009

tual contexts, then, we may have moved from a biologically based to a socially based construction of 'men' and 'women' as complex collective subjects, but subverting the binary introduced *through* (rather than by) labour has somehow been harder to achieve. As if proof of this binary was missing, when in 2016 the *pater familias* billionaire Donald Trump was elected president of the US, 'rust belt workers' were seen as an important constituency whose years of labour-related humiliation had led to this outcome.[7] Yet, what comes under the designation 'labour' is precisely what social-reproduction feminism strives to re-script today. And there are at least two ways to interpret the previous sentence: on the one hand, it points to a re-scripting that re-opens the file 'productive and unproductive' labour, asking whether the distinction should exist at all; on the other, it points to a re-scripting of what constitutes labour itself and whether it is still essential for the valorisation of capital in the always specific, yet changing, conditions of capitalism as an economy that is not just the economy.

Since the 1980s (yet much later in art theory), we have been accustomed to critical appraisals of capital's re-organisation of production under the umbrella term 'post-Fordism'.[8] Despite its definition, scope, and the periodisation that these introduce being still debated, post-Fordism is seen to display certain signal traits: computerisation-management and obsolescence of unskilled or even sectors of skilled labour;[9] flexibilisation and a consequently notable imbrication of 'work' and 'life' (the entry of private life into the formal economy); fragmentation and dispersal of the production process (from manufacture to the service industry); and a general weakening of the position of the individualised labouring subject that finds herself/himself often isolated in the transactions with capital as the economy.[10] The dissolution of the welfare state is not unrelated to this loss of power – if we are to follow the argument that regarded 'the welfare state as the Fordist state'.[11] But then, the paradigmatic affliction suffered by women under austerity capitalism is very closely connected with the question of the crisis of labour – which is, thus, *not* the sad prerogative of men. A number of recent feminist studies, among which we would highlight Nancy Fraser's and Hester Eisenstein's (both from 2009), have suggested that capital successfully (ab)used women's struggles for mass access to waged, productive labour (that is, for exiting the home) to push forth structural changes in production detrimental to the lives and work of most people, as experienced today.[12] The return to social reproduction is occurring in this dismal context, and it entails a rethinking of the *composition of a global working class*, such as that undertaken by Tithi Bhattacharya.[13] As feminism in the art field fought for women's recognition as creative subjects in a way that would also place them as productive subjects, initiating a dialogue on how social reproduction underpins practices and processes, as well as the articulation and reproduction of the art field as we know it, is topical and even urgent. Our aim in putting together this special issue is not then to merely align feminist art and visual culture theory with the concerns that presently define a broader, interdisciplinary feminist thought (though admittedly, this was a motive), or to bring together scattered instances of the subject's address that have considerably delayed social reproduction research in art, but to review and expand an apparatus of critique and strategic resistance to the ways in

13 See Tithi Bhattacharya, 'How Not to Skip Class: Social Reproduction of Labor and the Global Working Class', *Viewpoint Magazine* 5, 31 October 2015, https://www.viewpointmag.com/2015/10/31/how-not-to-skip-class-social-reproduction-of-labor-and-the-global-working-class/, accessed 24 March 2017. See especially the section headed 'Social Reproduction Framework as Strategy'.

14 Vishmidt's previous publications on this topic include Marina Vishmidt, 'Counter (Re-)Productive Labour', *Auto Italia South East*, 4 April 2012, http://autoitaliasoutheast.org/news/counter-re-productive-labour/, accessed 21 June 2017.

15 Indicatively, see the publication of Silvia Federici's anthology of essays tracing four decades of her work in this area, *Revolution at Point Zero: Housework, Reproduction, and Feminist Struggle*, PM Press, Oakland, California, 2012, and the 'Special Issue on Social Reproduction', *Historical Materialism*, vol 24, no 2, 2016.

16 See Griselda Pollock, 'Whither Art History?', *Art Bulletin*, vol 96, no 1, 2014, pp 9–23 where on p 10 Pollock notes that she was introduced to the work of Federici in May 2012 'by a younger feminist art historian, Jaleh Mansoor'. However, Pollock mentions 'social reproduction' in connection with Luis Althusser's work in her influential 1980s essay 'Screening the Seventies: Sexuality and Representation in Feminist Practice – A Brechtian Perspective', in her *Vision and Difference: Feminism, Femininity and Histories of Art*, Routledge, London and New York, 1988, pp 155–199, p 164.

17 On the proposition to approach feminism as fans, see Catherine Grant, 'Fans of Feminism: Re-writing

which capitalism uses the racialised gender divide that it relentlessly brings forth.

Social Reproduction in the Expanded (Art) Field

In her contribution to this special issue, Marina Vishmidt, whose work in connecting art and social reproduction has been foundational, calls attention to distinct paths by which 'social reproduction' becomes relevant to an analysis of the art field overall.[14] Discussing both the thematisation of reproductive labour in art *and* the institution of art as a form of reproduction, she points to the contemporary re-invigoration of debates that originate in the early 1970s.[15] We wish, however, to clarify a point that Vishmidt does not stress; that at its crucial point of formation, its genesis in the 1970s, feminist art history and theory does not, with few exceptions, engage 'social reproduction' as a core, rigorously examined concept within its complex analysis of the private/public divide, despite the partial grounding of some of its key texts in Marxist theory.[16] Our contention here is that bringing a social reproduction perspective to the art field prises open alternative lineages, reuniting us with the 1970s in quite a different way than as 'fans' of a concluded struggle.[17] In what can be described as a *first current*, Silvia Federici, one of the figureheads of social reproduction feminism, described the 'labour of love' that capital expects for free and with a smile. From an 'ideological' perspective this labour's non-remuneration or low pay ensures its successful presentation as non-work, or its irrelevance to an economy split between finance and the high street. That a more integrative and expansive account of 'social reproduction' has been in demand of late – one capable of passing *beyond* the household and the domestic to incorporate public services such as healthcare and the (re)production of social values – is indicative of a pressing requirement for access to a bigger picture which is nevertheless capable of rendering visible the nuanced dimensions of capitalist social relations (indeed, of capital as a social relation). This demand finds resonance with current developments in Marxist and decolonial interventions in art history where similar calls are made. And so, while Vishmidt's enquiry implicitly calls attention to the notable lack of traction that discussions on social reproduction have secured in the fields of art history and art theory, this special issue begins to address this absence in asking, first, whether such a perspective can, and should, instigate *a rethinking of art history in terms of a history of labour*, and second, what methodologies would be required for such a paradigm shift.[18]

What insights can then be gained from embedding the concept of social reproduction in art's critical lexicon for the twenty-first century? The short answer to this is: more than we could accommodate in a journal issue, especially one that happened to coincide (though maybe there is no such thing as coincidence) with a new intensity in the clash of racialised patriarchal capitalism and feminist consciousness. We write these lines shortly after the International Women's Strike on 8 March 2017 voiced the demand for, and invoked the possibility of, a transnational, if not global, counter-offensive in defence of feminism – indeed, a 'feminism of the 99%'.[19] Inspired by Poland's Black Monday (3 October 2016) where women went on strike against a threatened

Histories of Second Wave Feminism in Contemporary Art', *Oxford Art Journal*, vol 34, no 2, 2011, pp 265–286.

18 It is notable that art did not feature in either *Historical Materialism*'s or *Viewpoint*'s special issue on social reproduction, from 2016 and 2015 respectively.

19 See Angela Davis et al, 'Beyond Lean-In: For a Feminism of the 99% and a Militant International Strike on March 8', *Viewpoint Magazine*, 3 February 2017, https://www.viewpointmag.com/2017/02/03/beyond-lean-in-for-a-feminism-of-the-99-and-a-militant-international-strike-on-march-8/, accessed 24 March 2017.

20 Indicatively, see Coco Fusco, 'Why an Art Strike? Why Now?', *Hyperallergic*, 10 January 2017, http://hyperallergic.com/350529/why-an-art-strike-why-now/, accessed 24 March 2017; Yates McKee, *Strike Art: Contemporary Art and the Post-Occupy Condition*, Verso, London, 2016; the panel 'Artistic Strike' (16 January 2015) at the Radical Philosophy Conference 2015 at Haus der Kulturen der Welt in Berlin, available at https://www.hkw.de/en/app/mediathek/audio/38263, accessed 24 March 2017.

21 Nat Raha, 'Queering Marxist [Trans]Feminism: Queer and Trans Social Reproduction', paper presented at the *First Centro Interuniversitario di Ricerca Queer Conference*, L'Aquila, Italy, 1 April 2017; on the Anthropocene debate, see, indicatively, Donna Haraway, 'Tentacular Thinking: Anthropocene, Capitalocene, Chthulucene', *e-flux journal* 75, September 2016, http://www.e-flux.com/journal/75/67125/tentacular-thinking-anthropocene-

total ban on abortion, the 8 March 2017 strike also sought to connect women's power in production with women's power over reproduction. Women were to strike from paid work and from 'emotional labour'. Predictably, the issue of striking has been salient in recent debates on artistic labour, which revisit a relatively obscure(d) past of art militancy just as conditions of labour in the art field are deteriorating.[20] But although this special issue concludes with a conversation on labour in the art field among a curator, a theorist, and an artist (Helena Reckitt, Danielle Child, Jenny Richards), we were unable to include an article-length interrogation of strike in the gendered field of cultural work, despite social reproduction feminists having questioned the efficacy of a transposition of an industrial method of militancy to a field where lives are dependent on the unbroken continuation of labour. We were also unable to include a contribution on the social reproduction of LGTBQ lives, which, as Nat Raha observes, remain neglected in the literature; or an analysis tackling practices that address the environmental catastrophe perpetrated by capital, despite the fact that this concern – exemplified by the dispute over whether 'anthropocene' or 'capitalocene' is the apt name of the catastrophe-in-progress – has been central to social reproduction feminism for years now.[21] Other gaps include work that addresses the political principle of the common in relation to institutional critique and the flourishing of an informal art economy as a troubled commons sustaining the social reproduction of the art field today – though we do touch on this later in this introduction. Yet if we feel compelled to name some notable omissions, we see this collection of texts as a first step in research to come. The thematics traced in this special issue – the artist's home as the hub of social networking; the intimacy tales woven into the division of labour in radical moments of filmic representation; takes on, and protest over, social reproduction in urban space; practices of collecting the remains of appropriated life; questions on the difficulty of refusal in the art field; readings of social reproduction in the artwork or in the instituent practices of 'useful art' – certainly testify to a possibility of a radical re-scripting and re-mapping.

That said, it should by now be obvious that Vishmidt is right to caution in her article here against the infinite expansion of social reproduction to encompass the (in)conceivable range of practices that construe the gendered social field, the art field, and their dynamic interconnection, which does not of course arise in theory but is experienced as a material fact. This material fact, and its gendered history, is not a new feature of capitalist modernity, as shaped in the nineteenth century. But as Lara Perry's article suggests, the strong connection between the social field and the art field enabled by the gendered 'spheres' can illuminate in surprising ways the differentiated positions of 'women artists' as a crucial category of feminist art history. Given that social reproduction has mainly been connected with the contemporary art field, Perry's analysis is an opening towards a much needed, in our opinion, re-conceptualising of art history as a history of labour that stretches 'from industrialisation to globalisation', to quote the title of the 2016 Association of Art Historians annual conference strand on which this special issue has drawn. Perry's most notable finding for anyone working on the contemporary (where social networking and free labour are key) would be the amount of social labour (if we can call it that), straddling the 'affective'

capitalocene-chthulucene/, accessed 24 March 2017. Numerous studies connect social reproduction and the environment. Indicatively, see Wendy Harcourt and Ingrid L Nelson, eds, *Practicing Feminist Political Ecologies: Moving beyond the 'Green Economy'*, Zed Books, London, 2015, as well as the landmark Maria Mies, *Patriarchy and Accumulation on a World Scale: Women in the International Division of Labour* [1986], Zed Books, London, 1998.

22 Lise Vogel, *Marxism and the Oppression of Women: Toward a Unitary Theory*, Pluto Press, London, 1983, p 177

23 On these suppressed calls see Binna Choi, 'Introduction – Reproducing Revolution', in Binna Choi and Maiko Tanaka, eds, *Grand Domestic Revolution Handbook*, Casco, Utrecht and Valiz, Amsterdam, 2014.

24 Gregory Sholette, *Dark Matter: Art and Politics in the Age of Enterprise Culture*, Pluto Press, London, 2011

25 The term is almost always connected with Mario Tronti's book *Operai e Capitale* (*Workers and Capital*, 1966) though as Federici notes the term is not actually mentioned in this work. See George Souvlis and Ankica Čakardić, 'Feminism and Social Reproduction: An Interview with Silvia Federici', *Salvage*, 19 October 2016, http://salvage.zone/online-exclusive/feminism-and-social-reproduction-an-interview-with-silvia-federici/, accessed 24 March 2017.

and the 'material', that London-based artists' careers required in the nineteenth century, and the exemplary role that rigid combinations of class and gender played in the realisation of such labour as the invisible art-world infrastructure located in the artist's home. Here, we are returned to Lise Vogel's earlier identification of a need for historical work to be undertaken from a social reproduction perspective on the precise character of women's complex and differentiated oppression in class societies.[22] Reading Perry's account made us wonder how, upon the loss of that human infrastructure, women in the contemporary art field (especially those with children) can achieve at least partial visibility. The domestic technology revolutions in the second half of the twentieth century have been unable to replace the labour of care and sociality provided in the nineteenth-century artist's home. Rather, they have been used to help women forget earlier radical calls for the collectivisation of housework.[23] Gregory Sholette's oft-mentioned 'dark matter' of invisible art labour or 'participation' sustaining the contemporary artworld must, at some point, be connected with the history of a long artistic modernity as a terrain of hierarchised labour that exceeds even what 'dark matter' (referring to labour and participation *in* the art field) can encompass.[24]

Elisa Adami and Alex Fletcher's take on Anne-Marie Miéville and Jean-Luc Godard's *Numéro deux* (1975) testifies, however, on the significance of technological imagination for radicalising the analysis of the home as the faux-comfort-zone of the private/public divide on which industrial capitalism thrived. In the West, the 1970s is the moment not only of feminism but also of the popularisation of the 'social factory', a key term we inherit from Operaismo (Workerism).[25] In *Numéro deux*, we are no longer in the artist's home but in the working-class home located in social housing in some European city edge. Today, a father coming and going to the apartment and a stay-at-home mother most likely connote the lost ideal of the 'family wage' – of which the film, treating the home as a depressing yet inevitable extension of the factory, offers a most powerful subversion. The home as part of an encroaching social factory economy figures both in the film's logic of production (the home-movie) and the representation of working-class life as a gendered everyday. *Numéro deux* revels in dualisms and dualities – all, predictably, in need of 'deconstruction', to recall a buzzword of feminist critique both in film theory and art history. Yet the film's investment in the everyday of a 'white' working-class family places a wedge between the possibility of deconstruction in representational spaces and in 'real life' where doing the washing is – as the father explains to his daughter – the mother's 'factory' while for him it is the opposite: the 'home'. Acknowledging the spread of factory logic to relations and interacting subjects of intimacy (the couple, parents and children, the 'nuclear family') does not lead to this logic's abolition but just to conceding to the existence of different/gendered 'automated' subjectivities. These persist.

The requirements of a nineteenth-century artworld, where women's *immaterial and material* labour in the home provided the invisible infrastructure to careers and the marketing of artworks (and which sustained the 'family wage' dream even in the 1970s), find their antithesis in the twenty-first-century 'useful art' – that is, useful artistic (and not least curatorial) labour, which now enters the art institution as the latter attempts to become a *visible* infrastructure. Usefulness, in this case, is not about the valorisation of capital but about sustaining the fabric of 'life', and so, with Arte Util (Useful Art) we are properly in the territory of a truly expanded art field. Useful Art brings forth 'use value as an indisputably moral good', to quote Larne Abse Gogarty in this special issue, who also notes the *political* stakes in art drawing society's attention to use value against the hegemony of exchange value in historical and contemporary capitalism. Abse Gogarty's critique focuses on art institutions as sites where the conflict between utopianism and utilitarianism is played out in, and as, social reproduction. It is not so much that the art field becomes the outsourced site of social reproduction duties on which the state has given up, but that, in its experimentation with the avant-garde's wish for 'art as life', the art institution 'confronts' the state and its limitations. However, Abse Gogarty also identifies limitations in Useful Art, guided by this question: how can the political-ethical intentions of practising the alternative avoid becoming useful to the 'enemy' – a word encountered in the opening of her analysis and betraying the sense of urgency that permeates overall the post-2000 revival of social reproduction debates. One of the most engaging issues Abse Gogarty raises is the art institution's experimental appeal to the military as a context of useful tools and tactics. Yet three years after Nato Thomson discussed the intersections between 'military methodology' and art in *e-flux journal*, Fredric Jameson proposed the army as a viable candidate to manage the transition out of capitalism.[26] Published in 2016, Jameson's landmark manifesto *An American Utopia: Dual Power and the Universal Army* provides the core to a book where a number of critical Marxist and radical left theorists address the prospect of society organised on a military model. As Kathi Weeks notes in the volume, the army is brought forth to address the need to collectivise social reproduction in order to reduce social reproduction labour to a minimum.[27] We can surmise that in utopia there will be no other labour than social reproduction labour – indeed, utopia is a post-work society (Weeks herself epitomises this position in her feminist theoretical project overall) where the only labour left is social reproduction.[28] But the *means to an end* narrative is what catches our attention in this turn to the army, for this is where the military and its connotation of violence come in. The decoupling of social reproduction from a discourse of (feminist or other) pacifism is worth stressing.

The Violence of Reproduction

Deeply imbricated with reproduction, the concept of care (and its associated activities) has historically been drained of political relevance and import in the long modernity. In its recent rise to prominence, attention has been focused on the potential of care to counter the extractive, individualising pressures wrought by capitalist globalisation's processes of accumulation through new forms of 'care communities', 'reproductive commons' or, in the art field, instituting through strategies of taking 'care to power'.[29] While continuing to affirm the primacy of reproduction, others have pressed more prosaic survival strategies to the fore, a perspective encapsulated in what, for Malcolm Bull, remains the defining

26 Nato Thomson, 'The Insurgents, Part I: Community-based Practice as Military Methodology', *e-flux journal* 47, September 2013, http://www.e-flux.com/journal/47/60048/the-insurgents-part-i-community-based-practice-as-military-methodology/, accessed 29 March 2017

27 Kathi Weeks, 'The Seeds of Imagination', in Slavoj Zizek, ed, *An American Utopia: Dual Power and the Universal Army*, Verso, London, 2016

28 Kathi Weeks, *The Problem with Work: Feminism, Marxist, Antiwork Politics, and Postwork Imaginaries*, Duke University Press, Durham, 2011

29 Isabell Lorey, *State of Insecurity: Government of the Precarious*, Verso, London, 2015; Federici, op cit; 'Instituting for the Contemporary', BAK Public Editorial Meeting, Utrecht, 11 April 2016

question of the times, namely 'how to extract from the global economy the means to stay alive' when globalisation is articulated in relation to biopolitics.[30]

For many women, this increasingly necessitates dislocation and migration from the global south to take up caring positions in the north – poorly remunerated work that Rosemary Hennessy refers to in terms of 'abjection'.[31] Analysing the cycling of the female labour force, this time in factories across Mexico and China, Melissa Wright has challenged the myth of the disposable 'third-world' woman. Predicated on the worker's capacity to generate value and facilitate the *reproduction of capital* through her own *de*valuation towards worthlessness, such 'flexible' production conditions radically diminish the prospect of effective struggles over workers' capacity for regeneration. The undergirding narrative that Wright questions yokes apparently necessary – or even natural – destruction to capitalist development and modern progress.[32] Though her subject is women, the connection she makes is a familiar one found in justifications of ecological decimation and of colonialism, as seen in Manon Gaudet's contribution here. Connecting Indigenous dispossession through the systematic disruption and forced reformulation of traditions of social reproduction (both daily and generational) to settler-colonial collecting practices, Gaudet attends to contradictions of care, reproduction and violence in early twentieth-century Canada. Hers is one of two texts that engage these contradictions through 'the domestic' that is hardly contained as a small-scale event cut off from the metanarrative of colonial dispossession. What kind of solidarity – of friendship, or of guilt, or of hierarchy? – can ameliorate this metanarrative as women's lived reality remains a question that far exceeds the framework of 'cultural heritage'. Approaching Lizzie Borden's cult film *Born in Flames* (1983) from the standpoint of social reproduction, Beth Capper discusses its multiple portrayals as a site of both labour and struggle. On the one hand, the film underscores the structural exclusion of women of colour and black women from specific (hegemonic) domestic and familial imaginaries while also stressing the dependency of these very imaginaries on their maintenance labour. On the other, household interiors in the film play host to the Women's Army as the women plan for insurgency, and Capper foregrounds the connection drawn by the film between militancy and care-orientated social reproduction.

A key point stands out for us with respect to Borden's vision of struggle in the analysis offered by Capper. First, its implicit framing as a mechanism not only of social transformation but of self-defence – a perspective powerfully captured in a scene depicting a gang of whistle-blowing feminist vigilantes amassing on their bicycles to thwart street harassment and sexual assault. The urgency of this requirement to 'fight back' finds contemporary relevance in increasing rejections of a liberal feminist commitment to non-violence – or, in the words of Dilar Dirik, 'passive-ism' – that insist upon the class and racial privilege of such positions and instead advocate self-protection as an indispensable modality of resistance.[33] Dirik draws on the experience of Kurdish women fighters in Rojava in Northern Syria, maintaining that, first, nothing less than a social revolution structured around the position of women is required to defeat the deep patriarchy represented

30 Malcolm Bull, 'Introduction, Special Issue on Biopolitics', *New Left Review* 45, May–June 2007, p 1

31 Rosemary Hennessy, *Fires on the Border: The Passionate Politics of Labor Organizing on the Mexican Frontera*, University of Minnesota, Minneapolis, 2013

32 Melissa W Wright, *Disposable Women and Other Myths of Global Capitalism*, Routledge, New York and London, 2006, p 6

33 Dilar Dirik, 'Feminist Pacifism or Passive-ism?', *Open Democracy*, 7 March 2017, https://www.opendemocracy.net/5050/dilar-dirik/feminist-pacifism-or-passive-ism , accessed 21 March 2017

by ISIS; and, second, that the conscious move to seize the means of reproduction and to experiment with alternatives must be at the core of this social revolution. Although a focused analysis of Rojava as a social revolution is regrettably absent from this special issue, the major issue it introduces – the question of insurgent violence – is structural to Capper's reading of *Born in Flames*. In this sense, Capper can be seen to reflect on a largely forgotten – and indeed delegitimised in liberal feminism – thread of the feminist imaginary, thought and, ultimately, struggle: that which has sought to spell out the violence that inheres in women's servitude as well as revolutionary counter-violence as a proposition that negates the parochial illustration of the apparatus of care as a non-site for materially articulated insurgency. But whether, and how, the recognition of this double connection to violence through social reproduction will inform subsequent research remains to be seen.

At the same time, through this route we are allowed to ask whether challenging the naturalised connection of care culture with peace and comfort can be an opening towards understanding more broadly the connection of the social division of labour and violence. But this is just one debate; there are more, including on the thin line that may separate consent to maternal and parental subjectivity and coercion to reproduction. Ideology is not free from violence. The question of care labour alone in relation to a perceived sanctity of reproduction fuels major debates on queer parenthood that, as Maggie Nelson (citing Susan Freiman) notes, 'places femininity, reproduction, and normativity on one side and masculinity, sexuality, and queer resistance on the other'. But does the 'succinct slogan: Don't produce and don't reproduce', attributed by Nelson to a 'queer artist friend' belong exclusively to queer politics?[34] No, is the short answer. And apparently, queer politics is not necessarily and always emancipated from gendering as ideology. Confronted with the mutation of patriarchal traditionalism into both neofascism and strands of seemingly emancipatory polemics, the feminism of the early twenty-first century cannot afford the accommodation and perpetuation of 'taboo' issues, and in so far as its struggles cross through art history (as a history of the division of labour), neither can the latter.

We imagine that Sheila Rowbotham's *Women, Resistance and Revolution*, first published in 1972 and available in a new edition in 2013, can be infinitely expanded, but stress that in this imagined struggle without end, we pay greater heed to her words from 1971, 'we walk and think and talk in living contradiction', reiterating them as a question:[35] why, and for how long? A number of works associated with a loose feminist counter-canon engage or allude to individualised women's violence – Chantal Akerman's Jeanne Dielman, *23, Quai du Commerce, 1080 Bruxelles* (1975), Martha Rosler's *Semiotics of the Kitchen* (1975), Pipilotti Rist's *Ever Is Overall* (2005), not to mention Orlan's and Gina Pane's undoing of their own corporeal space. The image of Ene-Liis Semper having her open mouth filled with soil and a flower planted in it (*Oasis*, 1999) lingers from the annals of post-Soviet, Estonian art – an image that may or may not be read politically, that is, in terms of a public discourse on power and its enforcing silence and suffocation as the price that women must pay for 'life' to go on. But connecting the

34 Maggie Nelson, *The Argonauts*, Melville House, London, 2015, pp 93–94

35 Rowbotham cited in Vinaj Bahl, 'Reflections on the Recent Work of Sheila Rowbotham: Women's Movements and Building Bridges', *Monthly Review*, vol 48, no 6, November 1996, https://monthly review.org/1996/11/01/reflections-on-the-recent-work-of-sheila-row botham/, accessed 25 March 2017. See Sheila Rowbotham, *Women's Liberation and New Politics*, Pamphlet n. 17, May Day Manifesto Group, London, 1971, p 10.

realm of private disarticulation of the gendered self, no matter how historically grounded, with feminist solidarity as insurgent violence is, for now, a 'forgotten relation', to borrow Helena Reckitt's phrase from another context, yet one which also contributes to a history of memorial excisions that feminism has lived through.[36]

The Feminist Commons/
The Social Reproduction Commons

It is indeed of major interest that Dirik talks also about the self-management of co-operatives, communes and centres as a form of self-defence. The focus on the potential of feminist collectivity and – implicitly or explicitly – the possibility of a feminist commons is not new but such prospects remain severely marginalised in a society where social housing signifies (demonised) poverty rather than a social movement against capital and where mortgages signify upward social mobility as the petite bourgeoisie's ideal. Worse, so far there is much unclarity as to whether, in collectivising the domestic, women would still continue to carry the burden of that sphere or whether, and how, such a reconfiguration of the everyday would be tied to the end of the gender division of labour. Perhaps worse still, we are nowhere near reconfiguring the *feminist desire* for such a future into the political articulation of a *social need* that should be seen as merely identified by feminism but of pressing relevance to all.

The problem is hardly new. In her article for this issue, tellingly titled 'Losing Ground?', Victoria Horne discusses the activism of the Hackney Flashers in 1970s London, opening her examination by pointing to the collective

> concentrating on the structural difficulties of organising childcare in an exploitative urban environment where the necessary reproduction of life was coming into increasing conflict with the productivity demands of capitalism.

We can compare this assessment with Brian Holmes's statement from 2016:

> For the people, a crisis is measured by the lack of social welfare and civil liberties. For capital, a crisis is measured by the inability to manage a liberal free-trade regime.[37]

How can we approach instances of 1970s feminist art activism tackling the urgency of rethinking social reproduction from its future as our present? The struggle does go on but what are the questions to be asked that might allow us (feminists) to speak of a defeat that must be overcome without converting feminism into a gradual loss of ground, into a social form of progressive compromise? What about art? Horne goes on to stress the importance of holding on to the Hackney Flashers' commitment to agitprop. Their determined opposition to an 'art' frame resonates with current tensions aroused

36 Helena Reckitt, 'Forgotten Relations', in Angela Dimitrakaki and Lara Perry, eds, *Politics in a Glass Case: Feminism, Exhibition Cultures and Curatorial Transgressions*, Liverpool University Press, Liverpool, 2013

37 Brian Holmes, 'Live Your Models: Self-Orientation and Social Form', in Hlavajova and Sheikh, op cit, p 695

through 'artwashing', which has seen those artists taking advantage of low-cost space accused of complicity with speculative developers now well-versed in the 'fine art of gentrification'.[38] When communities organise against the incursions of artists and galleries in order to maintain and protect their own capacities for home- and place-making, how can we grasp the complex intersections between different social practices of reproduction, with art as one among many? What kind of 'social' is being reproduced, and what is being erased? We ask these questions while we note that at least two of the contributors to this special issue – Horne and Elke Krasny, who discusses VALIE EXPORT's *Transparent Space* (Vienna, 2001) – have orientated their critique in relation to practices that may implicate care but directly address public space. In the case of Krasny, the artwork-cum-exhibition space of EXPORT's room-size glass cube named *Transparent Space* is found to be dependent on a hidden care infrastructure that threatens to reveal the work's title as a misnomer. The work's function as a public artwork and exhibition space intended to increase the public visibility of women artists' work is also a testing ground for what actually enters public space as one still associated with state funding and subsidies and what is left out – in this case, to be managed by the loose collectivism of what we might call a feminist commons: the women whose informal labour in looking after the glass cube complements formal (public) care provision. The debates on the triangulation of care at present – split between private/capital enterprise, public/state provision and (an implicitly independent from both) care as commons – are proliferating to an extent that makes any meaningful summary impossible to undertake here.[39] But the problem of disentangling the radical potential of the commons from their fate as a 'commons fix' within the increasingly conservative and oppressive alliance of capital and the state remains.[40] It also remains a problem for feminism. How 'women's work' – never meant to be 'done' – might *avoid being* approached as a commons only to be liberally transformed into a resource appropriated by racialised patriarchal capitalism would be one way of expressing the problem. Something worries us when we read that today in the emergent 'commons studies' there is a prevalent tendency towards 'the articulation less of a physically existent "commons" and more of a performative claiming of the common'.[41] We hope that the case studies drawn from the art field and examined in this special issue might provide a degree of insight into the ways in which the real-time articulations of a feminist praxis might be addressed rather than looping feminist efforts into such performative claims. Finally, although we understand the symbolic value of 'political *commoning*', we remain sceptical about whether this symbolic operation is in fact, as we are told, 'enacting "another world" within the neoliberal landscape, and in so doing altering subjectivities, relations, and spaces'.[42] Both Krasny's and Horne's analyses suggest that women's role in care (and its private enclaves) is also a complex position in urban struggles where capital and the state enact their untiring appropriation of commoning and the commons, and that these vectors of alienation operate also through art.

38 Magally Miranda and Kyle Lane-McKinley, 'Artwashing, or, between Social Practice and Social Reproduction', *A Blade of Grass, Fertile Ground*, 1 February 2017, http://www.abladeofgrass.org/fertile-ground/artwashing-social-practice-social-reproduction/?utm_content=bufferdff48&utm_medium=social&utm_source=twitter.com&utm_campaign=buffer#_ftn3, accessed 14 February 2017

39 Indicatively, see the seventy-three essays in David Bollier and Silke Helfrich, eds, *The Wealth of the Commons: A World beyond Market and State*, Levellers Press, Massachusetts, Amherst and Florence, 2012.

40 See Massimo de Angelis, 'Economy, Capital and the Commons', in Angela Dimitrakaki and Kirsten Lloyd, eds, *Economy: Art, Production and the Subject in the 21st Century*, Liverpool University Press, Liverpool, 2015, pp 198–213. In an earlier iteration de Angelis considers the issue as a question. See Massimo De Angelis, 'Does Capital Need a Commons Fix?', *Ephemera: Theory & Politics in Organization*, vol 13, no 3, 2013, pp 603–615.

41 Leila Dawney, Samuel Kirwan and Julian Brigstocke, 'Introduction: The Promise of the Commons', in their *Space, Power and the Commons: The Struggle for Alternative Futures*, Routledge, New York, 2015, p 4

42 Ibid

Concluding: The Feminist Struggle in 'The Tragedy of the Totality'

'The kainos of labor in the twenty-first century is labor as intra-action, entanglement, the tragedy of the totality', writes McKenzie Wark in commenting on the importance of naming and, we surmise, of concepts.[43] We see the concept of social reproduction as crucial in grasping the parameters of capital as a totalising social relation, as also noted by Vogel.[44] In 2017 we have learned not only that you cannot have socialism in one country, as Stalin imagined, but that you cannot have capitalism in one country either, as imperialism and globalisation have demonstrated. We have also learned from the containment of feminist separatisms that a critical mass, relative to the scale of forces opposing women's and feminised subjects' emancipation, is required for any meaningful strategies and tactics of refusal. We have learned already from Marion von Osten's revisiting of Helke Sander's exemplary 1978 film *Redupers. Die allseitig reduzierte Persönlichkeit* a few things about the predicament of the activist working single mother:

> The protagonist is not only photographer, feminist activist, and theorist, that is, cultural producer, but also a product of emancipatory demands and capitalist impositions, a subject who has pulled away from wage labor and its regulatory apparatus in the factory or in the office, as the Autonomia Operaia called for. At the same time, she is a *Reduper* (an all-around REDUced PERson) – a figure who cannot be located biographically, and instead requires a new form of subjectivity to be realized in the contradictions of capitalist socialization. In this way, *Redupers* marks the post-Fordist convergence of work relationships, subjectivity, desires, and political demands that has consequently brought about a multitude of all-around reduced personalities.[45]

Have we learned that! We have learned that gender is 'a real abstraction' made operative and concrete in the question of value for capital: 'There must be an exterior to value in order for value to exist', say Endnotes, continuing: 'Similarly, for labour to exist and serve as the measure of value, there must be an exterior to labour.'[46] And as all historians know, there is only one time for the actuality of struggle: now. What we, as feminist art historians, need to learn, however, is which narrativisation of production and reproduction can reveal excisions (or, for that matter, inclusions) that remain central to the perpetuation of gendering as exploitative oppression and how the actually existing art field participates in *this* reproduction. In this special issue, we have striven to indicate the possibility of a feminist art history that departs from the monocausal endeavour of putting more women into capitalist art institutions where workers' rights are undermined and where even the wage relation has come to be perceived as a 'right' under threat by the internship culture.[47] Rather, the broader, underlying question here is: to the extent that this endeavour has been successful (the art market tells another story),[48] on what terms has 'success' been achieved? In short, you cannot have a successful feminism in just one sector either, and the art field is a 'sector' within the totality constituted out of capital as a

43 McKenzie Wark, 'Chthulucene, Capitalocene, Anthropocene', *Public Seminar*, New School, 8 September 2016, http://www.publicseminar.org/2016/09/chthulu/#.WNVPRI6kKCQ, accessed 24 March 2017

44 Vogel, *Marxism and the Oppression of Women*, op cit

45 Marion von Osten, 'Irene ist Viele! Or What We Call "Productive" Forces', *e-flux journal* 8, September 2009, http://www.e-flux.com/journal/08/61381/irene-ist-viele-or-what-we-call-productive-forces/, accessed 29 March 2017

46 Endnotes, 'The Logic of Gender: On the Separation of Spheres and the Process of Abjection', *Endnotes 3 – Gender, Race, Class, and Other Misfortunes*, September 2013, https://endnotes.org.uk/issues/3/en/endnotes-the-logic-of-gender, accessed 29 March 2017

47 See Precarious Workers Brigade, 'Training for Exploitation? Politicising Employability and Reclaiming Education', *The Journal of Aesthetics & Protest*, Los Angeles, 2017.

48 Maura Reilly, 'Taking the Measure of Sexism: Facts, Figures, and Fixes', *Artnews*, 26 May 2015, http://www.artnews.com/2015/05/26/taking-the-measure-of-sexism-facts-figures-and-fixes/, accessed 27 March 2017

social relation. The feminist struggle that now crosses through the art field cannot but be expansive, especially as the activist impulse sweeping the art field necessitates a re-thinking of how 'doing' traverses both working (for need) and participating (for love). The question is hardly one of aesthetics, given the latter term's perennial return to some 'sphere' of its own, no matter its appropriation by commodity fetishism and the 'packaging' of our discontent. Rather, the question is one of radical feminist praxis. To what extent can we undertake this without reproducing the totalising capital relation as we reproduce ourselves and our resistance?

CLEANING CONDITIONS
eepin...contin g da
Allan Kaprow

Third Text, 2017
Vol. 31, No. 1, 15–29, https://doi.org/10.1080/09528822.2017.1362788

The Artist's Household

On Gender and the Division of Artistic and Domestic Labour in Nineteenth-Century London

Lara Perry

Suzanne Lacy with Meg Parnell, Cleaning Conditions, 2013, (detail), Manchester Art Gallery, (painting in background: *Captive Andromache*, Sir Frederic Leighton, c 1888), image courtesy: the artists, photo: Alan Seabright

1 Angela Dimitrakaki, *Gender, ArtWork and the Global Imperative: A Materialist Feminist Critique*, Manchester University Press, Manchester, 2013; Marita Flisbäck, and Sofia Lindström, 'Work-family Conflict among Professional Visual Artists in Sweden: Gender Differences in the Influence of Parenting and Household Responsibilities', *Nordisk Kulturpolitisk Tidskrift*, vol 16, no 2, 2013, pp 239–268

Contemporary art and art histories are currently having a productive reckoning with the material demands of domestic work and parenting, considered as both a stimulus and constraint to art production. Resonating with the concept of 'immaterial labour' that has become prominent in explorations of the structures of contemporary art, feminist artists and critics have exposed the important gendered dimension of the immaterial and social-reproduction labour involved in the career of the contemporary artist. Art projects such as CASCO's long-term programme (2009–) *User's Manual: The Grand Domestic Revolution* and *The Mother House* project in London (2016) have picked up where Mierle Ukeles Laderman's performance works of Maintenance Art in the 1960s and 1970s left off, and analysts have similarly refocused their efforts to include considerations of the gendered impact of parenthood on art production. For example, in her book *Gender, ArtWork and the Global Imperative: A Materialist Feminist Critique* (2013), Angela Dimitrakaki explored the impact of constant travel and around-the-clock schedule on women's art careers; that this is more of an issue for mothers than for fathers was confirmed by a survey of Swedish artists made by Marita Flisbäck and Sofia Lindström (also published in 2013), which offered evidence that the careers of male artists benefit from a greater degree of freedom from the work of the household.[1]

All of this activity is associated with the investigation of contemporary rather than historical art practices. The reasons for that association are several and importantly include the predominance of performance and 'socially engaged' art as the forms through which domestic and maternal labours have been addressed by artists. The shift of art practice in the 1960s away from the production of artefacts to include performance,

Suzanne Lacy with Meg Parnell, *Cleaning Conditions*, 2013, Manchester Art Gallery, (painting in background: *Captive Andromache*, Sir Frederic Leighton, c 1888), image courtesy: the artists, photo: Alan Seabright

service and networking activities has latterly been approached in relation to patterns of labour in capitalist economies after globalisation by Luc Boltanski and Eve Chiapello, among others, while the connections between art, immaterial labour and globalised (post-1989) capitalism have formed the dominant lens through which these questions have been enunciated.[2] Of course, the problems of social reproduction in art are not indicated in the form or content of a nineteenth-century painting such as Frederic Leighton's *Captive Andromache* (1888), in the way that they are in the artwork shown in the foreground of that image, Suzanne Lacy with Meg Parnell's *Cleaning Conditions* (2013). But to explore the gendered labour of social reproduction *exclusively* in the context of contemporary art does not account for gender difference in art production before the innovations of the 1960s, although studies of women artists of earlier periods (particularly those which focus on Britain and France) have disclosed women artists' careers that were constrained by gender categories which typically excluded women from access to professional life.

Art historians have explained this older pattern with reference to women's exclusion from art educational institutions and professional associations, and with contextual ideological, psychic and spatial boundaries that sustained those barriers; but the examination of institutional barriers to women's careers as artists before 1968 also needs to be extended to the institution of the family. Art history, particularly the history of modernism, pushes back against such an enquiry. Flisbäck and Lindström's 2013 study connects the pattern of the divisions of family/professional labour to a historical legacy in which art is designated as 'autonomous'.[3] It is this quality of 'autonomous' practice which studies such as Christine Battersby's powerful *Gender and Genius: Towards a Feminist Aesthetics* (1989) and Linda Nochlin's answer to her question

2 Luc Boltanski and Eve Chiapello, *The New Spirit of Capitalism*, Gregory Elliott, trans, Verso, London, 2006. On the importance of gendering these discussions see Helena Reckitt, 'Forgotten Relations: Feminist Artists and Relational Aesthetics', in Angela Dimitrakaki and Lara Perry, eds, *Politics in a Glass Case: Feminism, Exhibition Cultures and Curatorial Transgressions*, Liverpool University Press, Liverpool, 2013, p 138.

3 Flisbäck, and Lindström, 'Work-family Conflict among Professional Visual Artists in Sweden', op cit, p 243

Census year	Borough	Head of household	Occupation	Spouse	Occupation	Dependents	Non dependent family	Visitors	Servants
61	Marylebone	Mary Osborn	Clergymans Widow	Nil		daughter 12 grandson 9, great-niece 8	Emily Mary unm age 30. Sons 27. 23 unm	female 23	2 - servants
61	Freshwater	Charles Cameron	State member of Council. Calcutta	Julia M	&		son 19	4	3 - parlourmaid, housemaid. cook
71	Chelsea	John Millais	Artist Royal Academician	Effie	Wife	sons 16, 7; daughters 12, 10, 2	Brother living on income		5 - servants
71	Finsbury	Ellis Williams	Stockbroker	Anna	Wife	daughters 22, 19, 5, 2, 1; sons/stepson 16, 6, 3, 12		Louise [R]omer	6- 5 servants, cook
81	Chelsea	Wm Allingham	Artist/poet	Helen Allingham	artist/watercolours	Child 5. Child 4			3 - nurse, cook, housemaid
81	Fulham	Edward Burne Jones	Artist/painter of pictures	Georgiana	Nil		son 19, daughter 14	Elizabeth, 14	3- parlourmaid, housemaid, cook
81	Chelsea	Frederic Leighton	Painter. ARA	Nil					3 -butler, kitchen domestic. housemaid
81	Chelsea	Valentine C Prinsep	ARA Artist	Nil					4 -butler, housekeeper (m. couple with 3 under 5s), housemaid, nurserymaid
81	Chelsea	John Millais	RA Painter	Nil (away visiting?)		son 17	m. daughter 18, brother 'artist' 53		6- nurse; 2x housemaids; kitchenmaid; butler; footman
81	Chelsea	Thomas Thornycroft	Sculptor	Mary	" (sculptor)	Nil	Mary A, unm, 35, painter/artist; Teresa 18 unm artist; William 37 Artist		3 - housemaid, cook, studio sweeper
81	Chelsea	Luke Fildes	artist - painter A.R.A.	Fanny	Nil	son 1	brother in law Henry Woods artist		4 -cook, housemaid, parlourmaid. nurse
81	Chelsea	Edward L. Sambourne	Artist	Mary Ann	Nil	daughter 5. son 2			3 - nurse, cook, housemaid
81	Chelsea	Adrian Coiffier (b. France)	Artist, painting	Alexandrine (b. France)	Nil	daughter 18 (b. France)			Nil
81	Chelsea	Joseph Jopling	Ret. Civil Service Clerk	Nil (Louise Jopling - away from home)	Nil				3, cook/domestic. housemaid, stonemason (listed as servant- m. cook?)
81	Chelsea	William Bell Scott	Historical painter and author	Letitia Scott	Nil			Alice Boyd	3 ladies' maid, housemaid. cook
81	Chelsea	Anna Lea Merritt	Artist in Oils and Colour	Nil					2 - butler, female domestic servant
81	Marylebone	William Ouless	Painter of RA	Lucy	Nil	daughter 1			5- nurse, 2x housemaids; parlourmaid. cook
81	Marylebone	Rebecca Solomon	Artist painter	Nil					Nil
81	Streatham	William Strudwick	Drawing Artist (photographer)	Julia Strudwick	Nil			Boarder - unemployed clerk 21	1 servant
81	Marylebone	Lawrence Alma Tadema	artist - member RAA	Laura	Nil	daughters 15, 13			4 - cook, housemaid, kitchen maid, parlourmaid
91	S. Kensington	George K. Rowe	Solicitor	Louisa J. Rowe (Jopling)	Artist- sculpt	son 8		Catherine Valliant visitor (27)	3 -cook/domestic; housemaid; general
91	Chelsea	Anna L. Merritt	Artist (sculptor)				Marion Lea, 26, actress		2 general servants
91	Kensington	Luke Fildes	Artist painter RA (sculptor)	Fanny		daughters, 7,7 sons 2, 1	brother in law Henry Woods artist		6, cook, housemaid, parlourmaid, nurse, under nurse, underhousemaid
91	Chelsea	Sir John E. Millais	Artist painter (sculp)	c. c.		grandsons. 1.2	daughter 31, brother in law Albert Gray		9 - butler, footman, Chef de Cuisine, housemaids x2, upper nurse, undernurse, kitchen maid, scullerymaid
91	Fulham	Edward Burne Jones	Sculpt/artist-painter				Philip (son, 29) artist-painter; Stanley Baldwin (nephew, 28) ironmaster		4 - parlourmaid, housemaid, cook, butler
01	S. Kensington	George K. Rowe	Solicitor	Louisa J Rowe (Jopling)	artist - paint				3 - servant

Summary of the census records for some artists' households 1861–1901

4 Griselda Pollock, 'Modernity and the Spaces of Femininity', *Vision and Difference: Femininity, Feminism and the Histories of Art*, Routledge, London and New York, 1988, pp 50–90

5 The census was first taken in 1801 and then every ten years thereafter, and from 1841 it created a centralised record of the names, ages, places of birth, relationship of the individual to the head of household, and the occupation and birthplace of every person who was in residence at a given address on the census day.

6 The 1881, 1891 and 1901 records for Louise Jopling were kindly provided to me by Patricia de Montfort, author of *Louise Jopling: A Biographical and Cultural Study of the Modern Woman Artist in Victorian Britain*, Routledge, London, 2016.

7 The information about occupation and the constitution of the household has been drawn from digital copies of enumerator's records, which Edward Higgs and Amanda Wilkinson, 'Women, Occupations and Work in the Victorian Censuses Revisited', *History Workshop* 81, 2016, p 22, conclude should be seen as a reliable source for information about women's occupations. However, neither Emily Osborn, Julia Margaret Cameron, Georgiana Burne-Jones, nor Laura Alma-Tadema were listed as having an occupation although known to be practising artists. A large number of women are named as artists in the census records (Pamela Gerrish Nunn's *Victorian Women Artists*, The Women's Press, London, 1987, reports 278 women listed as artists in the census of 1841 and 1069 in 1871, p 3), although the entries for occupation seem incomplete when it comes to women artists.

'Why have there been no great women artists?' identify as inaccessible to women because of their attachment to the mundane work of (aesthetic) imitation and routine household labour. As Griselda Pollock argued in her chapter on 'Modernity and the Spaces of Femininity', the motifs of domesticity are precisely those which have been rejected by scholars such as T J Clark as instances of emergent modern art.[4] The pressure to dissociate the production of art from the material context of family life has been tremendous.

Establishing the importance of the family in the history of art practice requires a method of enquiry which shifts the focus from the artist and her products to the artist's total engagement with labour both artistic and domestic. While Flisbäck and Lindström devised questionnaires which asked artists to self-report their participation in domestic duties, this is, to state the obvious, not a method which can be used retrospectively. Yet we do have access to a significant and extensive source of data about the constitution of households in Great Britain from the middle of the nineteenth century to the present, which is the decennial census.[5] The census form used from 1841 onwards collected information about the names, ages, occupations and birthplaces of householders, their families, visitors and resident servants, thus providing a snapshot of the household and its total capacity for labour. Historians frequently use census data in conjunction with other kinds of primary documents to evidence labour history; in this article, I have adopted their methods in relation to a small sample of census records from artist families/households of later nineteenth-century England.

Above is a summary of the twenty-six census entries referred to in this article, which represent the census records for eighteen artists' households (some artist's households are represented more than once). The table draws most extensively from the 1881 census, and was produced by searching for the names of specific artists (the easiest way to access the machine-searchable enumerator's records). I was conscious of building a sample of records that included different kinds of households, as well as artists practising in different media including photography, sculpture, painting and graphic art, and with greater and lesser degrees of commercial success.[6] The artist or artists in the household are denoted by their names appearing in colour – men in blue and women in red. Most of the artists in the sample are at least a little known and some of them were among the most prominent artists of the period, including two presidents of the Royal Academy (Frederic Leighton and John Everett Millais).[7] The resulting list should not be understood as a representative sample of all practising artists, and it must be noted that the records (bar that for Julia Margaret and Charles Cameron in 1861) are for families resident in London. So while the sample represented here is not an adequate representation of British artists in general, it does include a variety of artist circumstances within London.

I have interpreted this data to explore three different topics in the relationship between the artist and household labour: the first section deals with the intimate spatial relationship shared by art, work and family life; the second section explores some of the expanded labour associated with art making which was taken on by members of the artist's household (especially social or entrepreneurial labour of the type that interests many contemporary theorists); and the third section discusses mundane domestic work. Each section seeks to establish the significance of gender (and, to a lesser extent, class and rank) in ordering the labour that was performed by each member of the household, whether explicitly artistic or not. In the conclusion to this article, I use these findings as the basis for some speculation as to the reasons for the continuities between this apparently remote artistic scene and art's present concerns.

Working at Home: Art Work

Art historical methodologies tend to separate the artist from the family in which she or he worked, but the empirical evidence provided by the census, biographical accounts and architectural histories suggests that in London at least, nineteenth-century artists' work remained firmly located within family life. In this respect, artists' families were not an exception to the working patterns of professionals more broadly. While the transformations of the industrial revolution are often characterised through the idea of the separation of 'spheres' into distinct spaces for family and affective life (the domestic) on the one hand, and the places of productive labour (paid work), on the other, historians now recognise that this division was normative but invariably compromised in practice, because every home was somebody's workplace.[8] Artists' families were among those least likely to absolutely separate the domestic labour of the household from the productive labour of its commercial undertakings, because those occupied through self-employment – whether in the professions or in small business – often involved the combination of employment and domestic life in one building, where whole 'families', including servants, lodgers and children, lived out their daily lives.[9] While the places where artists were trained and where artworks were exhibited for sale were, like products manufactured in more obviously industrial ways, increasingly migrating to specialised commercially run exhibition spaces, the *production* of artworks remained spatially intertwined with domestic life.

An impressive home with a studio was a status symbol for artists and often provided a semi-public space which could accommodate both the production of artworks and *the social interactions* that were part and parcel of publicising and selling artistic outputs. From the middle of the nineteenth century, homes which were purpose-built or adapted for artists included studio space as part of the house or grounds. The house constructed for Valentine Prinsep in 1864 dedicated the first floor to the studio with the relatively modest domestic accommodation on the ground floor; that commissioned by the prominent Thornycraft family of sculptors and painters in the 1870s included ample domestic accommodation plus an elaborate network of studios dedicated to different kinds of art labour (a sculpture yard, a painting studio) including a gallery which sat between the reception rooms and the studios, providing a space for exhibiting work to visitors.[10] Linley Sambourne, who as a 'black and white' artist/illustrator earned a much more modest income than did a fine artist, set up his drawing board in the (remodelled) drawing room of his ordinary Kensington terraced townhouse, and frequently used both interior and exterior space as a photography studio for the production of reference works.[11] In these cases, the artists'

8 Moira Donald, 'Tranquil Havens? Critiquing the Idea of Home as the Middle-Class Sanctuary', in Inga Bryden and Janet Floyd, eds, *Domestic Space: Reading the Nineteenth-Century Interior*, Manchester University Press, Manchester, 1999, pp 103–120

9 The authoritative work on this topic is Leonore Davidoff and Catherine Hall, *Family Fortunes: Men and Women of the English Middle Class, 1780–1850*, University of Chicago, Chicago, 1987, see pp 364–374.

10 Giles Walkley, *Artists' Houses in London 1764–1914*, Scholar Press, Aldershot and Brookfield, Virginia, p 50, pp 67–68

11 Shirley Nicholson, *A Victorian Household*, Barrie & Jenkins, London, 1988, pp 14–15

homes reflect the principle of the period that dirty or noisy work was ideally conducted at a distance from social and domestic activities, but that professional or business activity was acceptable and indeed would take precedence in the allocation of the space commanded by any household.[12]

While the creation of substantive studio space within the homes of many of the artists in my sample provides a useful corrective to a model of a studio practice isolated from domestic life, in most cases the whole or primary space for artistic practice was allocated to the 'head of the household', usually a man. This allocation of space within a family property typically reiterated the privileging of adult males as economic subjects during the nineteenth century. The prioritisation of domestic space allocation tended to follow a hierarchy according to which status accrued to the oldest male in the household who was expected – and enabled – to pursue the family income. While men and women were understood to need segregated space within the home for activities ranging from personal washing to entertaining friends (even though some activities such as dining involved the whole family), the allocation of work and leisure space within the home privileged the male 'head of the household'. Only in some circumstances (most often widowhood) might women hold this status in their home. In consequence, women's entitlement to space for art work in the household would not be guaranteed, especially in households where there was competition for space.

The detailed evidence provided in architectural histories and biographical material bears out this proposition. In the large home built for the Thornycroft family, space for artistic practice was allocated to several members of the household. The primary studio was occupied by the family head, Thomas Thornycroft, and the plans for the home show the 'Miss Thornycrofts' Painting Studio' and a 'private studio' adjoining the Gallery which, according to Giles Walkley, was used by Mary Thornycroft.[13] Laura Alma-Tadema too had studio space in her home, although as Deborah Cherry notes, the small suite of rooms at her disposal did not compete with the palatial studio in the prized first-floor location, which was her husband's.[14] On the other hand, Louise Jopling's autobiography reveals a picture of studio access in which the designation of her husband as 'head of household' in the 1881 census is at odds with her role as a successful artist and family breadwinner. According to her autobiography, throughout the 1870s she had financial responsibility for her household including two young children, and she worked in a studio located in the front room of her rented houses; later, she had a studio built in the garden of a home in West London, which upon her marriage to Joseph Jopling she shared with her husband. When the studio-sharing arrangement proved impracticable, her husband moved his work to a rented studio in Trafalgar Square, leaving her as sole occupant of the garden studio; when they moved to Chelsea, around 1880, they built separate but adjacent studios in the garden.[15] The Joplings married after Louise had established her commercial career, and their marriage accommodated her continuing in that work: if Joseph Jopling was the nominal head of the household, Louise Jopling maintained a privileged position in respect of the organisation of family life to sustain her artistic practice.

12 Hannah Barker and Jane Hamlett, 'Living above the Shop: Home, Business, and Family in the English "Industrial Revolution"', *Journal of Family History*, vol 35, no 4, 2010, pp 311–328

13 Walkley, *Artists' Houses*, op cit, p 68

14 Deborah Cherry, *Painting Women: Victorian Women Artists*, Routledge, London, 1993, p 42

15 L J M Jopling-Rowe, *Twenty Years of My Life 1867–1887*, John Lane/the Bodley Head, London 1925, see pp 30, 51, p 125, pp 134–135

These examples show that during the period in which modern art was emerging, its products were typically, or at least ideally, made in a workshop arrangement that combined both domestic and working life. An artist's home, like that of a physician or a writer, was not necessarily separated from his or her place of work, and access to dedicated or private space for work within the home and its grounds seems to have been the ideal to which successful artists aspired. The allocation of that space normally followed a gendered order that prioritised access for the (prototypically male) head of the household, with adult children and spouses occupying secondary spaces for art working where they were available. Louise Jopling's household reversed the normal gendered order of this arrangement; but even in the case of such a role reversal, conventional patterns of gendered labour persisted in the undertaking of social duties associated with art practice.

Working at Home: Labouring for Art

The artist was not the only person in his or her household who contributed to the labours involved in art making, and members of artists' households made tangible contributions to artistic production in practical ways. Here, I am going to chiefly consider the social labour associated with the entrepreneurial side of artistic careers and, briefly, modelling, as two aspects of art production in which the artist relied on contributions from members of her or his household. These activities were typically performed in the service of the 'head of the household' and have largely remained invisible as elements of artistic practice because their contribution to the production of the artwork is not immediately evident in the end product. Current debates around the formations of art practice in the contemporary art world have focused on the central role occupied by the performance of social labour as a novel form of art practice. But in the nineteenth century, perhaps even more than now, the work of forging and maintaining social connections was essential for artists; this work relied in a material way on the participation of the artist's entire household.

The art market was being transformed by the emergence of the independent art dealer and the expansion of print culture in the third quarter of the nineteenth century, and artists were experimenting with varied ways of selling their work: traditional patronage which involved direct sales was still important as was selling to private collectors through an intermediary dealer; mounting paid exhibitions of spectacular paintings; and selling copyright for reproductions of popular works to print-sellers. Women were explicitly disadvantaged in these relationships since, as Maria Quirk has written, the expectation that women should exist in a state of economic dependence compromised women's negotiating position with some dealers and patrons.[16] This is not to say that women were innocent of commercial knowledge: Malcolm Warner, writing on the prominent artist John Everett Millais, can only reconstruct the commercial history of Millais's career because much of the detail was reported in letters to his wife, who would have been personally acquainted with Millais's patrons and business partners and was seemingly his greatest confidante in his business affairs.[17]

16 Maria Quirk, 'Portraiture and Patronage: Women, Reputation, and the Business of Selling Art, 1880–1914', *Visual Culture in Britain*, vol 17, no 2, 2016, pp 181–199

17 Malcolm Warner, 'Millais in the Marketplace: The Crisis of the Late 1850s', in Pamela Fletcher and Anne Helmreich, eds, *The Rise of the Modern Art Market in London, 1850–1939*, Manchester University Press, Manchester, 2011, pp 216–236

The rituals that governed social interactions among middle- and upper-ranking families in the nineteenth century were highly formalised, and the introduction of new acquaintances including patrons and other professional contacts was conducted on very prescriptive terms. Because a studio was often part of an artist's home, the reception of visitors involved professional entertaining. It was customary for artists to show works in their studio before sending them for a public exhibition in a gallery, and for this to have been a social occasion for the artists, their families and their visitors; Shirley Nicholson finds Marion Sambourne's diaries full of accounts of visits to artists' studios in the weeks leading up to the Royal Academy annual exhibition. The significance of this whirl of social activity was multiplied by being reported in the press. As Julie Codell has argued, the publication of artists' biographies and accounts of their studio homes was a key part of the diet of Victorian art journalism, and the publicity generated through these publications was, alongside the exhibition reviews, a tangible element of the emerging 'dealer-critic system'.[18] Transactions between dealers or collectors and artists may have taken place in private, but a wide range of social encounters, including those that involved the artist's home and family, were part of the wider context of those relationships.

The staging of all of these activities took place within a framework in which the adult women played a supporting role to the male head of the household in the conduct of his affairs. Women undertook to receive and entertain visitors to the home, and to pay the required reciprocal visits. The custom of the adult women of a family holding a day 'at home' to receive visitors was a routine mechanism for forging social bonds. The artist Anna Lea Merritt is now best remembered for this pithy reference to the importance of this work, which appeared in a 1900 essay counselling aspiring artists:

> The chief obstacle to a woman's success [as an artist] is that she can never have a wife. Just reflect what a wife does for an artist, Darns the stockings; Keeps his house; Writes his letters; Visits for his benefit; Wards off intruders; Is personally suggestive of beautiful pictures; Always an encouraging and partial critic. It is exceedingly difficult to be an artist without this time-saving help. A husband would be quite useless. He would never do any of these disagreeable things.[19]

Merritt's insight into the requirement for social labour (letter writing, visiting patrons, diverting unwelcome visitors) performed by the artist's wife, but not an artist's husband, suggests how unequal were the structures that organised the social labour necessary to the artist's career. It was not only the unequal balance of expectations between husband and wife that disadvantaged the woman artist; as Merritt observed in her autobiography, even fashion favoured the men:

> A portrait painter must associate with his patrons – unless he knows their ways and surroundings, it is not possible to give the right atmosphere. A man can do this at far less cost than a woman. His evening dress is far less expensive and it is possible at night to go in a bus, which is impossible for a lady's dinner dress.[20]

18 Julie F Codell, 'The Art Press and the Art Market: The Artist as "Economic Man"', in *The Rise of the Modern Art Market in London, 1850–1939*, ibid, pp 136–44

19 Anna Lea Merritt, 'A Letter to Artists: Especially Women Artists', reprinted from *Lippincott's Monthly Magazine* 65, March 1900, pp 463–469, together with her 1892 autobiography, *Love Locked Out: The Memoirs of Anna Lea Merritt with a Checklist of Her Works*, Boston Museum of Fine Arts, no date, p 237

20 Merritt, *Love Locked Out*, ibid, p 192

This startling observation suggests not only the extent to which entertaining and visiting was an integral part of the professional life of the artist, but how differently women were given access to that social scene.[21]

The importance of the wife (or adult daughter) in performing the supportive social activities that were required by the artist is also suggested by what happened in her absence: two male bachelor heads of household in my sample (Frederic Leighton and Valentine Prinsep) and, in 1881, the widowed artist Anna Lea Merritt, were all named as the head of a household that included a *butler*. It seems that Merritt, Leighton and Prinsep found in a butler the answer to the problem of not having a wife.[22] The designation of butler suggests the performance of *social* duties as opposed to manual ones (Millais retained a male footman, and the Thornycrofts a fourteen-year-old male 'studio sweeper'). The presence of any manservant in an urban household is now interpreted as a signifier of social status, but it is to be remarked that artists availed themselves of a butler in the absence of a literal or metaphorical 'wife'. This pattern indicates the importance of otherwise feminised *social* labour in the artist's household.

The complex interactions between class and gender that shaped the social engagements which sustained art practice are perhaps at their most poignant in relation to modelling. Studio models were still an integral part of the artistic process for artists whose work included figures, as many artworks then did. Employing workers paid on a daily basis as needed was the normal route through which an artist obtained a model, and models could enjoy the status of a skilled worker if they were a particular favourite. The work of models in the nineteenth century is a complicated and fascinating topic because of how the physically intimate relationship between model and artist frequently challenged the conventional spatial arrangements that divided professional from labourer, and women from men.[23] While the intimate relation between artist and *muse* is often regarded as a privileged relationship, it appears that family being called to the often menial work of modelling was commonplace: John Everett Millais, father to a large family, reportedly posed his children, wife and sister-in-law as models for his paintings; Nicholson recounts Edward Linley Sambourne directing children and visitors in the frequent production of reference photographs; and Julia Margaret Cameron's reliance on her domestic servants and family members as models for her photographs is well-documented[24] Modelling was clearly one area where the labour of the whole household could be put at the disposal of the artist in the development of their work, and no doubt one of the distinctive, intimate domestic chores associated with living in an artist's family.

Working at Home: Labouring for the Artist's Family

The work which artists' households devoted to the chores associated with artistic life, such as modelling, receiving and paying visits with other artists and patrons, as well as painting, drawing and building maquettes (or sweeping the studio after), took place alongside a huge amount of

21 See also Quick, 'Portraiture and Patronage', op cit, p 186.

22 Edward Burne Jones's household also shows a butler in 1891. His wife Georgiana was by then more often living at their house in Rottingdean, near Brighton, than in London.

23 Martin Postle, 'Behind the Screen: The Studio Model', Martin Postle and William Vaughan, eds, *The Artist's Model from Etty to Spencer*, Merrell Holberton, London, 1999, pp 55–79. See also Alison Smith, *The Victorian Nude: Sexuality, Morality and Art*, Manchester University Press, Manchester, 1996, pp 196–202.

24 On Sambourne's photography practice see footnote 10. Cameron's practice of posing her grandchildren and servants for the allegorical and biblical subjects for which she was most famous is documented in every discussion of her work, including a recent exhibition catalogue, Marta Weiss, *Julia Margaret Cameron: Photographs to Electrify You with Delight and Startle the World*, London and Tonbridge, MACK in association with the Victoria and Albert Museum, 2015.

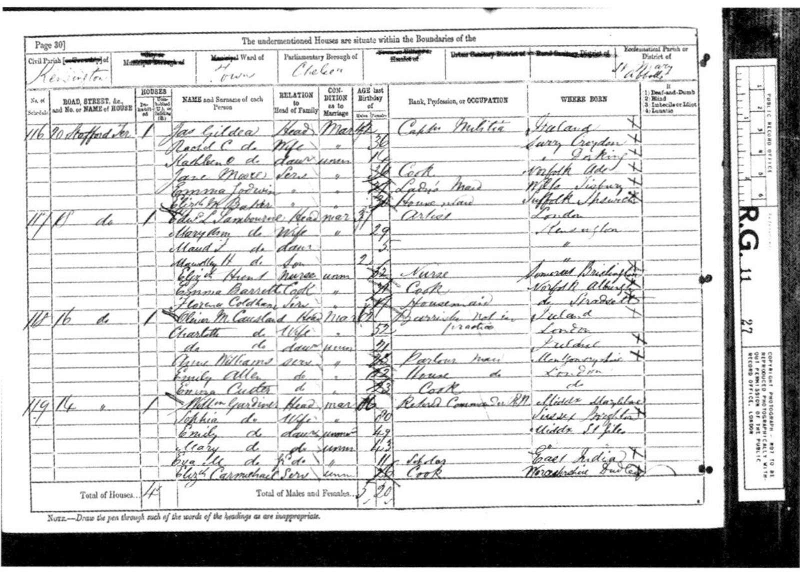

Census record for Linley Sambourne's household, 1881, copyright The National Archives

domestic labour that was essential for the functioning of the household. While the work of maintaining the home and the people who lived in it was of a generic sort which all families required, the census records make clear that artist families relied on an extensive network of paid and unpaid labour to perform essential household work: in contrast to the art labour to which men had privileged access, this domestic work was primarily allocated to women. That women were given the job of maintaining the home followed, as Leonore Davidoff discusses in her study of housekeeping as paid work, from

> the division of the sexes and the creation of a special domestic sphere with higher standards of cooking, cleaning, laundry and mending, [which] promoted male expectations of being 'serviced' by women, whether wives or daughters, employees or neighbours.[25]

The utilities in nineteenth-century homes were typically still supplied room by room, and materials such as coal, candles and water had to be carried in and out as they were used. Sewing machines and ready-to-wear manufactured clothing were only invented around this time, and without washing machines, the maintenance as well as the production of clothing was burdensome. The tasks were many and the standard of execution mattered: the cleanliness of homes and family members were essential to social success.[26] The use of paid domestic labour to perform the work was extensive.[27] Across the United Kingdom, the number of people whose formal employment was domestic work constituted an army: Moira Donald suggests that ten to thirteen per cent of the working population was employed in domestic service in the second half of the nineteenth century, more than was employed in factories.[28]

The census records allow us to ascertain the number of domestic workers resident with the families of artists, and usually identify

25 Leonore Davidoff, 'The Separation of Home and Work? Landladies and Lodgers in Nineteenth- and Twentieth-Century England', in Sandra Burman, ed, *Fit Work for Women*, Australian National University Press, Canberra, 1979, p 76

26 Davidoff and Hall, *Family Fortunes*, op cit, pp 380–388

27 Edward Higgs, 'Domestic Servants and Households in Victorian England', *Social History*, vol 8, no 2, 1983, pp 201–10

28 Donald, 'Tranquil Havens?', op cit, p 104

(through employment titles) the kind of work that servants were assigned to perform. The summary of the census records indicates the number and duties of servants listed on the household census form, and codes them red/blue for female/male in order to allow a visual indication of the prominence of female servants. A common pattern was to have at least two women servants (cook, housemaid); and sometimes further women servants and a childminder or 'nurse' for small children. Male servants are much rarer; that artists' homes serviced their domestic needs with predominantly female servants is consistent with patterns of labour in urban households from the late eighteenth century onwards.[29] The employment of domestic servants itself created additional work for the family in the management of the servants; this task normally fell to the head of household's nearest female relative (wife, mother or daughter). Nineteenth-century families were concerned to regulate the standards of performance and behaviour of their domestic staff, seen as reflecting on themselves, and the complaints of middle-class women about the burdens of managing servants are extensive.[30]

One way of rationalising the quantity of labour required to maintain a household was by adults sharing an existing home, an arrangement which increased the work of the women responsible for maintaining it.[31] In working-class South London, the photographer William Strudwick and his wife took in a boarder, whose contribution to the net family income probably offset the cost of the single, young female servant who lived in the house; more genteel versions of the same principle pertained where bachelor family members resided with their relatives' established families. In the Summary of the Census Record, we find Edward Burne-Jones's nephew, John Everett Millais's brother, and Luke Fildes's brother-in-law Henry Woods all affording themselves of the comforts of their married relatives' family homes. In the case of Henry Woods and Millais's brother, the arrangement was in place on two census dates, suggesting that it was permanent. In addition to four instances of male family members sharing the houses of their relatives, we find adult children, male and female, living with their parents, and in 1871 we find Louise Jopling (then Romer) residing in the very large household of a married couple described in her autobiography as 'kind friends', though her two small children and their nurse Emily Baldwin were then 'boarded out' with Emily's aunt and uncle in rural Kent.[32]

That Louise Jopling would not have wanted to impose on her friends by bringing her two children and their nurse to a house which already included nine children of various ages and six servants is not surprising. Although by her own account she was very attached to her children, they also often lived apart from her. Young children require attention from adults which prevents the latter from engaging in other pursuits: in the families in my sample, this was compensated for by recruiting additional paid domestic help. All the families with children under five years of age – the Williams family, the Oulesses, the Sambournes, the Millaises, Louise Rowe/Jopling, and the Allinghams – employed at least one nurse. As the Fildes family grew from one young child in 1881 to four in 1891, their household grew to include an 'undernurse' as well as an 'underhousemaid'. In the 1891 census records, John Millais's household included both nurse and undernurse, presumably the carers for two grandchildren also recorded at the address on census day. In 1881,

29 Male servants appear in six of the census records studied here. I have excluded W Reynolds living with the Joplings in 1891 and listed as a stonemason; he was probably the husband or brother of their cook Emma Reynolds and not working for the family. The gender of those in domestic service has been widely debated by historians, especially of the eighteenth century. For a discussion of the issues and a summary of some of the data, see Leonard Schwarz, 'English Servants and Their Employers during the Eighteenth and Nineteenth Centuries', *Economic History Review*, vol 52, no 2, 1999, pp 236–256.

30 See Barker and Hamlett, 'Living above the Shop', op cit, for a detailed discussion of the moral governance of the household. Hamlett, *Material Relations*, op cit, contains a general discussion of social relations between servants and employers pp 55–59; Nicholson in *A Victorian Household*, op cit, writes about Marion Sambourne's trials with servants on pp 65–66.

31 Davidoff, 'The Separation of Home and Work?', op cit, pp 83–89

32 Percival and Hilda Romer are listed on the 1871 census record for the Sevenoaks Road (Kent) household of Thomas Usherwood, together with their nurse, his niece, Emily Baldwin. The Usherwood household also included Thomas's wife, Susanna, and their three daughters, but no servants.

Valentine Prinsep employed a married couple as butler and housekeeper; they had three children under five years of age, and in turn employed a nursery maid. Working mothers, regardless of the nature of their employment, needed help with their children.

The nurse would normally cohabit with young children in a designated part of the house (the nursery) away from the adult rooms: a typical arrangement was to have the nursery at the top of the house, with the family's adult bedrooms and the living and working rooms on the lower floors.[33] This separation of young children from adults within the home was sometimes replicated out of it. The Sambournes, who would not have considered themselves to be very well off, rented separate accommodation for their children and nurse during family holidays at Marion Sambourne's parents' second home in the Kent countryside, so that the children could visit or be visited while the adults were left to enjoy their own company.[34] Children of school age may have been educated away from their parents' home. Louise Jopling's autobiography records that her first income from her painting was immediately spent on 'a little daily nursemaid to take my two little boys out walking, and... the necessary materials for study'.[35] The demands of childcare were the first to be given over to paid domestic labour.

While artist families routinely employed domestic help to care for their children, and normally had between two and six additional domestic servants living in, in order to attend to housework and meal preparation, two households in my sample recorded no domestic servants on the day of the census. These are Rebecca Solomon's residence at Great Tichfield Street in 1881, a flat in a building occupied by working-class tenants (other heads of household include a master builder, a courier and a general labourer). The other is the Chelsea home of French painter Adrian Coiffier and his wife and teenage daughter in the same year. Either case may reflect happenstance of the servants being away from home on census day, but we should take seriously the possibility that these families availed themselves of daily (rather than residential) domestic help, or none at all: none of the other households in Rebecca Solomon's building recorded any servants living in. These two are exceptionally small households in the sample, and it was probably a complex relationship between gender, class and poverty that led to the absence of servants in the Solomon and Coiffier households.[36] In the absence of sufficient income to retain a servant, the adult women of the family were evidently tasked with undertaking the domestic work of the household.

Although these arrangements were not exclusive to artist families, artist households appear to have conformed to a pattern in which the adult women – regardless of their other commitments – were expected to devote daily more of their time than adult men to the needs of the household. This is suggested by all the evidence of women's contribution to the domestic establishment, but also by some simple comparisons: the two single male householders in my sample (Prinsep and Leighton) maintained the same numbers of resident servants as did the Thornycroft household of five adults, or that of Linley Sambourne, his wife and two small children. Who, then, must have provided the extra work involved in caring for a larger family? Families in which both the head of the household

33 Jane Hamlett, *Domestic Interiors and Middle-Class Families in England, 1850–1910*, Manchester University Press, Manchester, 2010, pp 111–120

34 Nicholson, *A Victorian Household*, op cit, p 30

35 Jopling-Rowe, *Twenty Years of My Life*, op cit, p 10

36 Little is known of Rebecca Solomon's life at this time, although her circumstances, following the death of her brother Abraham in 1862 and the imprisonment of her brother Simeon in 1873, seem to have been in decline. A serviceable biography of Rebecca Solomon and her family can be consulted at the Simeon Solomon Research Archive, http://www.simeonsolomon.com/rebecca-solomon-biography.html, accessed 28 February 2017.

and his wife were practising artists (the Thornycrofts, Allinghams, the Burne Joneses, Alma-Tademas, and the Joplings) did not employ larger domestic staffs than the households in which the wife was not listed as having employment; in fact, none of the two-artist families had more than three servants. Even in the absence of the labour of childcare (which was routinely allocated to servants) the conclusion that the women artists were normally bearing what is now known as the 'double burden' of paid work and domestic labour is indicated.[37]

Conclusions:
The Domestic Life of Modern Artists

Nineteenth-century artist families seem to have organised their overall labour according to typical patterns in which the greatest burden of the work of the household clearly fell on women. Most of the domestic labour involved in the care of infants, cooking and cleaning was devolved to paid female household labour; the census data shows that the employment of female domestic help by artist families was commonplace, although the number and kind of servants varied according to a family's income, composition and status. Men by default took the role of the 'head of the household', which was associated both with commercial activity and with the command of the household resources. While women could access the resources needed to practise as artists, it seems that they rarely inhabited the role of 'head of the household', which would have prioritised their art production: the exceptions in my sample are Jopling (who was separated/widowed then remarried), Anna Lea Merritt (who was widowed after a brief marriage) and Rebecca Solomon (unmarried). Within a marriage it was usual for the role 'head of household' to default to the man; but women sustained artistic production by contributing to the necessary (unwaged) social labour that supported a commercial career, as well as undertaking ancillary production in the form of journalism and criticism.[38] That all of that work is normally considered simply as 'service' or 'context' for the production of art proper is characteristic of a commercialised art world that fetishises the work of art as a (saleable) commodity.

So accustomed are we to proclaiming the autonomy of the artwork that the significance of domestic and social labour to sustaining the artist and his or her practice has largely gone unremarked in our histories, at least since the emerging market for 'modern art' proposed the alienation of the artist and *his* art from routine social life. The primary aim of Harrison and Cynthia White's account of the formation of the 'dealer-critic system' in the third quarter of the nineteenth century was to explain the aesthetic changes associated with modern art in relation to the changing structures of the art market; but the 'dealer-critic system' that they described also hints at why the family has been sidelined from accounts of art histories. Inspired in part by the statements of Daniel-Henry Kahnweiler, the prominent twentieth-century art dealer, the Whites suggested that '[t]he speculative motive reinforced the concern of the dealer with the total career of the painter',[39] and this

37 The Allinghams and the Thornycrofts are households where both husband and wife are listed as practising artists. While each of these households had three servants, the Sambourne, the Fildes and the Ouless families, in which only the husband is listed as having employment, had three or more servants.

38 Hilary Fraser, *Women Writing Art History in the Nineteenth Century: Looking like a Woman*, Cambridge University Press, Cambridge, 2014; Meaghan Clarke, *Critical Voices: Women and Art Criticism in Britain, 1880–1905*, Ashgate Press, Aldershot, 2005

39 Harrison White and Cynthia White, *Canvases and Careers: Institutional Change in the French Painting World*, John Wiley and Sons, London, New York and Sydney, 1965, pp 94–99

40 See for example Colleen Denney and Susan Casteras, eds, *The Grosvenor Gallery: A Palace of Art in Victorian England*, Yale University Press, London and New Haven, 1996; and, on France, Patricia Mainardi, *The End of the Salon: Art and the State in the Early Third Republic*, Cambridge University Press, Cambridge, 1993.

41 See Quick, 'Portraiture and Patronage', op cit, for example; Maura Reilly included women's secondary market earnings as well as other measures of commercial success in 'Taking the Measure of Sexism: Facts, Figures, and Fixes', *Artnews*, June 2015, http://www.artnews.com/2015/05/26/taking-the-measure-of-sexism-facts-figures-and-fixes/, accessed 7 June 2017.

42 Silvia Federici, *Caliban and the Witch: Women, the Body and Primitive Accumulation*, Autonomedia, New York, 2004

was most marketable when ornamented with a reputation for genius. It is one of the hallmarks of genius that it operates independently or in opposition to the ordinary, the routine, and particularly to the feminised sphere of the domestic.

The valorisation of the eccentric genius notwithstanding, women arguably fared better in the new patterns of exhibition making which emerged around 1875 than in the system of the Academies which it displaced, because commercial exhibitions were unregulated by formal structures of membership, and often integrated fine art with decorative concerns in a way that was more hospitable to women artists.[40] Establishing women's participation in the art market is the subject of a growing interest; but whatever we discover about women artists' place in the art market, its explanatory significance can only be developed in relation to an understanding of the complementary context of women's (and men's) participation in domestic work.[41] The significance of the division of 'public' (as in trade, business and politics) from 'private' life (as in the concerns of the nuclear family) alongside the emergence of modern capitalism in nineteenth-century Europe is well known and, as Silvia Federici's work reminds us, was an essential feature of the structuring of the industrial economy.[42]

A key suggestion that arises from this study is that the role and status of women in the history of art since the nineteenth century is aligned to the gendered structure of a capitalist economy which assigns to women undervalued (low-paid or unpaid) domestic labour; this structure is *continuous* rather than discontinuous, extending from at least the nineteenth to the twenty-first century. The fractures in art's history that are marked by the terminology of movements and periods underplays the importance of the more entrenched division of domestic from artistic labour that underpins the production of artworks and access to the professional identity of the artist in Euro-American cultures. Understanding the extent to which the work, as in the *labour*, of art is structured by a long-term, pervasive gendered division of labour invites a shift in art historical investigation away from the fetishised commodity (as the saleable output of artistic labour) and onto a complex economy of production found to be, perhaps remarkably, very close to home.

THIRD TEXT

CRITICAL PERSPECTIVES ON CONTEMPORARY ART AND CULTURE

Announcing our forthcoming Special Issue for January 2018

Ethico-Aesthetic Repairs

Guest Edited by Theo Reeves-Evison and Mark Rainey

Number 150, volume 32, issue 1, January 2018

The concept of 'repair' as it intersects with visual and material culture is the focus of this special issue. While 'repair' often suggests the restoration of a broken or damaged object, the majority of articles in this issue describe ways of modifying or mending that render objects and ideas operative in new ways. In this respect, repair is not a static 'fix' to a breakage or problem, but rather invokes the potential for modification, transformation and creative addition. This approach is born out across domains ranging from photography and informal economies to consumer electronics and breast reconstruction technologies. What emerges is not only a set of new understandings of the word 'repair' and the practices it designates, but a more fundamental ethico-aesthetic attitude that is weighted towards the future through movements of fracture and reweaving, breakage and re-assembly and the re-making and undoing of material and symbolic possibilities.

http://www.thirdtext.org
article downloads and subscriptions:
http://www.tandfonline.com/pricing/journal/ctte20
subscribe to Third Text table of contents alerting services:
http://www.informaworld.com/alerting
subscribe to eUpdates and e-newsletter:
http://www.tandf.co.uk/journals/eupdates.asp
Sales of single issues and Third Text Publications titles:
http://www.centralbooks.com/

Third Text, 2017
Vol. 31, No. 1, 31–48, https://doi.org/10.1080/09528822.2017.1362835

'Under Trying Domestic Circumstances'

Reproducing Settler Identity and Resisting Indigenous Dispossession in Twentieth-Century Saskatchewan

Manon Gaudet

… I had to write the story under trying domestic circumstances. At the lake, I always kept an Indian girl to help look after the children (Indian girls are perfect with children), but like all girls from the Reserves, she would leave, when the notion took her – and at the most awkward times – to go off with her people to a Pow-Wow or Municipal Fair, returning when the fun was over.[1]

On 21 August 1939, Mary Weekes (1884–1980) – an author and collector of Plains Indigenous material culture – recounted to her publisher the 'trying domestic circumstances' under which she wrote her best-known book, *The Last Buffalo Hunter*, the autobiographical story of an elderly Métis hunter named Norbert Welsh. Integral to Weekes's self-positioning as an author were the obstacles posed by her 'three vigorous children' – the youngest insistent on unlatching car doors on the eleven-mile drive from the family cottage to Welsh's home and the oldest all too willing to deliver disruptive punishments to his younger brother while their mother worked at eking out memories from an aged mind.[2] Exacerbating Weekes's challenging domestic circumstances was, as she suggests in the above excerpt, the lack of reliable domestic help that a white woman such as herself might expect. Weekes's domestic circumstances became trying when, according to early twentieth-century gendered distributions of labour, the care of her three children fell solely to her, and not her husband; and when her race and class failed to deliver on their associated advantages.

The conventional distribution of labour between Weekes and her husband ignored the unconventional extent to which Weekes pursued a career as a professional author. When domestic help was available,

1 Mary Weekes to Miss McEwen, 21 August 1939, Mary Weekes fonds, F106, V.14a, Provincial Archives of Saskatchewan (SAB)

2 Ibid

Photographer unknown, Mary Weekes in a field, 1938, reproduction courtesy of the Provincial Archives of Saskatchewan, copyright: courtesy Kathy Weekes Southee

3 Mary Weekes, feature biography, *Saturday Night*, undated, F106, SB 2, 1, SAB

4 Anne McClintock, *Imperial Leather: Race, Gender and Sexuality in the Colonial Contest*, Routledge, New York, 1995, p 6

5 Barbara Laslett and Johanna Brenner, 'Gender and Social Reproduction: Historical Perspectives', *Annual Review of Sociology* 15, 1989, pp 381–404, p 383

6 At the time of Confederation in 1867, the British government gave the Canadian federal government responsibility for administering policies regarding First Nations, Métis, and Inuit peoples under the Department of Indian Affairs (now Indigenous and Northern Affairs Canada). The Indian Act of 1876 consolidated previous colonial legislation encompassing land, status, governance, and education rights that shared a common purpose of eliminating Indigenous culture in favour of assimilation into the dominant Euro-Christian Canadian society. The Indian Act was a 'piece of colonial legislation by which, in the name of "protection", one group of people ruled and controlled another'. For a more detailed history of the Indian Act's role in the assault on Indigenous identity, see The Truth and Reconciliation Commission of Canada, *Honouring the Truth, Reconciling for the Future: Summary of the Final Report of the Truth and Reconciliation Commission of Canada*, Library and Archives Canada, Ottawa, 2015, pp 53–55.

7 Katherine Pettipas, *Severing the Ties that Bind: Government Repression of Indigenous Religious Ceremonies on the*

Weekes still recalled returning home to an 'exacting family', who complained, 'Mother, how can you waste your time so?'[3] What Weekes perceived as her family's apparent lack of respect and support for her work demonstrates the subordinate position of women's waged, or in this case unwaged, labour outside of the home. Weekes was nonetheless unapologetically ambitious in pursuit of her career as a professional author and seamlessly occupied what Anne McClintock identifies as the white woman's 'ambiguously complicit' position in colonialism, wherein she was both 'colonizer… and colonized, privileged and restricted, acted upon and acting'.[4]

Weekes was disadvantaged by gender but advantaged by race – an advantage she took in the hiring of young Indigenous women, most of whom were trained at the local Lebret Residential School, to help with domestic tasks while she pursued her interests outside the home. Weekes's dismissive portrayal of her 'Indian girl' helper as fickle for prioritising participation in a powwow over the care of her children further demonstrates the stratified nature of women's labour according to hierarchies of race as well as gender. The circumstances of her helper's absence tell of the different types of labour encompassed by some feminist scholars under the term social reproduction. Barbara Laslett and Johanna Brenner define social reproduction as the labours necessary 'to maintain existing life and reproduce the next generation', by which they mean not only procreative or demographic production, nor, as in some Marxist theory, the perpetuation of modes of production and class inequality.[5] Rather, by social reproduction they (and in turn, I) also mean the perpetuation of social relationships and traditions from one generation to the next within a given culture.

A powwow, for example, is a gathering of groups of Plains Indigenous people for the purposes of singing, dancing, celebration, socialisation and the perpetuation of cultural beliefs and practices – all key aspects involved in the intergenerational maintenance and reproduction of culturally specific ways of living. It is significant that at the time of Weekes's writing, Indigenous cultural practices including powwows and other ceremonies were considered hindrances to the Canadian government's assimilation project and required special approval from the Department of Indian Affairs.[6] The powwow to which Weekes dismissively refers was thus no doubt a rare occurrence.[7] Also part of the government's assimilation project was the training of Indigenous women to be domestic workers for women like Weekes. The Truth and Reconciliation Commission of Canada has identified 139 residential schools across the country which were

> created for the purpose of separating Aboriginal children from their families, in order to minimize and weaken family ties and cultural linkages, and to indoctrinate children into a new culture – the culture of the legally dominant Euro-Christian Canadian society.[8]

In other words, they intended to disrupt Indigenous traditions of social reproduction and the transmission of culture.

The simple argument to be made is familiar to third-wave feminists who critique their predecessors for treating women's rights as a racial category that privileged white women at the expense of those of other races. But, by considering Weekes's activities through the lens of social

```
Mary Weekes Collection of Beadwork
___________________________________________
4 Firebags                         a/c $20 ea         $ 80.00
21 prs moccasins                   a/c    $20 pr      $420.00
1 Floral handbag  - solid beaded                       15.00
1 Geometric design-  "        "                        20.00
3 Breastpieces        "        "   a/c    $30 ea       90.00
1 decorated parchment box                              15.00
1 Beaded vest                                          45.00
1 dancing fan                                          10.00
1 boys' beaded deerskin suit                           25.00
3 beaded clubs                     a/c    $15.00 ea    45.00
1 roach                                                 5.00
1 pr. deerskin leggings                                 5.00
1 solid beaded leggings(short)                         20.00
1 Indian rattle                                         6.00
1 knife sheath                                          6.00
1 solid beaded firebag with quill decoration           35.00
23  "        " belts               a/c $15 ea         345.00
4 Fine porcupine quill belts  ($60 the 4)              60.00
2 small wall pouches               a/c $5 ea           10.00
4 pr. solid beaded cuffs           a/c $10.00          40.00
1 Eskimo necklace                                      15.00
10 Beaded strips - various designs  a/c  $2.00 ea      20.00
1 coplete set beaded strips(6 pieces) for costume      40.00
8 Algonquian pieces                a/c $5              40.00
1 Beaded saddle                                        50.00
1 Crayon portrait Poundmaker                           30.00
1 Indian Head - Rockthunder, by Metzger - in frame     75.00
3 Navajo rugs - $25; 6; 5                              36.00
3 baskets - 2 Nootka, 1 Micmac                          4.00
1 Elaborate shelf piece worked in quills               50.00
A number of Indian photographs            (no charge)
A number of historical H.B. Company calendars    "
1 Navajo ring                                           5.00
1 shell earrings                                        4.00
1 pr. moccasins to be reapired                         10.00
140 pieces - each pair of moccasins and cuffs counting as 2 pieces

All museum pieces
```

'Mary Weekes Collection of Beadwork', 1947, typed list. Mary Weekes to Fred Bard, 25 September, 1947, photo: courtesy The Government of Saskatchewan, represented by the Royal Saskatchewan Museum, all rights reserved

Prairies, University of Manitoba Press, Winnipeg, 1994

8 The Truth and Reconciliation Commission of Canada, *Honouring the Truth, Reconciling for the Future: Summary of the Final Report of the Truth and Reconciliation Commission of Canada*, preface, p v

9 Patrick Wolfe, 'Settler Colonialism and the Elimination of the Native', *Journal of Genocide*

reproduction, I argue that we can more accurately capture what it means to be '*ambiguously* complicit' in colonialism or, more specifically, settler-colonialism. As Patrick Wolfe argues, the settler's 'invasion [of a territory] is a structure not an event' and 'settler-colonizers come to stay'.[9] The settler is therefore interested in reproducing his or her identity as native to the territory so as to claim a right to that land and, in the process, displace the right of Indigenous peoples.[10] The question I address is one of different types of reproduction. What was Mary Weekes reproducing through her writing and collecting activities? What was the residential school system reproducing? What about the Indigenous women who worked for Weekes? And the women whose beadwork she avidly collected? Were the intended products of these different reproductive labours mutually exclusive? If not, where are the overlaps, the sites of resistance and the ambiguities?

Research, vol 8, no 4, December 2006, pp 387–409, p 388

10 I use the term 'settler' after Patrick Wolfe, who observes the systematic and ongoing nature of settler-colonialism. I apply the term to descendants of original European settlers – people like Mary Weekes and myself – who continue to benefit from settler-colonialism's systematic stratification of rights and privileges. I use the term 'Indigenous' to be inclusive of the diverse and unique First Nations, Inuit and Métis peoples about whom Mary Weekes wrote, using specific group names where possible. When citing historical sources I retain use of the term 'Indian' to reflect its historical and semantic usage, although it is now largely considered outmoded and derogatory in Canada.

11 Mary Weekes, 'The Wedding Dress', *Prairie Sketchbook*, unpublished manuscript, c mid-1930s, Mary Weekes fonds, F106, I.143, SAB

12 Weekes was the daughter of Eliza Jane Reddy and the shipbuilder David Girroir.

13 Damian Skinner, 'Settler-Colonial Art History: A Proposition in Two Parts', *Journal of Canadian Art History*, vol 35, no 1, 2014, pp 131–145, p 139

This article is concerned with two types of labouring female bodies – non-Indigenous and Indigenous – and two aspects of social reproduction, one consisting of the manual tasks of cooking, cleaning and child-rearing, and the other consisting of the transmission of culture and social relationships. It is about the relationship between Mary Weekes and the Indigenous women on whose domestic labour she relied, but whose beadwork, culture and friendship she also immensely valued. It focuses on the exchange of different 'labours of love' that took place in the presence of radically asymmetrical power relations. I aim to understand how Weekes's 'trying domestic circumstances' offer insight into her reproduction of settler identity in twentieth-century Saskatchewan and her simultaneous and contradictory participation in the resistance of Indigenous dispossession.

Composing, Collecting and Choosing a Settler Identity

Food, shelter, the return of their hunting grounds was all these poor people wanted. These things had been wrest from them by the pioneers – by herself![11]

Save for those settlers who boarded boats in European harbours destined for North American shores, or those immigrating to Canada today, few of us *chose* to be settlers. Born in Tracadie, Nova Scotia in 1884, Mary Weekes (née Mary Loretto Girroir) had little say in whether she would occupy land that had been forcibly removed from its Indigenous forebears.[12] And yet, through her writing and collecting activities Weekes precociously chose to self-identify as a settler – one of the most important symbolic and significant choices that Canadians continue to struggle with today. In arguing for Mary Weekes's self-conscious settler-subjectivity, I do not ignore the complexities explored by Damian Skinner and other scholars, who observe the double identity of the settler as both coloniser (of the new world and its inhabitants) and colonised (by the old world). Adding the third layer of a gendered identity to Skinner's discussion of the settler 'who [just as much as the Indigenous person] mimics and negotiates unstable, hybrid, identities', I seek to explore the identity negotiations of a figure whose collecting activities and accompanying prose offer unique insight into the ambivalent self-definition of a twentieth-century settler woman.[13] Much of Weekes's writing is semi-autobiographical, featuring settler women strikingly similar to herself. It is a strategy that makes her quote, above, significant for its self-conscious recognition of her collusion in colonial violence. Recognition of such complicity, and her identity as a settler, did not, however, prevent Weekes's willing participation in systems of colonialism advantageous to her own interests – such as residential schools. Weekes was, as many of us still are, ambiguously complicit in both systems of colonial violence *and* Indigenous resistance.

While born unwittingly as a settler to North America, Weekes willingly moved around the territory. Her parents separated sometime around 1893 in light of her father's alcoholism and loss of livelihood. Financially insecure, Mary's mother arranged for relatives to care for her five children while she relocated to Boston.[14] A young Mary was left in Tracadie under the care of prosperous relatives of her father, overseen by her maternal grandparents. Her mother had arranged for her accommodation and care in exchange for extra household duties, but insisted that Mary also attend school, where she excelled. After high school, Mary rejoined her mother and three sisters in Boston. There she completed her training as a registered nurse and went on to serve as Superintendent of Nursing at the Boston Psychopathic Hospital for four years.[15] In 1914, she married Melville Bell Weekes, a thirty-eight-year-old land surveyor from Regina, Saskatchewan.[16] With her new husband and a new surname, Mary Weekes relocated to Regina, where she gave birth to three sons – Henry (1915), John (1919) and Richard (1925). Despite settling into motherhood and domestic life, Weekes insisted on maintaining a professional identity by self-identifying as a nurse on the 1916 census although she never practised in Canada.[17] She further pursued her identity outside the home as a member of the Local Council of Women and as an author and collector.

By the end of her life, Weekes had published approximately 140 short stories and articles (of the over 170 that she wrote), eleven books, and was included in ten different anthologies. Her foremost literary inspiration was the history and traditions of Saskatchewan's Indigenous peoples. The monikers 'Lady Buffalo' and 'Lady of the White Wampum', bestowed upon Weekes by her friend and fellow author Ethel Kirk Grayson, demonstrate the extent to which she became associated with Indigenous subject matter.[18] Weekes also acquired a 140-piece collection consisting primarily of beaded work, including: twenty-three beaded belts, twenty-one pairs of moccasins, ten beaded strips, four firebags (Indigenous crafted bag, used to carry fire-starting flints), three beaded clubs, two handbags, and one beaded saddle, among other items.[19] According to Weekes's own records, the pieces originate from eight nearby communities, with a particular strength in materials from the Muscowpetung (Saulteaux) and Standing Buffalo (Dakota) communities.[20] Exceptions include a selection of Northwest Coast and Mi'kmaq baskets, Navajo blankets and jewellery, and a selection of Algonquin artifacts. The majority of the collection consists of pieces produced in the first half of the twentieth century (although Weekes had a fascination with what she called, but failed to precisely date, 'antique Indian beadwork').[21] Weekes's records indicate that her judiciously selected pieces entered several prominent Canadian museum collections.[22] She also frequently exhibited her collection to local clubs and at venues such as the Canadian Handicrafts Guild's 1946–1947 *Indian Arts of Canada* exhibition in Montréal. In 1947, the Provincial Museum of Natural History in Regina (now the Royal Saskatchewan Museum) purchased her collection for $1,000.[23]

As is the case with much of Weekes's life, her collecting activities are contradictory and would appear to be at odds with what I argue was her self-conscious position as a settler. Collecting in settler-colonial contexts is widely understood as a strategy of dispossession and an attempt to salvage the remains of a perceived naturally disappearing culture (whose disappearance was in fact federally enforced). Additionally, settler-colonial collecting is itself a socially reproductive process that seeks to reproduce the settler as native to the territory and capture the

14 It is unclear whether Jane Reddy brought any of her children – Mary (Weekes), Winifred (Cregg), Ida, Beatrice and John – with her to Boston or if all were placed in the care of relatives. Kathy Weekes Southee, interview with the author, 17 November 2015.

15 Ibid

16 The origin of Mary and Melville Bell Weekes's acquaintance is unclear; whether at a tuberculosis institution where Melville's first wife was being treated in 1874 (unlikely) or while Melville was vacationing in Boston. Kathy Weekes Southee, interview with the author, op cit; Catherine Higgins, interview with the author, 3 December 2015.

17 Government of Canada, *1916 Census of Manitoba, Saskatchewan and Alberta*, District 27, S District 3, Enumeration District 4, p 22. Weekes further maintained her identity as a nurse by establishing a branch of the Victorian Order of Nurses in 1929 and volunteering her services to the American Red Cross at age fifty-five during World War II (they were never needed). Annotation made by Weekes on 'Annual Meeting of the VON', *Leader Post*, 11 February 1965, Mary Weekes fonds, F106, SB 3, p 71, SAB; Weekes to American Red Cross, undated, Mary Weekes fonds, R-395, 4a, SAB.

18 EKG (Ethel Kirk Grayson) to Lady Buffalo, no date, Mary Weekes fonds, F106, XII.9k, SAB; EKG to Lady of the White Wampum, no date, Mary Weekes fonds, R-395, VII.8, SAB

19 Three pieces have been designated by museum officials as sacred and are cared for accordingly. While some of what Weekes collected was likely made for sale or trade, she was preoccupied with a type of intimacy she considered integral to

authenticity. For example, she writes: 'When an Indian woman fashions garments for her husband or sons and embroiders designs on them in beads or quills she blends the colors with all the artistic skill of her race and in her work expresses all the love of her heart. But when she makes moccasins to sell to the White Campers she weaves no sentiment or tenderness into her work, consequentially it lacks that true Indian feeling.' See Weekes, 'Antique Indian Beadwork', *Canadian Home and Gardens*, December 1927, republished in the *Nurses Alumni Quarterly*, April 1928, Mary Weekes fonds, F106, I.1 and F106, SB 3, p 16, SAB.

social reproductive processes of Indigenous peoples in an ethnographic present best viewed and understood through a glass vitrine.[24] While I do not discount the extent to which cultural dispossession characterised Weekes's collecting practice, I argue that the circumstances of Weekes's collecting – viewed through the lens of social reproduction – indicated that Weekes was possessed of a tentative identification as a settler-ally who saw her collecting and writing practices insisting upon the perseverance rather than preservation of Indigenous culture. The cottage where Weekes acquired most of her collection was an important facilitator in defining her unique perspective.

Writing in 1939 to Alice MacKay, acting editor of the Hudson's Bay Company magazine *The Beaver*, Weekes reflected on the importance of her cottage and the social ritual of tea in producing relationships with Indigenous peoples from communities surrounding her cottage:

> …at my cottage there is always tea and cakes… from the time my smoke splits the April air I am 'at home' to my Indian friends. My cottage on the Qu'Appelle Lakes lies between two Indian Reservations – a Cree and a Sioux. It is twenty years now since I first began to 'put the kettle on'.[25]

According to a chronological narrative based on Weekes's acquisition records, she first purchased pieces of Indigenous material culture at Glacier National Park, Montana in 1914 and at the Panama-Pacific

Artist unknown, *Many Maples* (the Weekes family cottage), date unknown, painting (detail), photo, Manon Gaudet with the permission of Vicky Weekes

Beaded belts from the Weekes Collection, date unknown, reproduction: courtesy the Royal Saskatchewan Museum, all rights reserved

20 These communities include: The Piapot First Nations, Muscowpetung Saulteaux First Nation, Standing Buffalo Dakota First Nation, Okanese First Nation, Little Black Bear First Nation, Star Blanket Cree Nation, Peepeekisis First Nation, and Carry the Kettle First Nation. I use the term 'Dakota' here to reflect the contemporary name of the Standing Buffalo Dakota First Nation. The name Sioux was a French translation of the Ojibwe name for the Dakota people meaning 'snake or enemy', and is considered by some to be derogatory. For the sake of clarity and to reflect the historical discourse of the time, I henceforth retain Mary Weekes's use of the term Sioux.

21 Weekes, 'Antique Indian Beadwork', op cit

22 Her records indicate that pieces from her collection entered the Victoria Provincial Museum, McCord Museum, McGill University Museum, the permanent collection of the Canadian Handicrafts Guild, and the Hudson's Bay Company collection now in the Manitoba Museum. Mary Weekes to Fred Bard, 25 September 1947, Mary Weekes papers, Royal Saskatchewan Museum (RSM).

23 Fred Bard to Mr E E Eisenhauer, Deputy Minister, Department of Reconstruction and Rehabilitation re: Weekes collection, Indian beadwork, 4 December 1947, Mary Weekes papers, RSM

24 Johannes Fabian describes the ethnographic present as a distancing device. See Johannes Fabian, *Time and the Other: How Anthropology Makes Its Object*, Columbia University Press, New York, 1983, p 31.

25 Mary Weekes to Alice MacKay, undated

Exhibition in San Francisco a year later. Despite evidence of this early impulse to collect, she narratively identified a handwoven Cree belt acquired at her B-Say-Tah point cottage in the Qu'Appelle Valley as 'the first piece of Indian work I bought'.[26] By delaying her self-identification as a collector until 1918, Weekes constructed a narrative of collecting whose personal significance was rooted less in the exchange of the physical product itself and more in the social circumstances of exchange produced at her summer cottage and absent from the tourist market. Weekes's display practices (or lack thereof) further contributes to the argument that she dynamically considered the *process* of collecting as potentially more significant and rewarding than the *products*. Unlike her contemporaries who were wont to construct 'Indian corners' in their homes – lavishly decorated bric-a-brac collections of Indigenous material culture – Weekes seems to have been uninterested in using her collection as decor.[27] Only once in her writing does she reference its domestic display when she commented that 'high on my wall [an Assiniboine belt] hangs with my other pieces, and the sun striking through the window makes the colors live and glow'.[28] Her elevated presentation of belts and other pieces, together with an absence of the family recollections one might expect of such an avid collector, indicates a deliberately inconspicuous and restrained display practice that suggests a greater appreciation for the immaterial aspects of collecting.[29]

Most immaterial of all were the friendships she made with the Indigenous peoples at her cottage, which Weekes considered inseparable from her collecting activities, and which, I argue, had an impact on her ability and willingness to confront colonial realities. In my analysis of Weekes's friendship with Indigenous peoples I am, with a few exceptions, limited by a one-sided description of the relationship.[30] I do not redress this imbalance by validating or discrediting Weekes's claims to friendship. Instead, as Vanessa Smith models in her analysis of the Pacific colonial encounter, I 'focus not on what particular friendship claims [whether real or imagined] represent, connote or imply, but rather what they enabled'.[31] The emphasis Weekes put on the development of social relationships with the Indigenous sources of her collection reflects Sharon Macdonald's observation that collecting 'not only produces knowledge about objects but also configures particular ways of knowing and seeing'.[32] The interpersonal relationships Weekes cultivated with members of source communities influenced her attitude towards their financially and culturally impoverished situation (a result of centuries of colonial rule). Pieces of her prose demonstrate her self-conscious recognition of her role (as a settler and as a collector) in reproducing colonial conditions; however, her insistence that her self-awareness set her apart from other settlers and redeemed her behaviour reinforces the ambiguous nature of her position. Her consciousness of colonialism did not negate, and nor did she abdicate, the material advantages associated with her racial position. What follows is an interrogation of the relationships facilitated by the particular social and geographic circumstances of Weekes's cottage and the resulting attitudes demonstrated in her prose.

The Weekes's affectionately named summer cottage, 'Many Maples', bordered Echo Lake in the Qu'Appelle Valley. The Valley had rapidly become a major tourist destination for the growing urban populations of Regina and Moose Jaw in the 1920s. For many Saskatchewan settlers,

correspondence, 19 September 1939, Mary Weekes fonds, F106, III.37, SAB

26 The list reads: 'bought at my cottage at B-Say-Tah 29 years ago'. While undated, the list accompanied the collection Weekes donated to the RSM in 1947. This suggests that the Cree belt must have been purchased in 1918. Weekes, 'Item 47', Handwritten list of objects donated to the Royal Saskatchewan Museum, Mary Weekes papers, RSM.

27 Elizabeth Hutchinson, *The Indian Craze: Primitivism, Modernism, and Transculturation in American Art, 1890–1915*, Duke University Press, Durham, 2009, p 2

28 Weekes, 'Gone Is the Old Trail', op cit

29 All of Weekes's grandchildren were born shortly before or after the collection's donation (the first in 1946). The private and inconspicuous nature of her collection differs from those belonging to collectors such as David Ross McCord, whose family was driven out of various rooms in their home because of his collection. Moira T McCaffrey, 'Rononshonni – The Builder: David Ross McCord's Ethnographic Collection', in Shepard Krech III and Barbara A Hail, eds, *Collecting Native America, 1870–1960*, Smithsonian Institution, Washington, DC, 1999, p 61.

30 Letters exchanged between Weekes and Kennedy offer an exception to this bias. Dan Kennedy was an Assiniboine Chief from the Carry the Kettle Reserve. He served as a source of historical and cultural knowledge for Weekes as well as inspiration for at least one story. In 1941, Kennedy recounted how his own ancestry was bound up in settler-Indigenous relations but requested that

the Qu'Appelle Valley offered 'a respite from the dry and sunburnt open spaces to the north and south, east and west'.[33] In considering the appeal associated with cottage life, Patricia Jasen proposes that tourism is a state of mind in which imagination and romanticism play key roles.[34] Weekes certainly viewed her cottage experience romantically. As she wrote of her return to the cottage:

> In the kitchen, the kettle, which I had put on the stove, began to sing. The cottage, as if by a miracle, came alive. It returned our voices. It answered our footfalls. I glanced out of the window that looked up the valley. Mystery enwrapped the long smooth Western hills.[35]

While the surrounding hills were enwrapped in a romantic mystery, the familiar whistle of the kettle seems to domesticate the cottage with the social mores of hospitality and with the comfort that the sound connotes. Weekes's granddaughter suggests that the cottage, where Weekes 'kept a large teapot at hand and a good supply of tea and cakes especially for [her] Indian visitors', may even have felt more like home to Weekes than her house in the city.[36] Many of the people Weekes invited in for tea were, as she recalls in her eloquent farewell to 'the old trail' torn up by government engineers, those from whom she collected beadwork. As Weekes wrote:

> often, down this old luring trail came, on moccasined feet, Indian women to my cottage door. Bits of beadwork they brought – treasured pieces worked in tribal patterns by the artistic beadworkers of the past. Carefully, they'd have them wrapped in new-washed flour-sacks and tied just so, lest the beads, or porcupine quills should get broken.[37]

The threshold at 'Many Maples', where Weekes met these women, is thus a significant physical and symbolic boundary in Weekes's collecting narrative.[38] In 'The Buffalo Skull', Weekes writes about an encounter between an Indigenous man named Standing Deer and a settler woman named Belinda:

> At the door of the cottage [Standing Deer] paused, then walked over and sat under a maple tree that commanded a view of the porch. How would Belinda receive him? She was a good woman, but hard.[39]

The threshold of the cottage in this story seems to symbolise the uneven possession of power in the encounter between Mary Weekes and her Indigenous neighbours. Standing Deer (and thus Weekes herself) is conscious that the cottage and porch are symbols of the asymmetrical distribution of power in their encounter, over which Belinda has significantly more authority as a gatekeeper.

Victor W Turner's anthropological analysis of the liminal period in *rites de passage* offers a helpful conceptual framework through which to situate the symbolic emphasis on boundaries and the value Weekes ascribed to the cottage. Turner expands on Arnold Van Gennep's 1909 pioneering analysis of what he defined as 'rites which accompany every change of place, state, social position or age'.[40] According to this definition, the transition from urban to rural space for the cottage vacation can be understood as a *rite de passage* bestowed upon Weekes and her family by the privilege of their class and race. In moving from Regina to B-Say-Tah Point, Weekes crossed a spatial boundary physically and ideologically constructed both by the settler's assertion of territorial rights and the imagination of an idealised, 'primitive', Indigenous Other. As Patrick Wolfe argues, the settler's construction of Indigenous authenticity depends on spatial separations that locate Indigeneity 'somewhere else'.[41] Weekes's own prose demonstrates these spatial separations, incorporating Indigenous peoples as an integral part of the rural Prairie landscape while, more often than not, remaining silent about their urban presence. Weekes's denial of urban Indigeneity confirms a colonial insistence on contemporary Indigenous invisibility through policies of assimilation and of controlled movement.[42] The privilege of a cottage vacation and the transgression of these spatial boundaries is thus both a rite and a right through which middle-class Canadians could entertain themselves by flirting with wilderness and bearing witness to a perceived Indigenous past.

Although associated with her colonial privilege, Weekes's cottage is also a space of separation and liminality, both important phases in the *rite de passage*. Separated from urban social structures, the cottage offers the possibility for the relaxation of some social boundaries and the maintenance of others. As Turner observes of the liminal condition, it is 'one of ambiguity and paradox, a confusion of all the customary categories'.[43] In the case of Mary Weekes, the cottage threshold is the site of this potential confusion. While the threshold symbolises the uneven power relations between Weekes and her Indigenous friends (as demonstrated in 'The Buffalo Skull'), the invited transgression of this rural spatial boundary for tea and cakes allows for an unconventional exchange. Together, these transgressions provided a framework that 'temporarily suspended the constraining rules of [colonially prescribed] social behaviour', enabling the development of unusually familiar relationships that went beyond the impersonal commercial relationships fostered by ethnographic and tourist collecting.[44] Importantly, the relationships Weekes cultivated over the exchange of material culture influenced her writing, which frequently provided a platform for the complaints of her Indigenous friends. For example, Frank Isnanna, then the Standing Buffalo Sioux Chief, is a recurring figure in Weekes's extensive archive and characterised as a close friend of hers and a valuable source of historical and cultural knowledge. Weekes's text 'Gone Is the Old Trail', functions momentarily as a platform for Isnanna's condemnation of his people's colonial condition:

> Sixty years have I lived in this place. I am a Canadian. Long ago, my people the Great Sioux Nation owned all the country to the East. Silver medals have we from King George III. Now I am old and poor. My woman, too, is old and poor. The Government will not give me a pension. New people have come to this country and the Government gives them money and houses to live in. My people are sad. We should not be sad. This is our country. I am a Canadian. Canada is the country of my people.[45]

Weekes not share these details at least until after he had passed, a request she respected. Dan Kennedy to Mary Weekes, 16 January 1941 and 11 December 1945, Mary Weekes papers, RSM.

31 Vanessa Smith, *Intimate Strangers: Friendship, Exchange and Pacific Encounters*, Cambridge University Press, Cambridge, 2010, p 14

32 Sharon Macdonald, 'Collecting Practices', in Sharon Macdonald, ed, *A Companion to Museum Studies*, Wiley-Blackwell, Oxford, 2006, pp 94–95

33 Dan Ring, 'Qu'Appelle: Tales of Two Valleys: An Introductory Essay', in Dan Ring, ed, *Qu'Appelle: Tales of Two Valleys*, Mendel Art Gallery, Saskatchewan, 2002, p 13

34 Patricia Jasen, *Wild Things: Nature, Culture, and Tourism in Ontario, 1790–1914*, University of Toronto Press, Toronto, 1995, p 4

35 Weekes, 'Summer Cottage in Saskatchewan', *Saturday Night*, 17 May 1941, Mary Weekes fonds, F106, SB 3, p 19, SAB

36 Weekes, 'Paper delivered to the Regina Natural History Society', 21 February 1949, Mary Weekes fonds, F106, XII.1, SAB; Kathy Weekes Southee, interview with the author, 17 November 2015

37 Weekes, 'Gone Is the Old Trail', op cit

38 While I identify the cottage as the crux of Weekes's collecting narrative, she did actively seek pieces for her collection elsewhere. In a 1927 article Weekes advised that 'one never knows where [antique Indian beadwork] may be found' and suggested that one must look in 'the homes of old settlers and pioneers', 'in the possession of storekeepers, in the small towns', and in the possessions of postmasters who often 'have fine

Saddle from the Weekes Collection, date unknown, reproduction: courtesy the Provincial Archives of Saskatchewan, copyright: courtesy Kathy Weekes Southee

pieces of Cree beadwork lying in neglected places'. Mary Weekes, 'Antique Indian Beadwork', op cit.

39 Weekes, 'The Buffalo Skull', *Saturday Night*, 29 March 1947, Mary Weekes fonds, F106, SB 2, p 22, SAB

40 Arnold Van Gennep, *Les Rites de passage*, Emile Nourry, Paris, 1909, quoted in Victor W Turner, 'Betwixt and Between: The Liminal Period in *Rites de Passage*', in Arthur C Lehmann and James E Myers, eds, *Magic, Witchcraft, and Religion: An Anthropological Study of the Supernatural*, fifth edition, Mayfield Publishing, Houston, 2000, p 49

41 Patrick Wolfe, 'Nation and Miscegenation: Discursive Continuity in the Post-Mabo Era', *Social Analysis* 36, October 1994, p 110

42 By 'controlled movement' I refer to the pass system, initiated on a large scale during the 1885 North-West Rebellion. Never codified under the Indian Act, the policy required those who wished to leave their reserves to obtain a pass from the agent or farm instructor declaring the reason and length of their absence and whether or not they had permission to carry arms. Sarah Carter, *Aboriginal People and Colonizers of Western Canada to 1900*, University of Toronto Press, Toronto, 1999, pp 164–166.

43 Turner, 'Betwixt and Between', op cit, p 48

44 Carol Duncan, 'The Art Museum as Ritual', in *Civilizing Rituals: Inside Public Art Museums*, Routledge, London, 1995, p 11

45 Weekes, 'Gone Is the Old Trail', op cit

46 Elizabeth Cromley, 'Masculine/Indian', *Winterthur Portfolio*, vol 31, no 4, winter 1996, pp 265–280, p 280

Elizabeth Cromley suggests:

> for both men and women in mainstream culture, using Indian goods in domestic space for decoration narrowed their encounter with Indians, protecting them from fully connecting with the tragic life Indians endured at the turn of the century.[46]

In contrast, for Weekes, the incorporation of Indigenous goods (and by extension the invitation of Indigenous peoples into the domestic sphere) expanded her encounter and her understanding of the harsh realities of Indigenous life.

Elsewhere, Weekes's prose demonstrates recognition of her complicity in the colonial systems Isnanna critiques. Her unpublished story 'These Summer Women – Such hurry, hurry!' is narrated from the perspective of Moses, a Cree man of sixty summers who is envious of the 'paleface summer women' whose money flows in and out of their purses like water, while he struggles to sell a pair of moccasins for the meat his sick grandson needs. One such 'summer woman' is Miss Norah, a collector (like Weekes), who Moses reflects has been trying to buy his saddle for many years despite his insistence that it is a saddle for an Indian only. Weekes's self-conscious recognition (through Moses) that some elements of Indigenous culture are not for sale, and yet her alter-ego's insistence upon ownership, demonstrates her own conflictual relationship to collecting. Nonetheless, Moses sets Miss Norah apart from other summer women, reflecting that 'when times were hard, she had paid him handsomely for his work and never did she bargain as sharply as other white folk for moccasins or other articles.'[47] The story thus both implicates Weekes and excuses her from any guilt associated with her settler-status and role as a collector.

In one regard, Weekes appears to be reproducing herself – through her writing and collecting activities – as a self-conscious and conscientious settler, both of which challenge the settler's conventional attempt to reproduce his or herself as unquestionably native to the land. Even more than reproducing herself through repeated literary motifs, Weekes also sought to alternatively reproduce settler children by encouraging more critical reflections on colonialism and more respectful interactions. Of the eleven novels she published, seven were for children, within which she did not shy away from language asserting Indigenous rights and condemning their dispossession. In a 1941 paper delivered at the Canadian Author's Association convention, she began by admiring how discerning the juvenile audience is: 'there are perils and problems and modest rewards for those who recognize that the juvenile, on his own ground, is as exacting a critic as his elders'.[48] Weekes's confidence in her young readers' astuteness makes her candid writing about Indigenous peoples all the more notable. For example, the introduction to her novel *Indians of the Plains*, used in Saskatchewan social studies curricula, refutes the production of colonised space through the assumption of uninscribed land. Unlike other school textbooks, which, for instance, claimed that 'people are not native to America, but horses and other animals are', Weekes asserted the widespread and immemorial presence of Indigenous peoples:

47 Weekes, 'These Summer Women – Such hurry, hurry!', unpublished manuscript, date unknown, Mary Weekes fonds, F106, I.148, SAB

48 Weekes, 'Writing for the Young', Canadian Authors Convention, 1941, Mary Weekes fonds, F106, XV.1, SAB

49 Marion J McVeety and Anne MacMillan, *Friends – Far and Near: Grades 3 & 4 Social Studies: 'B' Course in Saskatchewan*, School Aids and Text Book Pub, Regina, 1943, p 34, quoted in Mary Lynn Gagné, 'Print, Profit and Pedagogy: School Aids and Text Book Publishing Company', *Saskatchewan History*, vol 60, no 1, 2008, p 23; Weekes, *Indians of the Plains*, School Aids and Text Book Pub, Regina, 1950, p 6

50 Ibid, p 20

51 For example, 'The Crees have from the earliest times been generally friendly with the French and English who invaded their country, first to trade goods of little value for their priceless furs, and later when the Canadian government took over their vast lands.' Ibid, p 9.

52 Turner, 'Betwixt and Between', op cit, p 48

53 Weekes, 'Paper delivered to the Regina Natural History Society', op cit

We do know definitely that long before [the] white man came, the North American continent was inhabited by numerous bands of Indians who lived in every part of the country from the Atlantic to the Pacific coasts and from the barren northern wastes to the waters of the southern shores.[49]

By insisting on Indigenous sovereignty and refuting some of the presumed truths upon which denial of settler status relies, Weekes encouraged her young audience to self-identify as settlers to an inhabited land. She further cultivated respect and tolerance among her audience by insisting on the heterogeneity of Indigenous peoples and criticising insincere colonial engagements with Indigenous culture. For instance, she began *Indians of the Plains* by carefully distinguishing four major groups in Western Canada (although there are in fact many more), and later in the text decried the display of ceremonial costumes in parades 'for the entertainment of white men', noting that this custom is 'regarded by thoughtful people as degrading to the descendants of the proud people who once ruled the plains'.[50] Elsewhere she openly referred to land appropriation and the inherent asymmetry of colonial trading practices.[51]

At the same time, however, Weekes perpetuated a version of settler society in which the white man (or woman) is at once the source of Indigenous struggle and the saviour. Miss Norah, for example, is complicit in her culturally insensitive desire for Moses's saddle, but also responsible for saving his grandson. So too does Weekes, along with her other female protagonists, occupy this ambiguous position. The coexistence of Weekes's condemnation of the colonial system and yet her participation in it is evidence of the tentative nature of her transformation and the only partial applicability of the concept of liminality to the cottage – it is a space of 'ambiguity and paradox', but it is not, after all, completely free from the prevailing rules of social behaviour in settler–Indigenous encounters.[52] While some of the social hierarchies governing the interaction between races were relaxed, those governing gender remained intact, presenting a barrier against which Weekes's racial privilege was an ideal weapon. While the introduction of Indigenous women into her home for the exchange of beadwork and conversation inspired much of Weekes's writing, it was still the introduction of Indigenous women as domestic labourers that provided Weekes with the leisure time she needed to write her progressive prose.

The Indigenous Role in (and Resistance to) Settler Reproduction

They became my friends. When Chief Standing Buffalo heard that I was looking for a nursemaid for my small children, he brought his daughter Vitaline, just out of the Lebret Mission school. She was a splendid girl. She worked for me for several summers. When she got married, her sister Annie came to me. When she got married, Jacob Leswiss brought his Eve, and later her sister. Always at the lake, I had fine Indian girls.[53]

While Weekes helped Norbert Welsh preserve, or reproduce, his life story for his community, her activities were simultaneously enabled by

54 Andrew Woolford, *This Benevolent Experiment: Indigenous Boarding Schools, Genocide, and Redress in Canada and the United States*, University of Nebraska Press, Lincoln, 2015, p 63

55 Ibid, p 167

56 Mary Jane Logan McCallum, '"I Would Like the Girls at Home": Domestic Labor and the Age of Discharge at Canadian Indian Residential Schools', in Victoria K Haskins and Claire Lowrie, eds, *Colonization and Domestic Service: Historical and Contemporary Perspectives*, Routledge, New York, 2015, p 193

57 Ibid, p 195

58 Ibid, p 196

59 Shellee Colen, '"Like a Mother to Them": Stratified Reproduction and West Indian Childcare Workers and Employers in New York', in Faye D Ginsburg and Rayna Rapp, eds, *Conceiving the New World Order: The Global Politics of Reproduction*, University of California Press, Berkeley, 1995

60 The term 'Sixties Scoop' is used to refer to the disproportionate numbers of Indigenous children removed from their homes and placed in the care of white families after the federal government amended the Indian Act in 1951, making responsibility for Aboriginal health and welfare a provincial concern. Resulting adoptions and removals are widely viewed as a continuation of the policies of forced assimilation that characterised the residential school system. Raven Sinclair, 'Identity Lost and Found: Lessons from the Sixties Scoop', *First Peoples Child & Family Review*, vol 3, no 1, 2007, pp 65–82.

61 Taking Indigenous girls into domestic service also

participation in a harmful residential school system that sought to distance young Indigenous students from their traditions and histories such as those told by Welsh. Education in residential schools was one component of the settler government's multivalent approach to solving the 'Indian Problem'.[54] A key element included the policing of gender. Male and female students were divided into strictly separated spheres of activity where girls were taught 'sewing, plain and fancy, cutting out and making up their clothes, darning, knitting, laundry work and scrubbing, and other domestic work'.[55] A young girl's experience of domestic labour at the residential school was intended to prepare her to have a 'civilising' influence on her community and future family.[56] Her domestic labour also helped maintain underfunded schools and prepared her for entrance into the labour market as a domestic servant, a menial role for which biased school administrators understood Indigenous women to show considerable aptitude.[57]

Weekes, importantly, prefaced her own use of Indigenous domestic labour with friendship, disassociating herself from the institutionalised market for Indigenous women's labour and also insinuating that the provision of labour was appropriate compensation for friendship. This is not to imply that Weekes did not pay the women on whose domestic labour she relied, but rather to comment on the societal value ascribed to this labour. Historian Mary Jane Logan McCallum observes that colonialism produced a system in which 'young Indigenous women [were] in fact only considered "useful" when their labour [was] harnessed to non-Indigenous projects', the extent of which is demonstrated by Standing Buffalo and Jacob Leswiss's voluntary displacement of their daughters' labour from their own communities to Weekes's home.[58] This is exemplary of stratified social reproduction – in which some categories of people are empowered to nurture and reproduce, while others are disempowered.[59] The removal of children to residential schools intended to isolate them from the influences of their families, traditions and cultures and assimilate them into the dominant culture – objectives based on the assumed inferiority of Indigenous cultures, spiritual beliefs and practices of social reproduction. Indigenous parents were disempowered from nurturing and socially reproducing their own children and cultures – a practice that continued well into the late twentieth century.[60] Instead, residential schools sought to make Indigenous men and women productive participants in the reproduction of the dominant Euro-Christian Canadian society. Consequentially, through the enforced initiation of Indigenous women into the so-called cult of domesticity, settler women were able to escape their own domestic obligations and therefore devote their time to other interests – in Weekes's case, the development of a professional writing career.[61] Thus, young Indigenous women were forced to participate in the social reproduction of settler society rather than their own.

However, as indicated at the beginning of this article, there were moments of resistance – such as attending a rarely allowed powwow. Indigenous beadwork produced for sale is another instance of resistance and a medium for Indigenous social reproduction. It strategically co-opted the settler's desire to own Indigenous culture as a means of dispossession. Despite seeking the assimilation of the cultures behind beadworking traditions, during the time that Weekes was an active

played an integral role in the system's 'training in dispossession under the guise of domesticity', which helped to develop a 'habitus shaped by messages about subservience and one's proper place'. See K Tsianina Lomawaima, 'Domesticity in the Federal Indian Schools: The Power of Authority over Mind and Body', *American Ethnologist*, vol 20, no 2, May 1993, pp 227–240, p 231.

collector, branches of the Canadian government encouraged beadwork production as a source for Indigenous economic self-sufficiency and as a solution to the large numbers relying on government aid. Unconcerned with the role of beadwork and other forms of material culture in Indigenous social reproduction, the Department of Indian Affairs prioritised marketability and economic relief over the preservation of culture. But while the initiation of Indigenous peoples into a capitalist economy and the commoditisation of women's labour was part of a larger project of assimilation and national appropriation of palatable motifs of Indigeneity, some scholars have argued that Indigenous women subversively used the commoditisation of their beadwork to their advantage. Discussing Haudenosone beadwork, for example, Ruth Phillips argues that bead workers used new commoditised art forms as 'repositories of artistic traditions that could not be easily expressed in other formats during this repressive age'.[62] Indigenous beadwork was thus a site for cultural transmission that was non-threatening to government officials. Through the voracious appetite of settlers for vestiges of Indigeneity, Indigenous women created what Sherry Farrell Racette has called an artistic legacy and repository for contemporary Indigenous artists.[63]

Weekes's own writing recognises the strategic role of Plains beadworking in the social reproduction of their traditions, observing, 'now that their work has a definite commercial value, the old women are busy once again reproducing with great success their favourite patterns'.[64] Weekes assigns agency to bead workers in the strategic appropriation of the commoditisation of their beadwork to reproduce their own desired patterns and thus those they considered important for the perpetuation of their traditions. Although Weekes's reliance on Indigenous domestic labour demonstrates her complicity in the colonial project of assimilation and the stratification of social reproduction (processes within which the collection of Indigenous artifacts from a perceived disappearing culture was a common feature), her consciousness about the reproductive role of beadwork might also reveal her collecting practice as deliberately complicit in the subversion of the government's intended assimilation.

62 See Ruth Phillips, *Trading Identities: The Souvenir in Native North American Art from the Northeast, 1700–1900*, University of Washington Press, Seattle, 1998, p 259.

63 Sherry Farrell Racette, 'Looking for Stories and Unbroken Threads: Museum Artifacts as Women's History and Cultural Legacy', in Gail Guthrie Valaskakis et al, eds, *Restoring the Balance: First Nations Women, Community, and Culture*, University of Manitoba Press, Winnipeg, 2009, p 285

64 Weekes, 'Beadwork of the Prairies', *Canadian National Railways Magazine*, September 1931, Mary Weekes fonds, F106, SB 5, p 32, SAB

65 Weekes, 'Paper Delivered to the Regina Natural History Society', op cit

Coming to Terms with Complicity and Contradictions

I learned from a Yale University professor who was doing field work in the Sioux reservation one summer that the Indians of that reserve call me 'wagon-sida-winga', which meant, 'good woman, kindly woman, but exact woman', and they elaborated by saying that when they needed help I gave it to them, but that when I advanced them five dollars for a load of wood, I insisted upon them delivering the wood. They seemed to respect me for this trait.[65]

The complex and contradictory behaviours of Mary Weekes discussed in this article recall the name she claimed her Sioux friends called her and speak to its potential accuracy in encapsulating what it means to be ambiguously complicit in colonialism. *Wagon-sida-winga* exemplifies the closeness of Weekes to those Indigenous peoples she considered friends, while at the same time maintains colonial hierarchies and her perceived superior position as their necessary saviour. She was kind and empathetic, but methodical in regards to her relationships and how they benefitted her. By examining the complex networks of racialised, gendered and classed labour involved in making the Weekes collection, this article has sought to expand the usefulness of social reproduction as a critical term for examining collecting in settler-colonial art history.

Viewing the Weekes collection through the lens of social reproduction offers a fruitful opportunity to both broaden our assumptions about colonial collections and enrich our understanding about white women's active (yet ambivalent) roles in reproducing settler society. Narratives of settler-colonial collecting rightly argue that the twentieth-century settler's appropriation and consumption of Indigenous culture attempted to naturalise territorial rights and invent a sense of belonging.[66] While I do not dispute that the Weekes collection likely originated from similar impulses, I contend that its unusually intimate conditions of acquisition alternatively and somewhat paradoxically led to the denaturalisation of Weekes's perceived territorial rights and challenged her sense of belonging. Examining the exchange of socially reproductive labour between Weekes and her Indigenous friends deepens our understanding of the confrontation between the settler-self and Indigenous Other and illuminates how the encounter forced Weekes to acknowledge and confront her complicity in colonial norms. In so doing, Weekes precociously sought to reproduce a more empathetic, self-conscious and culturally aware settler society, while failing to more radically disrupt the reproduction of the settler's assumed socio-political superiority. The usefulness of social reproduction as a critical term in this case study of settler-colonial collecting lies, therefore, in revealing the contradictory self-positioning of Mary Weekes, who simultaneously admired, valued and exploited the artistic and domestic labour of her Indigenous friends and neighbours, while attempting to reproduce a settler majority that shared her values. Considering the so far little examined but important role that colonial collections continue to play in the social reproduction of contemporary Indigenous and settler societies and their interactions also offers a range of radical opportunities for decolonisation and reconciliation.

66 Ruth Phillips, 'Why Not Tourist Art? Significant Silences in Native American Museum Representation', in Gyan Prakash, ed, *After Colonialism: Imperial Histories and Postcolonial Displacements*, Princeton University Press, Princeton, 1999, p 111; Skinner, op cit, p 137

Third Text, 2017
Vol. 31, No. 1, 49–66, https://doi.org/10.1080/09528822.2017.1364331

The Two Reproductions in (Feminist) Art and Theory since the 1970s

Marina Vishmidt

Pilvi Takala, The Trainee, 2008, (detail), installation, image courtesy: Stigter van Doesburg and Carlos/Ishikawa

1 Elena Gorfinkel, 'The Body's Failed Labor: Performance Work in Sexploitation Cinema', *Framework: The Journal of Cinema and Media*, vol 53, no 1, 2012, pp 79–98

2 Louis Althusser, 'Ideology and Ideological State Apparatuses (Notes Towards an Investigation)', 1970, https://www.marxists.org/reference/archive/althusser/1970/ideology.htm, accessed 20 July 2016

3 See Marina Vishmidt, 'Between Not Everything and Not Nothing: Cuts Toward Infrastructural Critique', in Maria Hlavajova and Simon Sheikh, eds, *Former West: Art and the Contemporary after 1989*, BAK, Utrecht and The MIT Press, Cambridge, Massachusetts, 2017, pp 265–270.

This work, this labor – deskilled, untrained, and easily replaceable – matters the most because it is the most pervasive, but also because it makes itself visible by virtue of its capacity and inclination, at any moment, to stop working, to not work.[1]

This article will approach the optic of 'reproduction' in feminist theory and politics from two sides: (a) the discussion of social reproduction currently at the top of the agenda of materialist feminisms, that is as a *specific* modality of gendered, racialised and often unwaged labour; and b) the sense in which social reproduction can be taken as the 'reproduction of the conditions of production', as in Louis Althusser's analysis.[2] In this second instance, the perpetuation of capitalist society and the individuals in it makes reproduction continuous with social production. These two approaches to the question of reproduction will be used to open a path to a sample of historical and contemporary art practices, readable either in terms of a feminist notion of reproduction as a spectrum of gendered tasks, or in terms of performing the impasses of a kind of social 'non-reproduction' that belongs to the second type, with the social reproduction perspective assuming the function of institutional or, perhaps, 'infrastructural' critique.[3] The article covers the period between the 1970s and the present.

Through these two ways of looking at reproduction I aim to trace a politics of subjectivity reflecting the double dynamic of strategic affirmation and refusal of identity endemic to all movements of the oppressed. In these strategic affirmations and refusals, art does not behave simply as a mediating institution but as an *iterative* one. As a reproductive institution in its own right, art becomes a site of inventive and self-determined forms of work while also being traversed by class relations and, thus, class struggle. Throughout, I will contend that the separation of reproductive labour as a political matrix from its position in the reproduction of capital is a common *telos* of the feminist politics of social reproduction. This tendency can generate equivocal effects such as the moralisation of care work and the self-evidence of the need to manage crisis coupled with a de facto confirmation of gender roles, none of which diverge in any radical way from capitalism's own strategies for propping up its profit rates through the exploitation and deprivation of those least able to resist. Instead, it is to the negativity, waste and uselessness of reproductive labour that we might turn in order to see the vulnerability of the social whole in relation to which this work is *both* abjected and moralised. Specific feminist art practices materialise this turn by emptying out the 'value' of reproductive labour, highlighting the affective features of the kind of conceptual turn advocated here.

'Social reproduction' has gained traction as a key category of Marxist feminism amid the current resurgence both in radical queer and trans feminism as well as in related discourses and liberation movements whose strategies include affirming identity, such as the Movement for Black Lives, against its violent identifications by the state. This is largely because 'social reproduction' seems to go some way towards accommodating long-standing critiques of white, middle-class hegemony in Marxist feminism while enabling a more systematic framing than that afforded by the established discourse of intersectionality. Indeed, it is specifically within this expanded framing where a more global picture of diverse concrete positions of a population increasingly surplus to capital's valorisation requirements – those facing a real existential crisis in their possibilities of reproducing themselves and their communities – can be drawn. Here, identity claims are tendentially translated into devalued (racialised, gendered, classed) forms of labour. From this perspective, the socialisation of the financial crisis through an exacerbated politics of austerity, as we have seen since 2008, is a set of processes that trigger a crisis of social reproduction.

Social Reproductions

The concept of 'social reproduction' in feminist theory and feminist movements emerged in the 1970s, especially in Marxist and socialist feminism, coinciding roughly with a generalisation of a range of critiques of orthodox Marxism and highlighting the shortcomings of its analyses of labour and the blind spots in its conceptions of working-class struggle. As Rada Katsarova writes, 'social reproduction became both a standpoint of feminist critique of productivist Marxism and a lens for developing new critiques and theories of state power in the context of the liberal welfare and socialist states'.[4] Conceptualising feminist theory and struggle through the framework of social reproduction is thought to allow for a unifying approach, while sidestepping critiques aimed at 'legacy models' of Marxist feminism, including the methodological cul-de-sac of the 'dual systems' debate and some of its narrower assumptions, predicated upon a model of gender relations which universalised the predicament of white, middle-class women.[5] Contemporary articulations

4 Rada Katsarova, 'Repression and Resistance on the Terrain of Social Reproduction', *Viewpoint Magazine*, 2015, https://www.viewpointmag.com/2015/10/31/repression-and-resistance-on-the-terrain-of-social-reproduction-historical-trajectories-contemporary-openings/, accessed 23 March 2017

5 Most famously through texts like Betty Friedan's *The Feminine Mystique* (1963), but also more generally, diverse positions on the feminist spectrum then and now can universalise gender hierarchies ('patriarchy') without specifying its internal and historical relations to dynamics of biopolitical violence (not identities) such as race and class. It should be noted, however, that the mainstream historiography frequently omits the complexities of positions now understood to prioritise gender in a one-sided way; Friedan, for example, was a committed socialist activist.

6 Michael Denning, 'Wageless Life', *New Left Review* 66, 2010, pp 79–97; Susanne Soederberg, *Debtfare States and the Poverty Industry: Money, Discipline and the Surplus Population*, Routledge, London and New York, 2014; Endnotes and Aaron Benanav, 'Misery and Debt', *Endnotes* 2, London, 2010, pp 20–51; Endnotes, 'An Identical Abject-Subject?', *Endnotes* 4, 2015, pp 276–301

7 The notion of the 'hidden abode' comes from Marx, who writes of the site of production as a space quite other to the formal equality that reigns in the well-lit and above-board marketplace, a private domain where despotic capitalist holds sway. Karl Marx, *Capital: A Critique of Political Economy*, Volume One, Ben Fowkes, trans, Penguin Books, Harmondsworth, 1976, p 279. Since then development economists as well as feminist theorists have extended analysis of the 'hidden abode' to the site of reproductive labour, but for the purposes of Marxist feminism the key work is Leopoldina Fortunati's *The Arcane of Reproduction*, harbouring the concept already in its title. See William G Martin and Mark Beittel, 'The Hidden Abode of Reproduction: Conceptualizing Households in Southern Africa', *Development & Change*, vol 18, no 2, April 1987, pp 215–234; Leopoldina Fortunati, *The Arcane of Reproduction: Housework, Prostitution, Labor and Capital*, Hilary Creek, trans, Autonomedia, New York, 1995 (originally published in Italian as *L'Arcano della Reproduzione: Casalinghe, Prostitute, Operai e Capitale*, Marsilio Editori, Venezia, 1981); Maya Gonzalez, 'The Gendered Circuit: Reading the Arcane of Reproduction', *Viewpoint Magazine*, 2013, https://www.viewpointmag.com/2013/09/28/the-gendered-circuit-reading-the-arcane-of-reproduction/, accessed 23 March 2017.

of social reproduction feminism in the West often begin from the insights made available by these critiques but try to synthesise them from the standpoint of the totality of capitalist accumulation. Yet, overall, the category of 'social reproduction' has come to designate such different processes that it has grown prone to indeterminacy. 'Society' or 'the social' is a projected imaginary, and what actually counts as its reproduction is potentially open-ended and ambiguous.

During the 1970s and early 1980s, Marxist feminists emphasised the centrality of reproduction, arguing either that reproduction was value producing or else that it constituted the very conditions of the possibility of the production of value. But the concept of social reproduction can often be stretched, designating not the reproduction of a mode of production, but the reproduction of life per se, through which the capital relation is reproduced as though contingently. And as such, it becomes difficult to explain what distinguishes the terms 'life' and 'capital' in any determinate sense. However, when Marxist feminists speak of social reproduction they do often mean something quite specific: the production and reproduction of the special commodity of labour power ('special' because it adds more value in the production process than it costs). Yet what falls within the remit of the reproduction of labour power is itself still open to specification. This is then what makes it difficult to conceptually distinguish the reproduction of labour power from the reproduction of life per se – particularly when what has been called 'wageless life', or what other writers have called 'surplus population' (surplus to capital's valorisation needs, the redundant, the precarious, the expelled), becomes an experience increasingly central to the configuration of global societies.[6]

By analytically reinforcing the split between the so-called 'productive' and 'reproductive' spheres, Marxist feminists defined reproduction as a specific set of tasks. Struggle became conceptualised as the minimisation, socialisation or refusal of reproductive tasks. Many of these, however, could not be confined to unpaid work in the home. This has become particularly clear with the restructuring of capital to commodify more and more 'reproductive' activities, especially with the entrance of more women into the workforce, while welfare state institutions were also subjected to marketising logics. The 'hidden abode' of reproductive labour found advocates such as Wages for Housework who, in common with many in the Welfare Rights movement (especially in the US at the time), sought to politicise the reproductive sphere by claiming a 'wage' for subsidising the accumulation of capital, just like any other organised labour.[7] The demand was to extend the parameters of the workers' movements to include those who by dint of race and gender were marginal to the formal workplace, the wage, and the labour politics associated with them. Notably what has changed between the 1970s and now (the neoliberal and post-financial crisis period) is the state's disinvestment in the reproduction of workers and people in general. Thus, in some way, an extractive capitalist reality replicates the blind spot in Marx's analysis that the feminist theories of social reproduction developed to address.[8] Current debates such as the ones around Guaranteed Basic Income focus on the necessity of redistributive policies, acknowledging the

8 Saskia Sassen, *Expulsions: Brutality and Complexity in the Global Economy*, Harvard University Press, Cambridge, Massachusetts, 2014

9 Arguments have been made, however, that diagnose both the erosion and the steadfastness posited in such claims as misleading, and which instead assign the notion of an omni-productivity underlying Guaranteed or Universal Basic Income programmes to a misunderstanding of the nature of capitalist value production – measured by the market (abstract labour) and not in instances of concrete labour.

10 The concept of a directly market-mediated and an indirectly market-mediated sphere of labour is developed by Endnotes in order to overcome ambiguities in the private sphere/public sphere dichotomy which often appears in feminist accounts of the gender division of labour. Endnotes, 'The Logic of Gender', *Endnotes* 3, 2013, pp 56–91; also available at https://endnotes.org.uk/issues/3/en/endnotes-the-logic-of-gender, accessed 8 June 2017.

11 Marx, *Capital*, Volume One, op cit, p 711

12 Ibid, p 724

13 As Cinzia Arruzza contends, 'if we take into account the relations that exist in each capitalist society between social reproduction, the production of the society as a whole, and the relations of production, we can say that these relations of domination and power are not separate structures or levels: they do not intersect in a purely external manner and do not maintain a solely contingent relation with the relations of production'. See Cinzia Arruzza, 'Remarks on Gender', *Viewpoint*

erosion of once steadfast boundaries between work and life, production and reproduction.[9]

But what if we put reproduction on a continuum of capitalist productive relations and not in a 'separate sphere', whether mediated by the market or not?[10] Marx discusses reproduction in the chapter on 'simple reproduction' in the first volume of *Capital* in these terms:

> Whatever the social form of the production process, it has to be continuous, it must periodically repeat the same phases. A society can no more cease to produce than it can to consume. When viewed, therefore, as a connected whole, and in the constant flux of its incessant renewal, every social process of production is, at the same time, a process of reproduction.[11]

And, a few pages later:

> Capitalist production, therefore, under its aspect of a continuous connected process, of a process of reproduction, produces not only commodities, not only surplus-value, but it also produces and reproduces the capitalist relation; on the one side the capitalist, on the other the wage-labourer.[12]

If the process of capitalist reproduction is always a reproduction of its own preconditions, namely the means (including constant and variable capital) *and* the relations of production, no process of the reproduction of capital can fail to also be the reproduction of capitalist society, thus cannot fail to be, at one and the same time, 'social reproduction'. Keeping in mind the high level of abstraction in this phase of Marx's discussion, this acknowledges that there is a continuum and a unity between production and reproduction considered from the viewpoint of the 'totality', or, total social capital and its ability to maintain itself and expand. This makes the distinction between social production and social reproduction hard to maintain at the level of the social whole, but calls, rather, for a 'unitary theory' that some strands of social reproduction feminism have been advancing. This also necessitates a reckoning with the 'extra-economic' factors that feminism – from a plurality of viewpoints – has consistently addressed.[13]

In this light, we can turn to Althusser – a strong influence on much second-wave Marxist feminist theoretical work, including Michele Barrett, as well as Lise Vogel, whom I will discuss later. For Althusser, the reproduction of the relations of production (for example, an educated and compliant workforce) takes place outside the sphere of production proper, under the guidance of institutions of the state and civil society – schools, the church:

> To put this more scientifically, I shall say that the reproduction of labour power requires not only a reproduction of its skills, but also, at the same time, a reproduction of its submission to the rules of the established order, i.e., a reproduction of submission to the ruling ideology for the workers, and a reproduction of the ability to manipulate the ruling ideology correctly for the agents of exploitation and repression, so that they, too, will provide for the domination of the ruling class 'in words'.[14]

Magazine, 2014, https://www.viewpointmag.com/2014/09/02/remarks-on-gender/, accessed 23 March 2017.

14 Louis Althusser, 'Ideology and Ideological State Apparatuses (Notes towards an Investigation)', in *Lenin and Philosophy and Other Essays*, Ben Brewster, trans, Monthly Review Press, New York, 1971

15 Foucault's work as a whole can be considered within this frame, but see especially *Madness and Civilization: A History of Insanity in the Age of Reason*, Richard Howard, trans, Routledge, London and New York, 2009; *Discipline and Punish: The Birth of the Prison*, Alan Sheridan, trans, Vintage Books, New York, 2012; *The History of Sexuality, Volume One: The Will to Knowledge*, Robert Hurley, trans, Penguin, London, 2008, and in the lecture series collections, *The Birth of Biopolitics: Lectures at the Collège de France, 1978–1979*, Graham Burchell, trans, Palgrave Macmillan, Basingstoke, 2008; and *The Punitive Society: Lectures at the Collège de France, 1972–1973*, Graham Burchell, trans, Palgrave Macmillan, Basingstoke, 2015. For an interesting and little-known attempt to bridge Marx, Althusser and Foucault, see François Guéry and Didier Deleule *The Productive Body* [1972], Philip Barnard and Stephen Shapiro, trans, Zero Books, Winchester, 2014.

16 Jemima Repo, *The Biopolitics of Gender*, Oxford University Press, Oxford and New York, 2016

17 Pierre Macherey, 'The Productive Subject', *Viewpoint Magazine*, 2015, https://www.viewpointmag.com/2015/10/31/the-productive-subject, accessed 23 March 2017. The French text was originally published on the

Althusser tries to extrapolate and concretise the systemic explanation of the link between production and reproduction posited by Marx from the viewpoint of the totality, by bringing the state into the picture, in however rudimentary a fashion. He also does this by contesting the assumed dominance of the sphere of production in Marxist theory and political practice, pointing rather to how the formation of the subject requires collective and not primarily economic institutions (such as church, school, army and other entities) where the reproduction of the conditions of production would be ensured over time through the medium of a norm-producing and socialising ideology. Michel Foucault would later assign such institutions to the 'disciplinary regime'. Reproduction is then configured as the production of (materialised) ideology which works to render capitalism socially effective *over time* rather than a sphere of particular, gendered tasks that reproduce the conditions of life. The connection between the theories of social reproduction advanced by social reproduction feminism (SRF) since the 1970s and Foucault's work on biopolitics remains underdeveloped, even as both look beyond the sphere of 'production' to socialisation, tracking the development of mechanisms of 'extra-economic' coercion that produce the favourable conditions for the governance of capital and state over populations in the modern period.[15] The point here is hardly that the encounter between feminism and Foucault has been missed; decades of work have developed this dialogue, including the work of Judith Butler, Elisabeth Grosz and, recently, Jemima Repo.[16] The point is rather that there has been relatively little engagement with Foucault in SRF in particular – a gap possibly also traced to the not infrequent mutual suspicion entertained between scholars of Marx and scholars of Foucault in the academy. Foucauldian biopolitics is historically parallel to SRF however, both being theoretical projects that consider the 'reproduction of the relations of production' from a totalising standpoint, but also take into account the production of gendered and racialised divisions of social labour. Pierre Macherey has recently underlined that the analysis of the normalisation of the sale of labour power (and its unwaged and coerced counterpart) is an integral aspect of Foucault's conceptualisation of biopower. What Macherey calls the 'productive power' of capitalist society is perpetuated via wage labour relations.[17] And as we know from SRF, and more specifically the work of Silvia Federici and her cohort, wage labour relations structure the lives of everyone who cannot or does not work for a wage, hence 'wages against housework'.[18] Reading social reproduction through biopolitics, then, problematises the terrain of social reproduction as a plenum of activities and tasks positively coded as reproducing life tendentially *in itself* and only contingently within, and for, the capital relation: life does not exist outside the mode of production, which in our historical period is characterised by the wage relation, and, more lately, the generalisation of debt and other coercive financial measures which regulate access to the means of social reproduction.[19]

As we have seen, social reproduction was always a concept that remained open to radical indeterminacy, sometimes meaning a specified set of tasks,[20] and sometimes the reproduction of life insofar as it is useful as labour power to capital and indirectly in the production of docile bodies by, and for, the state. With the link to theorisation of the

website of a Macherey studies group as *Le Sujet productif*, 2012, http://philolarge.hypotheses.org/1245.

18 Silvia Federici, 'Wages Against Housework' [1975], in *Revolution at Point Zero: Housework, Reproduction, and Feminist Struggle*, PM Press, Oakland, 2012

19 Soederberg, *Debtfare States and the Poverty Industry*, op cit; Maurizio Lazzarato, *The Making of the Indebted Man: An Essay on the Neoliberal Condition*, Joshua David Jordan, trans, The MIT Press and Semiotext(e), London and Cambridge, Massachusetts, 2012; Ivan Ascher, '"Moneybags Must Be So Lucky": Inside the Hidden Abode of Prediction', *Political Theory*, vol 44, no 1, 2015, pp 4–25

20 Christine Delphy, *Close to Home: A Materialist Analysis of Women's Oppression*, Diana Leonard, trans, University of Massachusetts Press, Amherst, 1984

21 This refers to the thesis first elaborated by Antonio Negri and others in the mid-1970s that the law of value fundamental to the capitalist mode of production in Marxist analysis no longer applied due to the technologically complex and socially diffuse character of contemporary labour. While the debates on this hypothesis have been, and continue to be, extensive, the relevant point here is that the expansion of the categories of 'labour' and 'value' enables many kinds of activity, not traditionally recognised with a wage or a job description, to claim a space both in political economy and its critique. The rise of terms such as 'immaterial labour', 'affective labour', 'caring labour' etc, illustrates the often contradictory double heritage of feminism and autonomist Marxism, which has had an equivocal

biopolitical already apparent, we can note that in this, it also mirrors the expansive notion of value production we find in post-operaist theory and often draws on the same theoretical sources.[21] In some cases, the tendency to define all activity taking place in the home as 'labour' introduced a potential risk of equating gender oppression too narrowly with a set of tasks and of homogenising them as functionally equivalent. It also implicitly brought into play a distinction between the 'productive' and the 'unproductive' which tended to be read normatively: domestic tasks were often interpreted as 'labour' and as 'productive' to justify their accommodation in a working-class – or a socialist feminist – politics. More recently, Marxist feminist analyses have tended to include not just unpaid but also 'paid reproductive labour' outside the home, such as healthcare, care work, sex work, and so on.[22] And they have also been expanded to consider sexuality and race, bringing into visibility the technologies of racialisation and illegalisation that prop up accumulation through the economic and social de-valorisation of (the labour of) many, if not most, of the global population.

However, in this article I will stay chiefly with the Marxist feminist legacy of SRF, following it into the present and the junctures with contemporary art practices. Two key Marxist feminist theorists of social reproduction who have provided reference points for the current debate, and who have been active since the 1970s, are Lise Vogel and Silvia Federici. I will go on to provide short precis of their contributions before summing up the questions that attend the contemporary appropriation of these bodies of work before moving on to a consideration of the role of art in the landscape of SRF.

In *Marxism and the Oppression of Women*, Vogel rethinks women's oppression within the categorical framework of Marx's *Capital*, theorising the structural significance that reproduction holds for capital.[23] For Vogel, at the very heart of the conditions of possibility of the reproduction of capitalism is labour power, ie people with the potential to be waged workers. Due to the central role of labour power in producing surplus value for capital, the generation and maintenance of past, present and future workers is the necessary condition for capitalist accumulation per se. Yet, for Vogel, reproduction had a contradictory character. As reproductive work itself was not value producing, it would fall outside the ambit of capital's immediate prerogatives. It follows from this that social reproduction leads to a dilemma for capital, with the prospect that the sidelining of reproductive activities might undermine the population of wage workers that would be its own future basis. In outlining this apparent contradiction, Vogel was undertaking a Marxist critique of the social character of reproductive activities, interrogating them from the standpoint of their structural devaluation within capitalist societies, on the basis of their contradictory position within the process of accumulation. In grasping an expanded terrain of reproduction in these ways – including not just the domestic environment but also labour processes and migration patterns – Vogel's theory mobilised the concept of reproduction, subjecting it to broader shifts in the global economy. Although Vogel does not explicitly pursue this, her approach opened the possibility for an analysis of the devaluation of racialised labour and its connection to that of gendered labour. However, and in a way that highlights the indeterminacy which often

relationship to gender politics. For a cogent if polemical encapsulation of the latter critique see Silvia Federici, 'Precarious Labor: A Feminist Viewpoint', lecture, 28 October 2006, Radical Bookstore, New York City, available at https://inthemiddle ofthewhirlwind.wordpress. com/precarious-labor-a-feminist-viewpoint/, accessed 8 June 2017.

22 Endnotes 3, 2013, op cit. See also Federica Giardini and Anna Simone, 'Reproduction as Paradigm: Elements for a Feminist Political Economy'; Premilla Nadasen, 'Domestic Workers' Rights, the Politics of Social Reproduction, and New Models of Labor Organizing'; Morgane Merteuil, 'Sex Work Against Work', all in the above cited issue of *Viewpoint*.

23 Lise Vogel, *Marxism and the Oppression of Women: Toward a Unitary Theory* [1983], Brill, Leiden, 2013

24 Silvia Federici, 'Feminism and the Politics of the Commons', *The Commoner*, 2011, http:// commoner.org.uk/wp-content/uploads/2011/01/ federici-feminism-and-the-politics-of-commons.pdf, accessed 12 December 2016

attends the concept of social reproduction, Vogel's work exhibits a subtle elision between a *quantitative* sense of 'necessary labour' in the terms established in Marx's critique of political economy – the part of the labour expended in a working day in which the worker earns the wage necessary to reproduce her or himself (and, debatably, a family of non-workers) in order to return to work the next day – and a *qualitative* sense of necessary labour considered more generally as a *kind* (rather than a measure) of labour essential to life. Thus, the reproduction of the population of workers is not so clearly distinct from the reproduction of the species per se, and the problem of reproductive tasks becomes entwined not only with the reproduction of the capitalist mode of production but also with humanity as such. In this, her analysis enacts a blurring in the term 'social reproduction', as the latter comes to stand in for the high level of abstraction communicated by 'the reproduction of the conditions of production' and the gendered concreteness of *tasks* which reproduce either 'labour power' or 'social relations' or 'people', as it were.

Silvia Federici, on the other hand, has insisted upon a fundamental identity between reproductive labour and other forms of work as value producing for capital. She positions the former within the core of the capitalist mode of production and affirms reproductive labour as *the* key moment of potential autonomy and struggle, based on the quasi-universal link between women and the domestic and care work that reproduces actual and potential workers in the market:

> Capitalist accumulation is structurally dependent on the free appropriation of immense quantities of labour and resources that must appear as externalities to the market, like the unpaid domestic work that women have provided, upon which employers have relied for the reproduction of the workforce.[24]

From this sentence alone, it is clear how Federici's writing over the years has generated the *locus classicus* for the popularisation of the radical analysis of women's reproductive work as economically and socially crucial for the reproduction of not just workers but of capital, and hence of capitalist society. Federici extends the analysis of surplus value as unpaid labour to the whole of capitalist class society and its gendered, racialised and colonial divisions, not only building bridges between working-class politics and feminism but also to critical race theory and decolonising thought more generally. In *Caliban and the Witch*, the links between gender, race and class exploitation are compellingly drawn across time and space, from the European medieval community to the Nigerian village of recent decades, to show that primitive accumulation is a constant for capitalism, and that the dispossession of women by legal or extra-legal means is a keystone of this logic.

For all the clarity and relevance of Federici's analysis, there is a certain vulnerability that attaches to some of its core assumptions, predicated on a vision of reproductive relations that can be sustained within, beyond and against their capitalist context. This vulnerability is likewise tied to the imperative to locate a revolutionary subject who carries an objective centrality to the relations of capitalist accumulation. The reproductive sphere becomes the privileged site for the identification of this subject, envisioned as the agent of a revolutionary 'domestication' of the world:

> If the house is the *oikos* on which the economy is built, then it is women, historically the house-workers and house-prisoners, who must take the initiative to reclaim the house as a centre of collective life, one traversed by multiple people and forms of cooperation, providing safety without isolation and fixation, allowing for the sharing and circulation of community possessions, and above all providing the foundation for collective forms of reproduction.[25]

Through these steps, the social reproduction of the totality seems to become writ small in a specific set of tasks, and it is this that essentially justifies Federici's valorisation of women's particular role in performing these tasks – a valorisation that risks implicitly endorsing or naturalising the existing gendered division of labour.[26]

Social Reproduction from the Standpoint of Art

Reproductive labour, in the Marxist feminist narrative, is a category designed to recast as labour activities performed in private, and coded as 'natural', which enable the activities that go on in public and are coded as cultural. This is done as a means to move the private into the public and to politicise the enforcement of the distinction as a structural constant in gendered and (if, at first, less frequently in the analysis) racialised exploitation. The key question becomes how to situate reproduction in its gendered, racialised and colonial specificity without drawing from it an affirmative politics that valorises the 'subject of reproduction' and her activities, that neglects the dialectic between the reproduction of life and the reproduction of capital in favour of a benign autonomising vision, as if life and capital can go their separate ways, each engaged in a dynamic of self-valorisation, unmediated by the state and its mechanisms of coercion and consensus. There is a tendency here to (strategically) bracket political questions, leaving aside knotty dilemmas of antagonism, composition and subjectivation.[27] While there are more complex political genealogies and debates indicated here than can be explored in the remainder of this article, the key issue is how to extricate the politics of reproduction from the re-naturalisings that have developed in the wake of its denaturalisation as labour by Marxist and socialist feminists in recent and current times. I will now turn to how such a project of denaturalisation of reproduction – of gendered labour, as well as of gender – is pursued by a sample of historical as well as current and historically inflected art practices, whose take on 'reproduction' indexes a paradigm shift in the focal point of systemic feminist critique, from the housewife in the 1970s to the dispersal of this focus among the 'infrastructures' that determine the collective life chances for populations – and art's capacity to render these legible and transformable.

Given the above critical formulations about social reproduction feminism, can we look to art for models of anti-reproductive labour and gender practices? The motivation to ask this question comes from a number of places.[28] Initially, it is because art itself can be seen as a

25 Ibid

26 Indeed, Federici's valorisation of the reproductive commons carries no overt critique of existing gendered divisions of labour, in fact transvaluing them as anti-capitalist so long as they occur in subsistence economies.

27 See Bue Rübner Hansen, 'Surplus Population, Social Reproduction, and the Problem of Class Formation', 2015, https://viewpointmag.com/2015/10/31/surplus-population-social-reproduction-and-the-problem-of-class-formation/, accessed 23 November 2016

28 See Marina Vishmidt and Kerstin Stakemeier, *Reproducing Autonomy: Work, Money, Crisis & Contemporary Art*, Mute, London and Berlin, 2016.

Pilvi Takala, *The Trainee*, 2008, installation, image courtesy: Stigter van Doesburg and Carlos/Ishikawa

29 My concern here is not with the operations of art markets but rather with the role of art in capitalist political economy as a commodity not produced in ways analogous to other capitalist industries, hence with a different relationship to the capitalist form of value. This is a fairly standard account of the economics of art in relation to capitalist (re)production recently eclipsed by more expansive notions of value derived loosely from strands in Italian autonomist Marxism. Dave Beech has done much to try to correct this course, though I differ from him in his argument that art is not a commodity and question the weight he places on a disciplinary notion of economics to undergird art's

reproductive institution, in Althusserian terms: an institution not directly implicated in the reproduction of capital but which yet contributes to socialising that reproduction when capital is seen through the lens of the reproduction of the class relation, along with race and gender and other profitable systems of subordination. It does this primarily by seeming to stand beyond or above them (like education or religion or, indeed, the state itself), ergo 'ideologically', pointing to a space of autonomy from the consequences of those relations.[29] The relationship is ever more direct, particularly when modes of labour relations and subjectivity rooted in art become the economic norm, as in the figure of the creative entrepreneur imposed upon the indebted and self-investing/exploiting subjects of unending socio-economic crisis. Gender (and gendered labour) likewise signifies a form of unconditionedness, or nature, or even a psycho-social excess, that stands in complicated relation to 'structural imperatives'. This opens up a number of questions, for example, for enquiries such as those by the journal/collective Endnotes into the 'logic of gender', which finds itself in a productive bind between explaining gender in functionalist terms using Marxist categories and accounting for an 'accursed share' (which they call 'the abject') which positions 'gender' as a psychic-libidinal remainder outliving its ideological as well as economic utility but still 'stick[ing] to the skin'.[30]

Pilvi Takala, *The Trainee*, 2008, installation, image courtesy: Stigter van Doesburg and Carlos/Ishikawa

'exceptionality'. See his *Art and Value: Art's Economic Exceptionalism in Classical, Neoclassical and Marxist Economic*, Brill, Leiden, 2015.

30 Endnotes 3, 2013, op cit

31 With specific exceptions – see Angela Dimitrakaki, *Gender, ArtWork and the Global Imperative*, Manchester University Press, Manchester, 2013, and Angela Dimitrakaki and Kirsten Lloyd, eds, *ECONOMY: Art, Production and the Subject in the 21st Century*, Liverpool University Press, Liverpool, 2015. Siona Wilson, Julia Bryan-Wilson and Helen Molesworth are among the few other art historians who research the labour politics of art from a feminist perspective, though in distinction from Dimitrakaki, they do not consistently employ a Marxist feminist optic.

32 Mierle Laderman Ukeles, *Washing, Tracks, Maintenance: Outside*, 1973; Francis Alys, *Turista*, 1997; Pilvi Takala, *The Trainee* (2008)

33 The canonical emblem for all these works is undoubtedly the late Mladen Stilinović's *Artist at Work* (1978), which pictures the artist asleep on the couch.

The relationship between production and reproduction has been a core issue for feminist art practices in recent decades and in the present – though one not consistently attended to by feminist art history.[31] The depiction of working women or women's work, in and out of the market, constitutes a strong strand in the image politics of feminist art and film. Yet there is another, perhaps more oblique, strand wherein the artist identifies with being a worker, but it is not clear whether their work is productive, reproductive or simply unproductive. In this mode, art's relation to work may, at first, appear only mimetic. We can loosely periodise two (overlapping) phases of such gestures in the art of the twentieth century: a heroic one, often male (think Rodchenko in a production suit, or the appeals to industrial work, even if often ironised, made by people like Robert Morris, Edward Kienholz, Richard Serra and Andy Warhol) in which artists sought to identify with the worker as the agent of history; and an anti-heroic phase, taking hold in a period in which work and its logic had subsequently become generalised for all genders, where artists appropriate the gestures of 'work' to make subaltern forms of labour present and disruptive to the categories and institutions of art and labour (think Mierle Laderman Ukeles washing the steps of the Wadsworth Athenaeum, Francis Alÿs holding a placard renting himself as a 'Turista' amidst the other day labourers in Mexico City's Zócalo square, Pilvi Takala turning up to work as a marketing intern to conspicuously do nothing).[32] In a continuum with this relation to work in its de-heroicising phase are practices that emphasise lethargy, failure, entropy and boredom.[33] Of course, Soviet productivism also had its counter-tendencies, as do contemporary enunciations of futility and *paresse*.[34] Yet here I am mainly interested in the more specific question of how art practices have allegorised the entropic qualities of reproductive labour, denaturalising it by making it look foolish, futile or indeed grandly absurd. These kinds of portrayals denaturalise reproductive labour from both sides: they cut away its social embeddedness, showing it purely as an activity which can be de- and recontextualised while they highlight the social relationship within which this activity can either acquire or lose an aura of inevitability and necessity, with all the moral implications carried by those categories.

34 Kasimir Malevich, 'Laziness as the Truth of Mankind', http://shifter-magazine.com/wp-content/uploads/2015/05/malevich_laziness.pdf, on the one hand, and the collection of social justice projects as 'useful art' (*Arte Util*) by Tania Bruguera on the other.

35 Park McArthur, 'Ramps', 12 January 2013 – 23 February 2013, Essex Street, New York; Cameron Rowland, '91020000', 17 January 2016 – 13 March 2016, Artists Space, New York

36 The literature is extensive, including Orlando Patterson, *Slavery and Social Death: A Comparative Study*, Harvard University Press, Cambridge, Massachusetts, 1985. Contemporary theorists often grouped under the 'Afro-pessimism' rubric are Frank Wilderson III, Jared Sexton, Christina Sharpe and Saidiya Hartman. For 'gender abolition', see Endnotes and others in the 'communisation current' (journals/collectives including *Riff-Raff, SIC, Theorie Communiste*, etc). An interesting addendum to this debate can be found in a recent interview with Benjamin Noys, who distinguishes cinematic representations of the 'working class' (a sociological category) from representations of the 'proletariat' (a position of nothingness within the system). See Benjamin Noys and Ramin Alaei '"The Proletariat Is Missing": Representations of the Proletariat in Cinema', 2016, https://www.academia.edu/28620075/_The_Proletariat_is_Missing_Representations_of_the_Proletariat_in_Cinema_Interview_with_Ramin_Alaei_of_farhangemrooz_Iran_, accessed 23 March 2017. This line of thought can be traced back to Brecht's commentary on the limitations of

Entropy seems like the main modality through which we experience an alienation from the manifest or unarguable 'usefulness' of reproductive labour – 'a woman's work is never done', and so on. (And indeed, it can be offered that all 'socially necessary labour', wherever it is performed, waged or not, shares this entropic quality as a hallmark of the experience of alienated labour.) I have chosen to focus on reproductive labour for this reason. Nonetheless, we can begin by regarding practices that take the more Althusserian (or Foucauldian, since the biopolitical is never far away) stance of using the field of art to stake out embodied, affective and formal critiques of reproductive institutions, such as the carceral complex, racialised urban decline, and the infrastructural violence of physical and mental normativity. We can examine the practices of Park McArthur, Cameron Rowland, LaToya Ruby Frazer and Eva Kotatkova from this perspective. In McArthur's and Rowland's work especially, there is a coextensive dimension of immanent critique of the art institution, yet one which both absorbs and inverts the laminated lessons of institutional critique. It is the contingency and the overdetermination of the art institution and not its omnipotence that we are shown when wheelchair access ramps are harvested from nearby facilities and reappear as works in McArthur's 'Ramps' (2013), or when rented prisoner-made desks are put up for rent rather than for sale – evoking the system of convict-leasing – in Rowland's shows.[35] Stigmatised identity is articulated as a formal principle. The means used, however, turn back on the mechanism of representation itself insofar as representation can lend a phantom tangibility and fullness to that which, in terms explored in contemporary writing grouped under shorthands like 'afro-pessimism' and 'gender abolition', exists as a site of nothing, or of 'social death', within a system of social relations and the significations possible within it.[36] Thus, on the one hand, there is an evocation of biopolitics both within and beyond the institution of art while, on the other, there is a refusal to depict its subject in the available terms of aesthetic critique or polemic, to short-circuit the enunciative claims that such practices risk reproducing and thus legitimating for the platforms and consumers of such critique. Here, a reproductive focus implicates the art institution as a paradoxical 'state apparatus' which both normalises *and* de-functionalises, in Claire Fontaine's terms, allowing other potentials to emerge as material hypothesis. However, like all institutions whose economic significance is displaced or relatively indirect, art can also act to legitimise existing social arrangements by providing a space of indeterminacy and experimentation. The question of what traction the de-functionalisation of subjectivities and objectivities can have, just like who does the work, cannot be deflected for long. There is thus a way in which the first sense of 'reproduction' in this article aligns with the already cited legacy of institutional critique as a problematic for artistic practices, an implication (also in its connotation of 'folding') to be taken up on another occasion.

Going back in time and shifting category, the second 'reproduction', which connotes 'reproductive labour', presents a more clear-cut strand in feminist art histories. The 1970s saw a number of feminist art strategies which operated to denaturalise both art and work from the standpoint of gender politics, emptying feminised domestic tasks of natural content to fill them with social content in a way that also interrogated the normative aesthetic and institutional claims of art. In 1969, Ukeles's 'Maintenance

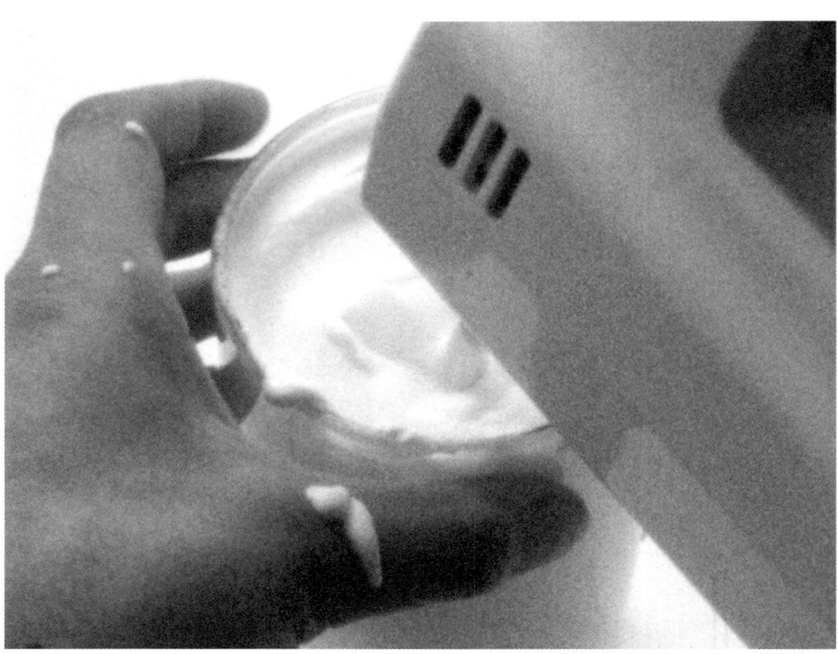

Margaret Raspé, *The Sadist Beats the Unquestionably Innocent*, 1971, image courtesy: Deutsche Kinemathek – Museum für Film und Fernsehen

representation – such as photographs of factories – to capture the rule of capitalist abstraction that organises the social conditions with respect to which such documentation would attempt to 'raise awareness'. Allan Sekula's writing has a great deal to contribute on this point as well. See Walter Benjamin, 'A Small History of Photography', *One-Way Street and Other Writings* [1931], Edmund Jephcott and Kingsley Shorter, trans, *New Left Review*, London, 1979; Allan Sekula, *Photography against the Grain: Essays and Photo Works, 1973–1983*, NSCAD Press, Halifax, Nova Scotia, 1984.

37 Andrea Phillips, 'In Service: Art, Value, Merit, and the Making of Publics', in Johanna Burton, Shannon Jackson and Domenic Willsdon, eds, *Public Servants: Art and the Crisis of the Common Good*, The New Museum and MIT Press, New York and Cambridge, Massachusetts, 2015

Art' dragged housework into the space of art, a now canonical feminist gesture of recasting (feminised) 'life' as work, upending the sovereign unconditionedness of the artistic 'work' in the process while exposing the gendered (and colonial) content of the 'separate spheres' principle which both insured this fragile autonomy and drained it of political force.

Ukeles may have spoofed the transcendent universality of the (male) artistic subject by proposing housework as art, but her targets were more extensive and, like the Italian feminists, these targets included revolutionary politics. In her *Maintenance Art Manifesto* (1969) Ukeles notes something that brings us back to what Claire Fontaine or Precarias a la deriva (the Spanish feminist collective) have, more recently, called the 'strike within the strike': can the labour that socially exists as the unacknowledged maintenance activity that goes on beneath and after work stoppages and revolutionary rupture ('the sourball of every revolution, who will clean up') also be suspended? And how would we envision the intensity and complexity of the challenge to established social relations introduced by a break in the continuity of care that precisely makes both alienated labour *and* its refusal possible? Thus, like Wages for Housework, Ukeles sought to valorise the excluded – here the excluded of the institution of art in its broadest sense, there of wage labour and the labour movement. In both cases, this valorisation is also a *de*-valuing, that is, a strategy which also challenges the institution that orders visibility and invisibility, inclusion and exclusion, as well as the larger system that it represents.[37] This is the dynamic of affirmation and negation that traverses social movements as well as the kind of politicised social practice for which Ukeles's work is often seen as emblematic.

Ukeles also introduced housework (or paid cleaning labour outside the home, as she does in other projects such as *Touch Sanitation*

(1977–1980) and *I Make Maintenance Art One Hour Every Day*, 1976) to the repertoire of feminist art as a comic medium; while in terms of the 'reproduction of the relations of production' art's reproductive role in society is also thereby highlighted, and its sovereignty exposed to its own abjection, by associating it with these activities. The comic horror of reproduction is famously taken up in Martha Rosler's *Semiotics of the Kitchen* (1975), but perhaps less well known are Margaret Raspé's camera-helmet films, also made in the early 1970s. Mounting a Super-8 camera on a hard hat, Raspé documented domestic tasks, mainly food preparation, at the same time as she was doing them. Unpicking the separation of spheres formally, but also performatively, she engaged the body-based aesthetics of feminist performance to estrange these prosaic activities by turning them into structuralist film. At the same time, the 'camera helmet' played on the affectation of industrial working-class masculinity so in vogue at the time among male artists such as Richard Serra and Carl Andre.[38] Apart from the collapse of action and documentation, and the displacement of humdrum women's activity into artistic action, there was also the idea of Woman as a domestic appliance, a fembot or, as Raspé called it, the Frautomat, where the discourse of reproduction veers into the technological.

This crossover between gendered labour, replication and ingestion can be picked out in recent work such as Wangechi Mutu's *The End of Eating Everything* (2013), where a fantasy creature performs the technologised reproduction of abjected black feminised (post-human) life.[39] Although extensively discussed in feminist art scholarship, most recently in Siona Wilson's monograph, it is also worth bringing in Mary Kelly's *Post-Partum Document* (first exhibited at the ICA, London, in 1976), since it presents such a fine dialectic with Ukeles's more performative work.[40] Focusing on biological and social reproduction in the figure of the mother-child couple, Kelly claimed the 'aesthetics of administration' for child-raising. Like Ukeles, she contaminated the sovereign body of art with invisible feminised labour, but rather than cleaning the museum, she contaminated it literally with the (dried) bodily fluids of her baby rendered onto plaques and charts. As the document and the chart was a form of heteronomous reproduction that had already infiltrated the museum under the sign of conceptual art, so Kelly's was a double pollution, of linguistically mannered, record-keeping conceptualism 'about' art, as well as the white cube. Rendering childcare and the social reproductive labour of being a mother as 'information that amounted to artwork', in the lexicon of the era, meant that the activities, the two parallel worlds, denaturalised and evacuated one another. The maternal virtues and the privilege of the artist neutralised one another in the space of the document. Finally, from this era we can mention the short performance films of Leticia Parente, such as *In* (1975) and *Task I* (1982), which dwell on the fungibility between the gendered body and housework, between subject and object. Parente hangs herself up in wardrobes, lays herself on an ironing board to be ironed by her maid. Parente's location in the Brazilian postcolonial context meant that any dramatisation of gendered labour could not help but disclose the racialised and classed 'Others' in the home, where much North American and Western European feminist art privileged the isolated 'housewife'.

38 Lynda Benglis's 1974 dildo-wielding advert in *Artforum* can be surveyed as the pinnacle of queer critique of such machismo, *avant la letter*.

39 Theodora Danylevich has published a fine experiential discussion of the piece: 'Beyond Thinking: Black Flesh as *Meat Patties* and *The End of Eating Everything*', *Rhizomes* 29, 2016, http://www.rhizomes.net/issue29/danylevich/index.html, accessed 15 November 2016

40 Siona Wilson, *Art Labor, Sex Politics: Feminist Effects in 1970s British Art and Performance*, University of Minnesota Press, Minneapolis, 2015

41 Barbara Ehrenreich, and Deirdre English, 'Microbes and the Manufacture of Housework', *Socialist Revolution*, vol 5, no 4, 1975, pp 5–40

42 Not to go without acknowledging the thematisation and theorisation of entropy in the work of Robert Smithson in that period.

43 Lacy's projects in this vein are too numerous to cite here, but the publication I refer to is *Mapping the Terrain: New Genre Public Art*, Bay Press, Seattle, 1995. More recent reflections are collected in Suzanne Lacy, *Leaving Art: Writings on Performance, Politics, and Publics, 1974–2007*, Duke University Press, Durham, North Carolina, 2010. Lacy may be considered one of a handful of progenitors of a feminist, performative public art, but there are many non-Western examples as well.

44 For the UK context see Josephine Berry Slater, and Anthony Iles, *No Room to Move: Radical Art and the Regenerate City*, Mute, London, 2010. The fundamental texts remain Rosalyn Deutsche, *Evictions: Art and Spatial Politics*, The MIT Press, Cambridge, Massachusetts, 1996 and Sharon Zukin, *Loft Living: Culture and Capital in Urban Change*, Johns Hopkins University Press, Baltimore, 1982.

45 Link TV, 'Art and Complicity: How the Fight Against Gentrification in Boyle Heights Questions the Role of Artists', 20 July 2016, https://www.linktv. org/shows/artbound/boyle-heights-gentrification-art-galleries-pssst, accessed 12 December 2016

Across these practices of staging, inversion and displacement, we also track the importance of the gesture of negation. We see waste as creative force, as a medium that propagates the destruction of representation. Older references here could be Marcel Duchamp's 'dust breeding', the social reproduction of dust on his *The Bride Stripped Bare by Her Bachelors, Even (The Large Glass)* (1915–1923), which can be read as an allegory of reproduction on a number of levels. Ukeles's 'dust paintings' then consolidate this entropic tendency, even as the re-presentation of housework as art also points to an entropic loss in art's heroic signifying power, which persists undimmed in its asseverations of uselessness and unproductivity: 'After a day's work, no matter how tiring, the housewife has produced no tangible object – except, perhaps, dinner; and that will disappear in less than half the time it took to prepare.'[41] As we see in Chantal Akerman's *Jeanne Dielman* (1975), entropy can become a source of psychic terror and disorganisation, which Akerman's protagonist tries to keep at bay with rules and routines, in an effort to make sense of this senseless, repetitive work, with diminishing success. In fact, entropy can be one of the key modalities through which we experience an alienation from the manifest or unarguable 'usefulness' of reproductive labour: maintenance as 'unworking'. Work that is not recognised as work meets its own unrepresentability as an image – it is that which disappears, which is consumed, which unravels into pathology rather than delivers a product. Performance coincides with its own negation. Akerman's first film, *Saute ma ville* (1968), directly collides domestic maintenance, absurdity and self-abolition: cleaning the kitchen is just a prelude to blowing up the apartment block, blasting all the housewives out of their kitchens.

These episodes from a reproductive history of entropy compel us to think not just about housework, even if women still do the majority of it, but the whole apparatus of gender which is being thrown open here.[42] It is the apparatus as reproductive and reparative of the gender relation that is denaturalised when gendered labour is depicted as something monstrous, abject but also prosaic and eccentric, and the domestic as a 'weird' or paradoxical space bereft of nature, nurture or hope. But we would also have to think about this kind of work not just as a spectrum of activities and the spheres to which they are assigned but also in terms of the general work allocated to women in the upkeep and maintenance of social bonds, which would be observed in the centrality of feminist practices to the genres of 'community' and 'social practices', both pioneered and theorised by Suzanne Lacy, to take one prominent example.[43] In an age where more and more of the population is deemed 'surplus' by the reproduction needs of capital, their own reproduction no longer the province of a functioning job market or welfare service, this institutionalised genre can begin to perform as a form of crisis management. Arguably, such a role had already been allocated to art by the introduction of socially engaged practice in the redevelopment and class/racial cleansing of deindustrialised but potentially lucrative urban areas. While exhaustively documented over the recent neoliberal decades,[44] the pattern of disinvestment, followed by speculative redevelopment and displacement, with artists and arts institutions as the mediating stage, is showing signs of being interrupted in locales like Boyle Heights, a working-class Latino neighbourhood in Los Angeles currently engaged in an anti-gentrification struggle that explicitly forces artists to take sides.[45]

Conclusion

As already discussed, there seem to be certain key conceptual tensions within the problematic of social reproduction. Is reproduction a total paradigm, incorporating not just the specific tasks traditionally allocated to women but the entirety of social production and consumption? Unifying formulations, like those of Cinzia Arruzza, present a conceptualisation of social reproduction as a totality like the one found in Marx, albeit more capable of grasping the function of gendered labour obfuscated in his work.[46] But the capacity for totalising, unifying theory that the concept seems to offer also brings with it a risk of indeterminacy in relation to concrete politics, as also suggested earlier. If 'social reproduction' comes to encompass the whole, it attains priority over the mode of production, and the reproduction of the relations of production comes to eclipse those relations themselves.[47]

A major source of indeterminacy in the social reproduction perspective comes from centring the elastic category of labour. Conversely, defining reproduction in terms of a set of gendered tasks runs the risk of naturalising a historically and geographically specific division of social labour. Proposals to resolve the current crises of reproduction in the self-management of reproduction stake all on the transvaluation of subsistence into practices of autonomy. Such a collapsing of ends and means is characteristic of a strong current of recent political thinking on the left, which often identifies self-organisation as the solution to all kinds of problems, conflating, as Jason E Smith writes, a 'vision of communism' with 'simple survival'.[48]

Marx talks about following the worker and the boss into the 'hidden abode of production' as where we really see what is going on beneath the apparent equality of contracts and exchange of labour time for money in the market, and where the domination and exploitation really unfold as an intrinsic part of capitalist production.[49] Leopoldina Fortunati talks about the 'arcane' of social reproduction, which is even more hidden as it is gendered, unmonetised and assigned to the 'private sphere' even more definitively than the private property of the factory floor.[50] Recent analyses of the household as a space beneath and beyond the contractual relations that structure the public sphere include Angela Mitropoulos's study or the queer theorist Miranda Joseph's anatomies of re-naturalisation in discourses of reproduction via their refusals of financial abstraction.[51] Both provide resources to unpick tendencies to valorise reproduction as a politics of life, in its understandably reparative desire to defend the many lives which are neither recognised nor sustained by the reproduction of capital.

Likewise, we have seen that feminist art practices have been and are performing the kind of denaturalisation of gendered domestic and social labour that contemporary politics of reproduction still finds a challenge. But for the larger scope of this enquiry, we have to establish the importance of an attitude of negation, or at the very least sublation, which recognises antagonism not just in these art practices but in the everyday life of gender in general. This cannot be an abstract challenge to a thinking or politics that valorises reproduction but to the reproduction of the gender relation as a relation articulated with, but not

46 Arruzza, 'Remarks on Gender', op cit

47 Kathi Weeks also asked: 'What happens when social reproduction is understood as the production of the forms of social cooperation on which accumulation depends or, alternatively, as the rest of life beyond work that capital seeks continually to harness to its times, spaces, rhythms, purposes, and values? What I am in search of is a conception of social reproduction – of what it is we might organize around – that can pose the full measure of its antagonism with the exigencies of capital accumulation, a biopolitical model of social reproduction less readily transformed into new forms of work and thus less easily recuperated within the present terms of the work society.' Kathi Weeks, *The Problem with Work: Feminism, Marxism, Antiwork Politics, and Postwork Imaginaries*, Duke University Press, Durham, North Carolina, 2011, p 29.

48 Jason E Smith, 'Since the End of the Movement of the Squares: The Return of The Invisible Committee', *The Brooklyn Rail*, 2015, http://brooklynrail.org/2015/06/field-notes/since-the-end-of-the-movement-of-the-squares-the-return-of-the-invisible-committee, accessed 15 December 2016

49 Marx, *Capital*, Volume One, op cit, pp 279–280

50 Fortunati, *The Arcane of Reproduction*, op cit

51 Angela Mitropoulos, *Contract and Contagion: From Biopolitics to Oikonomia*, Autonomedia, New York, 2012; Miranda Joseph, *Debt to Society: Accounting for Life under Capitalism*, University of Minnesota Press, Minneapolis, 2014. For the current feminist theoretical debates on contract, it helps to go further back to feminist legal scholars such as Carole Pateman, *The*

Sexual Contract, Polity Press, Cambridge, 1988, and to historians of the contract as equivocal instrument of emancipation and repression for women and slaves in the nineteenth-century United States, such as Amy Dru Stanley, *From Bondage to Contract: Wage Labor, Marriage, and the Market in the Age of Slave Emancipation*, Cambridge University Press, Cambridge, 1998. For a powerful and subtle excavation of enslavement as the premise of freedom of contract see Sora Han, 'Slavery as Contract: *Betty's Case* and the Question of Freedom', *Law & Literature*, vol 27, no 3, 2015, pp 395–416.

52 This is an argument made by K D Griffiths and J J Gleeson in '*Kinderkommunismus*: A Feminist Analysis of the 21st-Century Family and a Communist Proposal for its Abolition', *Ritual Magazine*, undated, http://ritualmag.com/kinderkommunismus/, particularly in relation to queer theory; accessed 8 June 2017. This argument is echoed in critiques of 'queer nihilism', often associated with the work of Lee Edelman, *No Future: Queer Theory and the Death Drive*, Duke University Press, Durham, 2004 as disregarding its own blind spots of race, class and gender, and arguing for an aestheticised conception of anti-family politics without a materialist analysis.

53 Karl Marx, 'Draft of an Article on Friedrich List's Book *Das nationale System der politischen Oekonomie*', *Marx and Engels Collected Works, Volume 4* [1845], Lawrence & Wishart, London, 2010, pp 278–279

54 Indicatively, Sue Ferguson proposes an 'integrative ontology of labour' which repeats the tendencies to indeterminacy in the concept of social reproduction by eliding the distinction

collapsible to, the reproduction of other social relations such as class and race.[52] To do that, we have to evacuate the work done by women of its necessity and naturalness, and to evacuate reproduction of its nobility, as the last vestige of, on the one hand, the goddess mythology of 1970s feminism that the politics of reproduction still cannot leave behind and, on the other, the myth of the revolutionary subject, which is (part of the reason) why domestic work had to be turned into productive labour by the theorists of Wages for Housework. Reproductive work is not exempt from what Marx had in mind when he wrote:

> It is one of the greatest misunderstandings to talk of free, human, social work, or work without private property. 'Work' is essentially the unfree, inhuman, unsocial activity, determined by private property and creating private property. The abolition of private property becomes a reality only when it is understood as the abolition of 'work'.[53]

Including reproductive work in this assessment prevents us from separating it from formally market-mediated capitalist labour as somehow more wholesome, more selfless (or, worse, more expressive of the self), more constitutive of social ties, simply because it seems to wear a badge of necessity which can never be completely abstracted into pointless and exploitative profit-making activity. It also allows us to sharpen the traction of 'social reproduction' as part of the project of constructing a 'unitary theory' without thereby repeating the problematic 'ontology of labour' that has been often (mis-)diagnosed in Marx and repeated by some social reproduction theorists.[54]

The 'two reproductions' delineated above allow us to think about reproduction at different scales, and here specifically to see reproduction as a *theme* and a *methodology* in art (reproductive labour in feminist art) as well as see *art as itself an institution of reproduction*, both normalising certain behaviours and bodies and putting these into question. The biopolitical efficacy of art cannot be divorced from its 'defunctionalisation of subjectivities' and uses, but neither can it be collapsed with it. Thus it is in art's suspension of necessity – contra to programmes such as Arte Util – and in its speculative relationship to social reality that imaginatively undermines a simple association between use and ethics; an association which can blind us to the more systemic beneficiaries of our useful activity.[55] The key question that emerges then is how to situate 'the hidden abode' of reproduction in its gendered, racialised and colonial specificity without drawing from it an affirmative politics in favour of a benign autonomising vision. As Jasmine Gibson writes,

> a mass movement with an analysis of what is happening in the U.S. today must endeavor to destroy what it means to be a 'woman' in the midst of the current recession, not to laud and valorize it.[56]

That is, following an older guideline, to show capital and the state what a real state of emergency looks like.

between labour and life: 'At the heart of social-reproduction feminism is the conception of labour as broadly productive – creative not just of economic values, but of society (and thus of life) itself.' Sue Ferguson, 'Intersectionality and Social-Reproduction Feminisms: Towards an Integrative Ontology', *Historical Materialism*, vol 24, no 2, 2016, pp 38–60. Some materialist feminist work that tries to present a totalising account of the persistence of gender and gendered labour in capital that does not take the 'ontology' path is the work of Endnotes, specifically in 'The Logic of Gender', op cit.

55 Stephen Wright, *Toward a Lexicon of Usership*, 2013, http://museumarteutil.net/wp-content/uploads/2013/12/Toward-a-lexicon-of-usership.pdf, accessed 20 November 2016

56 Jasmine Gibson, 'Fire This Time: Notes on the Crisis of Reproduction', *LIES Journal*, 2015

57 Angela Dimitrakaki, 'The Premise of Contradiction and Feminist Politics: Reflections on Arahmaiani's Art and Life' *Afterall* 42, 2016, pp 12–23

58 Griselda Pollock, 'Is Feminism a Trauma, a Bad Memory, or a Virtual Future?', *Differences: A Journal of Feminist Cultural Studies*, vol 27, no 2, 2016, pp 27–61. Importantly, Pollock, op cit, p 30, diagnoses the taxonomy of 'waves' used to historicise the feminist movement as an iteration of patriarchal generational logic, noting that this usage carries with it 'a false sequentiality, deceptive consistency, and obligatory ruptures along a line of time, rather than holding us to moments, flashes, constellations of unexhausted and unpredictable feminist potentiality'.

59 Vishmidt and Stakemeier, *Reproducing Autonomy*, op cit

Coda

There is still a distinct contradiction or, maybe more gently, paradox, in the preceding analysis, since I have been talking about practices that deflate the sovereignty of the artist, of art, of the autonomous individual and the creative genius which is as basic to feminist art as it is to feminist politics. Many of these practices have been increasingly 'rediscovered' and recuperated within the exhibition circuit and the market. It is primarily women artists who are being inscribed into the canon along the premises of a radical authorship based on a politics of recognition and representation, also very much driven by social media and the de-contextualised practices of subjectivation that are reinforced in that space. But how are these inclusions and historicisations being performed, when social movements – with feminism as a privileged instance – are showcased in art institutions embedded in the reproduction of capitalism? As Angela Dimitrakaki has asked, how do we square the radical projects of de-hierarchisation and collective separatisms those histories bring to light with the canon as a format of the competitive market in the exhibition venue and the academy?[57] If recent decades of postcolonial critique and globalisation have significantly dented the oedipal modernist genealogy of canon formation as the progressive transmission of culture down the male line that feminist art historians (most prominently Griselda Pollock) have trenchantly critiqued over the years,[58] institutions and markets continue to be actuated by an 'extractive gaze' which delivers a forceful impulse to canon formation in the present, just as it leaves the capitalist premises of artistic autonomy intact functionally, if not rhetorically.[59] With the proviso that there is an important pedagogical and consciousness-raising aspect to such mappings and recontextualisations, the composition of 'the viewers' (or the public) continues to be a difficult challenge. It remains an open question as to how one can shed light on important practices without casting their political contexts into the shadow or claiming to know where the context stops and the radical authorship begins, much less to prescribe how, or even if, they resonate in the present, and whose present that might be.

Third Text, 2017
Vol. 31, No. 1, 67–78, https://doi.org/10.1080/09528822.2017.1364333

Losing Ground?

A Note on Feminism, Cultural Activism and Urban Space

Victoria Horne

1 Moira Gatens, *Feminism and Philosophy: Perspectives on Difference and Equality*, Polity Press, Cambridge, 1991, p 129

2 Collective member Liz Heron writing on her personal blog: https://lizheron.wordpress.com/tag/agitprop/, accessed 15 August 2016

3 The artists would not grant permission to reproduce sections of the project needed to illustrate this article; however, interested readers can find the images online.

4 Victoria Horne, 'The Art of Social Reproduction', *Journal of Visual Culture*, vol 15, no 2, August 2016, pp 179–202

To effect the total insertion of women into capitalist society would involve the acknowledgment of the 'blind spot' of traditional socio-political theorizing: that the reproduction of the species, sexual relations and domestic work are performed under *socially constructed* conditions, not natural ones, and that these tasks are socially and economically necessary.[1]

Our intention was not to make art, but effective agitprop.[2]

Over an eighteen-month period in the late 1970s, the feminist collective the Hackney Flashers produced a documentary account of a community nursery in North East London, concentrating on the structural difficulties of organising childcare in an exploitative urban environment where the necessary reproduction of life was coming into increasing conflict with the productivity demands of capitalism. The project combined research on childcare facilities, and interviews with parents and workers at the nursery, alongside visual material including photographs, cartoons and appropriated advertising images. Hung on a series of twenty-nine laminated panels, *Who's Holding the Baby?* was available for hire and was exhibited at community centres, libraries and trade union events across the UK.[3]

I have written elsewhere about *Who's Holding the Baby?* in relation to the contemporary art museum, considering whether the project can continue to fulfil its pedagogic ambitions under altered social and economic conditions of display.[4] My intention here, however, is to comment in greater depth on how a historical consideration of the Hackney Flashers opens up pressing enquiries around activism and artistic practice in contexts of urban change or gentrification. Given that the collective's working life in the mid-1970s coincides with the beginning of a decades-long decline in welfare capitalism and we are currently negotiating the ruined aftermath of that decline, it is instructive to explore the salient features of urban change and social reproduction activism captured by the project. Consequently, rather than relinquishing the project to the sepulchral or spectacular effects of the contemporary art museum, by examining the complex social structure within which *Who's Holding the Baby?* was produced and now circulates, this article aims to separate the original cultural intervention from the art historical representation produced out of it. This would allow us to see how the project captures a moment of historical change in the organisation of social reproduction labour, and why its critique remains – or has become *increasingly* – relevant to contemporary debates about gentrification, gender and the possibility of labour withdrawal or collective resistance. What follows is a series of notes situating the social reproduction activism of the Hackney Flashers in relation to coexistent conditions of the period.

Feminism at Home

The critique of domestic space and its associated 'homemaking' tasks has long been a prominent feature of art informed by feminist politics. This tradition encompasses diverse examples, including the handcrafted environments of the LA *Womanhouse* (1972), Martha Rosler's seething video-performance *Semiotics of the Kitchen* (1975), the UK postal network *Feministo: Portrait of the Artist as a Young Housewife* (1975–1977), and Alexis Hunter's photographic series *The Marxist Housewife (Still Does the Housework)* (1978). For the second-wave feminist movement, emerging in the 1960s, this focus was a logical response to the phenomenon of suburbanisation, with its associated race, class and gender effects, that was taking place as a result of a postwar housing expansion.[5] Betty Friedan's book of 1963, *The Feminine Mystique*, gave expression to that generation's gathering discontent; the paradigm of the isolated and frustrated middle-class housewife was inaugurated, and the suburban home became the locus of women's emancipatory organising. As Kirsten Lloyd points out, however, recent conditions (most notably a financial crisis spurred by risky mortgage debts) demand a shift of emphasis in feminist art history '*from housework to housing*'.[6] Given the very visible absorption of reproductive work within the productive sphere and, consequently, the deepened imprecision of those already uncertain boundaries, such a shift is certainly required. However, we must be careful not to relinquish the great feminist gains that have been built upon the exaggerated (or at least in need of updating) division between the public and private, and we must remain cautious of hierarchising the public/urban and private/domestic figures once again.[7] This shift might also allow us to revisit historical moments, to trace more clearly how women's cultural activism in the areas of life labelled personal (including childcare and housework) was never secondary, but was deeply connected to public struggles around neoliberal economies and the right to the city.

5 David Harvey traces the history of suburbanisation in postwar America and argues that it served the ideological function of refocusing largely white, middle-class desires towards the private, individual and conservative; crucially absorbing surplus capital and assuring social stability. See David Harvey, 'The Right to the City', *New Left Review* 53, September/October 2008, pp 27–28.

6 See Kirsten Lloyd, '*If you lived here … A Case Study on Social Reproduction in Feminist Art History*', in Victoria Horne and Lara Perry, eds, *Feminism and Art History Now*, I B Tauris, London, 2017, p 183, emphasis added.

7 For more on this topic see Aruna D'Souza and Tom McDonough, eds, *The Invisible Flâneuse? Gender, Public Space, and Visual Culture in Nineteenth-Century Paris*, Manchester University Press, Manchester, 2006.

8 The commodification of maternity has reached exceptional levels today: see Victoria Browne, 'The Money Follows the Mum', *Radical Philosophy* 199, September/October 2016, pp 2–7.

9 Arlie Hochschild later described this phenomenon strikingly in *The Second Shift: Working Families and the Revolution at Home* [1989], Penguin Books, London, 2012, pp xii-xiii: 'I don't believe these lively, inquiring eighteen- to twenty-two-year-old students haven't thought about the problem. I believe they are afraid of it. And since they think of it as a "private" problem, each also feels alone.'

10 Glenda Wall, '"Putting Family First": Shifting Discourses of Motherhood and Childhood in Representations of Mothers' Employment and Child Care', *Women's Studies International Forum* 40, 2013, pp 162–171. I was directed to this essay by Littler et al, 'Life after Work: A Discussion', *Soundings: A Journal of Art and Culture* 56, spring 2014, pp 67–80.

11 Griselda Pollock and Janet Wolff have notably theorised gender, modernity and urban space. For more recent responses to these theories, see D'Souza and McDonough, eds, *The Invisible Flâneuse?* op cit.

12 Dolores Hayden, 'Claiming Women's History in the Urban Landscape', in Joan Rothschild, ed, *Design and Feminism: Re-visioning Spaces, Places and Everyday Things*, Rutgers University Press, New Jersey, 1999, pp 45–57

13 See, for instance, the pressure group 'Focus E15: Social Housing Not Social Cleansing'. As *The Independent* reported on 29 April 2015, over 50,000 families had been 'shipped out of London boroughs in

Who's Holding the Baby? was intended as an intervention into the moral ideologies giving shape to practices of motherhood and childcare rather than a straight documentary series. And although the collective called on men to share this care burden (by aiming critique at the interdependent structures of capitalism *and* patriarchy), the focus of the project remained on an urban female subject, recognising her primary role in reproduction and its associated relations of care. Read together, the textured display panels draw critical connections between a series of issues, including poor housing provision, a lack of childcare facilities, surviving on a modest income, and women's mental health. The critique mounted by the Hackney Flashers was especially prescient in targeting pharmaceutical companies and their individualised, medical solutions to what were undeniably public, structural problems.[8] This occurred within the context of a women's liberation movement that was loudly proclaiming maintenance labour, and reproductive health, to be falsely characterised as private, individual, even shameful problems, leaving women susceptible to those targeted corporate and promotional pressures.[9]

Who's Holding the Baby? asked how we might re-politicise the work of childrearing in the face of such powerful ideological adversaries, and presented viewers with a tangible alternative based on solidarity, relationality and collectivism. Regrettably, over the ensuing years, as sociologist Glenda Wall has shown, media representations of socialised childcare and nursery provision have significantly worsened. Wall's detailed analysis describes the cultural construction of 'child-centred' mothering which leaves little room for a mother's own needs and desires, and investment in other activities including paid work. This, coupled with the competitive language of neoliberal self-responsibility, has consolidated desires for individual solutions predicated on the private family unit.[10]

Care in the City

The subject of how sexual difference shapes experience of the modern city has historically formed a significant thematic within the development of feminist discourse. Cultural theorists have constructed valuable frameworks – concerning gender, the power of the gaze, and controlled access to social and representational space – to describe how women's urban experience has necessarily been very different to that of men's.[11] How women see and are seen has formed the core of these investigations; thus the urban specialist Dolores Hayden has examined ways of making women's elided history visible in the metropolitan landscape.[12] Such investigations cut to the core of contemporary struggles over gentrification, homogenisation, and the displacement of 'surplus' subjects who are no longer considered economically useful.[13] The position of culture within these issues is complex (not least in terms of art's well-known entanglement in processes of gentrification) but, as Rob Shields argues, representational strategies are vital:

> Without attention to gender there is a tendency to represent the city as a generally public space, that is to focus on its street life, leaving out home life within the tenements, flats, dwellings and backyards in which family

the past three years due to welfare cuts and soaring rents', which they also described as a form of 'social cleansing'. Available at: http://www.independent.co.uk/news/uk/home-news/over-50000-families-shipped-out-of-london-in-the-past-three-years-due-to-welfare-cuts-and-soaring-10213854.html, accessed 15 August 2016.

14 Rob Shields quoted in Janet Wolff, 'Gender and the Haunting of Cities', in D'Souza and McDonough, *The Invisible Flâneuse?*, op cit, pp 18–28, p 23

15 Liz Bondi, 'The Best of Times for Some and the Worst of Times for Others? Gender and Class Divisions in Urban Britain Today', *Geoforum* 31, 2000, pp 329–343, p 331. See also: 'Gender Divisions and Gentrification: A Critique', *Transactions of the Institute of British Geographers*, vol 16, no 2, 1991, pp 190–198; 'Gender, Class, and Gentrification: Enriching the Debate', *Society and Space* 17, 1999, pp 261–282. Thanks to Angela Dimitrakaki and Kirsten Lloyd for alerting me to Bondi's research.

16 Bondi 2000, op cit, p 335

17 Ibid

18 Bondi 1991, op cit

19 Larry Elliott and Dan Atkinson, *Fantasy Island: Waking up to the Incredible Economic, Political and Social Illusions of the Blair Legacy*, Constable, London, 2007, p 76. Emphasis added. The term 'New Labour' refers to the Labour Party's redefinition under the leadership of Tony Blair, in the run-up to the 1997 UK election. Although no longer in government, the legacies of that rebranding have been carried forward.

20 Ibid, p 89

life takes place. The domestic remains *invisible* in representations of the city as a public 'space' which is thought of merely as the built analogue or architectural concretisation of the public 'sphere'.[14]

The geographer Liz Bondi has worked assiduously to draw attention to the numerous ways in which the family, as a key mechanism of social reproduction, exists and thrives in an urban environment – and notably how, alongside class relations, 'gender relations are built into the organisation of the city and… continue to shape its development'.[15] Bondi's research establishes links from childcare organisation to gentrification and displacement; demonstrating that if campaigners want to combat the social cleansing of cities, some of the solutions will have to start at home. The geographer determines that young men and women may achieve relative parity across their waged and unwaged work, but this commitment to gender equality tends to last only *until the introduction of children into the household*.[16] At this stage, career-driven middle-class women may avoid the reassertion of a care disparity by displacing the burden onto paid professionals, usually other women. This implies that the historic focus on progressing women's working practices through improved access to childcare requires a more holistic reconception of the ethics and practices of 'work' overall.

Most vitally, Bondi points to the lack of a collective feminist voice in this housing debate; this is the 'best of times for some and the worst of times for others'.[17] Women are cast as simultaneously agents of gentrification (cities have provided emancipatory opportunities for waged employment, housing, and new levels of consumption) and, at the other end of the economic scale, as vulnerable casualties aggressively expelled from their homes as a result of those changes.[18] The aspirational ideology of liberal feminism finds a direct correlation here with that of the creative economy – as both 'success stories' are predicated on a fundamental clash between the domestic and the public, between productive and reproductive work. Larry Elliott and Dan Atkinson have hinted that Britain could today be accurately described as 'a servant economy', as 'there are at least four million people "in service" and the proportion of the population employed by the well-off to do their cooking, cleaning, childcare and gardening *is as high as it was in the 1860s*'.[19] Throughout their book, the authors excoriate New Labour's focus on the employment and regeneration opportunities presented by the so-called creative industries, pointing out that:

> A large number of people work in the creative industries, broadly defined, although not nearly as many as the hype would suggest. There are three times as many people working in domestic services as there are in advertising, television, video games, film, the music business and design combined; the creative industries represent around one in 20 of the people working in Britain today. Between them they account for 4 per cent of all UK exports of goods and services, but as the NESTA report made clear, it is hard to make serious money.[20]

These figures implode the myth of creative industrial regeneration, exposing at its core the replication of a characteristically bourgeois urban subject, one whose freedom is predicated on the unseen reproductive work of others. For Elliott and Atkinson's creative workers, and Bondi's middle-class mothers, achieving and sustaining a bourgeois social position is only possible by displacing what used to be called 'women's work' onto others. As feminists we need to further investigate how gender is entwined with this risk of being declassed.

Art in the City

Coincidentally, the very name chosen by the collective indicates some of the more excessive transformations to have sculpted London's landscape over the past four decades. The *Hackney* Flashers: during the 1970s this geographic signifier would have evoked a working-class periphery in the North East of the city, strewed with tower blocks and deserted warehouses left over following the deindustrialisation of the area. Indeed, Sheila Rowbotham tellingly recalls relocating to Dalston in the mid-1960s, the train journey seeming 'that we were heading for the end of the known world'.[21] At the other end of the spectrum, the borough has now become a byword for hipster chic, more likely to conjure the romanticised post-industrial design aesthetic of artisan coffee shops and the consumer lifestyle of affluent young professionals.

Cities change; and anti-gentrification struggles are not fundamentally opposed to change, or to development in the character of an area.[22] However, urban development does not occur organically but takes place within concrete historical conditions and uneven social relations. Timon Beyes reminds us that gentrification is not a benign process of urban revitalisation; instead, it involves 'the wholesale, and frequently shockingly brutal "cleansing" and "pacification" of inner-city areas to make them "safe" for middle-class residents'.[23] Rosalyn Deutsche and Cara Gendel Ryan, in their celebrated article 'The Fine Art of Gentrification', describe the victims of gentrification as the 'cast-offs of late capitalism', surplus subjects who are 'losing the right to survive in society at all'.[24]

A closer look at the exhibition history of *Who's Holding the Baby?* illuminates these transformations with striking accuracy, standing as a salient example of changes to the fabric of the city. Following its display at Market Nursery, the project was exhibited in 1978 at Centerprise Bookshop, a co-operative cultural centre situated on Dalston's bustling Kingsland High Street. '[T]he venue was important,' Rosemary Betterton writes, as 'Hackney had a thousand children on its daycare waiting list and the exhibition was linked to campaigns for nurseries in the borough.'[25] After touring various venues across the UK, in 1979 the project was included in the landmark show 'Three Perspectives on Photography' at the Hayward Gallery in London.[26] This exhibition was not without its tensions and, according to the collective, it 'attracted controversy and some criticism from the art establishment'.[27] The subsequent history of these two exhibition sites is valuable in that it points to forty years of mounting urban commodification, and the closure of non-institutional spaces for the dissemination of artistic activism.

From 1971, Centerprise provided an alternative cultural space for the local community, encompassing a bookshop, café, gallery and room for education classes. The bookshop and its associated publishing

21 Sheila Rowbotham, *Promise of a Dream*, Verso, London and New York, 2000, p 81

22 In 1964, Ruth Glass coined the term 'gentrification' to describe the injustice of displacement that she was witnessing in postwar London. See *London: Aspects of Change*, MacGibbon and Gee, London, 1964.

23 Timon Beyes, quoting Latham (2009), in 'Summoning Art to Save the City: A Note', *Ephemera: Theory & Politics in Organization*, vol 15, no 1, 2015, pp 207–220, p 213

24 Rosalyn Deutsche and Cara Gendel Ryan, 'The Fine Art of Gentrification', *October* 31, winter 1984, pp 91–111, p 96

25 Rosemary Betterton, 'Maternal Embarrassment: Feminist Art and Maternal Effects', *Studies in the Maternal*, vol 2, no 1, 2010, pp 1–18, p 3

26 'Three Perspectives on Photography: Recent British Photography', Hayward Gallery, 1 June – 8 July 1979

27 http://hackneyflashers.com/history/, accessed 15 August 2016

community has been especially noted for its dedication to recording and disseminating 'marginal' histories from the working-class and black British cultural spheres.[28] In 2012, however, Centerprise was forced to close after a lengthy legal battle with Hackney Council. The council insisted upon bringing annual rent on the property into line with commercial rates in the area rather than continuing the token 'peppercorn' arrangement that had been in place for forty-two years. It should be self-evident that non-profit community enterprises cannot compete at the levels established by the commercial sector, and are resultantly forced out of economically 'regenerated' areas. In 2015, however, *Who's Holding the Baby?* returned to the Hayward, included in a thorough survey exhibition intended to shed light on the cultural history of Britain since the postwar period. As Liz Heron writes:

> After much debate on the subject in the past, we have no objection to our work being seen in museum and gallery contexts, because we think it still raises questions about women's work and childcare within a wider political framework.[29]

Founded two years previous to Centerprise, and therefore sharing a historical ancestry, the Hayward nonetheless reveals a converse history of this period. The gallery was managed until 1987 by the Arts Council of Britain, after which it became part of the independent arts organisation the Southbank Centre. The Southbank has its origins in the Festival of Britain and in 2011 celebrated the bicentennial of that event 'with Mastercard', the tagline epitomising the shift from state-funded to corporately sponsored culture during half a century. The Southbank has also been engaged in a legal dispute centred on property rights, since its announcement in 2011 of a £120-million-pound development project that would see a historic community skate park transformed into corporate retail venues. The closure of non-institutional or non-commercial spaces (as I explore in the following section) raises concerns over where cultural activism and artwork can be shown, the ideological context of their display, and which visitors are likely to access them. Acknowledging significant changes within the London property market, this discussion is not intended as a unique criticism of the Hayward – the fate of Centerprise illustrates the outcome for cultural organisations that do not conform to competitive economic arrangements – but suggests that the altered landscape of contemporary, creative cityscapes must be a prime consideration when assessing the history and future of activist work. As Andrea Phillips reminds us, today 'museums and galleries must understand that their survival depends on collaboration with the private sector'.[30]

In a further twist, in 1984 Deutsche and Gendel Ryan alerted readers to the twinned 'renewals' of property (economic capital) and art (cultural capital) in New York City, suggesting that their probable interrelationship was an ethical concern for subjects working in the cultural sector. Since then, of course, a number of agents have sought to harness this correlation in order to 'improve' or regenerate specific urban landscapes. Timon Beyes distinguishes three modes in which 'art is summoned to save the city: as spectacle, as grassroots development and as social work'.[31] Most relevant here is the third of these; how art in its

28 For more details see Tom Woodlin, 'Working-class Writing, Alternative Publishing and Audience Participation', *Media, Culture & Society*, vol 31, no 1, 2009, pp 79–96.

29 Liz Heron's personal blog: https://lizheron.wordpress.com/tag/hackney-flashers-collective/, accessed 15 August 2016

30 Andrea Phillips, 'Art and Housing: The Private Connection', in Andrea Phillips and Fulya Erdemci, eds, *Social Housing– Housing the Social: Art, Property and Spatial Justice*, Sternberg Press, Berlin, 2012, pp 143–159, p 154

31 Beyes, 'Summoning Art to Save the City: A Note', op cit, pp 207–220, p 208

post-representational, socially engaged form today (wherein artists want to do something 'more social... and more real than art'[32]) instantiates a further phase of art's incorporation into a contemporary regime of urban development. With the commodification of housing and childcare intensifying, in confrontation with the withdrawal of state funding, to what extent does the autonomous organising of artists complement or subvert processes of urban renewal? Does liberal voluntarism simply assuage the fissures in state-supported social reproduction? And if that is indeed the case, as others have already discussed, how might it be possible to withdraw or refuse our reproductive and/or artistic labour in the face of a care deficit, or to move beyond enforced complicity?[33]

Alternative Spaces, Public Protests

The epigraph at the beginning of this article reminds us that the Hackney Flashers conceived of their photography practice principally in terms of cultural activism or 'agitprop' rather than fine art. The acronym agitprop emerged in use shortly after the October Revolution of 1917, to describe art and design projects explicitly 'applied to political and agitational ends'. But as John Milner puts it, 'Agitprop was not a stylistic term; it applied to various forms and... [t]hese new art forms were, crucially, defined as public, political and communal in purpose and execution.'[34] The criterion of municipal production and consumption is useful here (not only as it is so often in tension with the apparently private concerns of the reproductive sphere), as it points to resonances with recent scholarship on the politics of 'visual ephemera in public space'.[35] This facilitates an understanding of how the Hackney Flashers' work precedes, and corresponds with, civic modes of cultural activism that became popular within feminist and queer organisations of the 1980s. Moreover, while *Who's Holding the Baby?* has been limitedly historicised with reference to feminism and photoconceptualism, adopting a material culture framework enables us to trace more clearly the project's relation to the urban environment in which it was sited.

In the 1960s, London was home to an agitprop revival, with leftist workers' groups, anti-nuclear campaigners and student radicals experimenting with countercultural street actions and political performance. Rowbotham vividly recalls this artistic-activist milieu in her memoirs of the period; encapsulated in her account by an anti-corporate housing campaign modelled on Ken Loach's realist drama about homelessness, where the banners and circulated flyers cried, 'Cathy Come to Centrepoint: It's Empty'.[36] These performative actions harked back to 1930s political theatre, and sculpted the activist environment within which the Hackney Flashers would later emerge. The anti-fascist montages of John Heartfield and Hannah Hoch shared a locus with agitprop and were also an influence on the collective's cultural resistance, updated in the context of the women's liberation movement and its demands for revolution in women's labour conditions, both in and out of the home.

The liveliness of this oppositional culture was predicated, in part, on the availability of free time to organise politically and an abundance of space in which to do so. Kathi Weeks has noted the escalating constriction of such free time from the demands of waged employment during the late

32 Quoted in Harry Weeks, 'Ethics in Public', in Kathryn Brown, ed, *Interactive Contemporary Art: Participation in Practice*, I B Tauris, London, 2014, p 173

33 Silvia Federici, 'Wages Against Housework', 1975. Widely available, see: https://caringlabor. wordpress.com/2010/09/ 15/silvia-federici-wages-against-housework/, accessed 7 June 2017

34 John Milner, entry on Agitprop (1996) for *Grove Art Online*, unpaginated http://oxfordindex.oup. com/view/10.1093/gao/ 9781884446054.article. T001136, accessed 15 August 2016

35 See Kevin Murphy and Sally O'Driscoll's edited issue of *Space and Culture*, vol 18, no 4, November 2015.

36 *Cathy Come Home* (1966) was Ken Loach's hugely successful TV play that screened on BBC One (16 November 1966, The Wednesday Play) to 12 million viewers.

37 Kathi Weeks, '"Hours for What We Will": Work, Family, and the Movement for Shorter Hours', *Feminist Studies*, vol 35, no 1, spring 2009, pp 101–127

38 For a summary of recent publications, see Fiona Anderson, '[Review] Preserving and Politicising the Alternative Space', *Oxford Art Journal*, vol 38, no 1, 2015, pp 448–451. For more on NYC's alternative art system in relation to feminism, see Meredith A Browne's award-winning essay '"The Enemies of Women's Liberation in the Arts Will be Crushed": A.I.R. Gallery's Role in the American Feminist Art Movement', available at http://www.aaa.si.edu/essay/meredith-brown, accessed 15 August 2016.

39 'A Woman's Place' was recently commemorated in the exhibition '56 Artillery Lane', Raven Row, 21 April–11 June 2017. In 2012, squatting was re-categorised as a criminal rather than civil offence, which seems to have put an end to such creative housing alternatives.

40 Rozsika Parker (1975), reprinted in Parker and Griselda Pollock, *Framing Feminism: Art and the Women's Movement 1970–1985*, Pandora Press, London, 1987, p 200

41 Alongside Centerprise, London had a rich network of alternative bookshops at the time, including Walter Rodney Bookshop, Gay's the Word, Compendium Books, and Silver Moon. From 1975 to 1981, a Federation of Radical Booksellers even existed.

42 For more on this topic see Julia Bryan-Wilson, *Art Workers: Radical Practice in the Vietnam War Era*, University of California Press, Berkeley, 2009.

twentieth century and proposes the need for a shorter working-hours movement to carve out 'hours for what we will'.[37] However this temporal revolution would need to be matched by a spatial counterpart, at least in metropolitan centres where peripheral public sites have been likewise enclosed. The developmental history of postwar avant-garde art is greatly bound up with the availability of cheap or unoccupied urban space. And while the post-industrial caverns of New York City have been so well documented as to become familiar, the networks of alternative sites in other cities, including London, have been less well attended to.[38] It quickly becomes apparent from looking more closely at the history of feminist art and cultural activism that access to alternative spaces beyond the established gallery circuit was crucial to sustaining the movement. In 1972, the cohort of students at CalArt's Feminist Art Program was able to arrange the use of a condemned mansion at 533 Mariposa Avenue in Hollywood, the scale of the decrepit space enabling outsized experiments that swathed visitors within the students' crafted environments. A few years later Kate Walker spearheaded the collective installation *A Woman's Place* at the South London Women's Centre at 14 Radnor Terrace. This centre was in fact housed within a squat, a not uncommon option at the time when councils with unoccupied properties would turn a blind eye to squatters.[39] The exhibition generally presented a situation of 'sordid chaos', and in reviewing the show Rozsika Parker emphasised the necessity of such chaotic spaces beyond conventional art structures. As she describes it: 'They worked on the home as a group instead of in isolation, creating a public instead of a private environment.'[40] For the Hackney Flashers also, such spatial community-building was evident in not only the content of their project (the derelict building that the community nursery workers and families were able to occupy and renovate) but also in its dissemination at alternative exhibition sites including Centerprise.[41]

Histories of alternative networks have until recently tended to focus on spaces and processes of production at the expense of reproduction. Of particular relevance is an established account of postwar art's development that concentrates on the anxious relationship between art workers and blue-collar labourers in light of artists' occupations of post-industrial spaces and a number of artists (including Robert Morris and Chris Burden) collaborating with labourers or self-consciously performing manual activities themselves.[42] A consideration of the Hackney Flashers – or the Waitresses, or Martha Rosler, or Feministo – interrupts and expands such an account by refocusing attention on the maintenance function of feminised labour, making it clear that such work was always already there, but at the same time signalling a transformation in the organisation of that sphere of work. The feminist (art) movement probed the divisions between gendered domestic and public spaces (nursery, museum, squat, kitchen), simultaneously reflecting and impelling transformations in the organisation of work more widely, as the public and private, waged and unwaged spheres became increasingly indistinct.

In recent years, the rapid expansion of digital technology has generated great interest in the history of print culture, ephemera and the modes of collective organising associated with those older forms of media. Kevin Murphy and Sally O' Driscoll point to the historical right to speak or make noise as a manifestation of power.[43] They note that the popular introduction of cheap printing facilitated an expansion in seventeenth- and eighteenth-century print culture, with revolutionary words and images displayed in homes, taverns and other public spaces. Print ephemera later became central to the public performance of political resistance: from women's suffrage organising and their famous displays of banners, to the abundant leaflets, badges and flyers of 1960s countercultural movements. Moreover, Kate Eichhorn has pointed out how the accelerated development of reprographic technology, particularly xerography, in the late twentieth century, facilitated numerous artistic and political experiments.[44] Thus the second-wave feminist movement was marked by a vibrant print culture of magazines, posters, and the circulation of information through photocopies and reading groups.[45] The affective dimension of these materials should not be overlooked; and it is revealing that, in this later period of economic unrest and disillusionment with the political elite, the Brooklyn Museum mounted an exhibition entitled 'Agitprop!', collecting together creative paraphernalia agitating for social change, and including the Hackney Flashers' *Who's Holding the Baby?*[46]

The textured layers of images montaged across the display boards capture a range of ephemeral activist interventions, including political demonstrations, urban graffiti slogans, collective meetings and exhibition flyers. The incorporated leaflets and photographs of nursery marches, with banners and placards, are often set against professional advertising imagery. This exacerbates the collective's deliberately crude, deskilled aesthetic, which was an important preference (if not entirely optional due to production constraints), enabling the evasion of the commodified ideals of marketing imagery and crafting a non-hierarchical public discourse. Unlike later feminist-activist artists of the 1980s, such as the Guerrilla Girls, Jenny Holzer or Barbara Kruger, who exploited the graphic aesthetics of consumer culture, the grass-roots aesthetic of 1970s print resistance was not slick enough to be reproduced and circulated as spectacular posters (a method of mainstream dissemination that has both pros and cons). Instead, as Siona Wilson has suggested, the noticeboard arrangement of *Who's Holding the Baby?* draws on historical civic models, deriving

from the widely used practice of the wall newspaper. Common in factories and other contexts, the wall newspaper was a temporary makeshift collage of information and imagery that served as a leftist alternative to the mainstream press.[47]

One particular image summarises the Hackney Flashers' visual montage technique and hints at the public display practices of punk subculture and AIDS activism that would swiftly follow.[48] 'Who's still holding the baby?' exemplifies the DIY aesthetic of the collective, featuring a striking cut-and-paste collage of a wall in Dalston, sprayed with angry graffiti declaring: 'Where's my (free) nursery? STAND UP FOR YOUR RIGHTS'. This public intervention was created in the dead of night, and could be seen by members of the public at any time. (That the image was also reproduced on exhibition flyers for Cockpit Gallery

43 Kevin D Murphy and Sally O' Driscoll, 'The Art/ History of Resistance: Visual Ephemera in Public Space', *Space and Culture*, vol 18, no 4, 2015, pp 328–357

44 Kate Eichhorn, *The Adjusted Margin*, The MIT Press, Cambridge, Massachusetts, 2016

45 Prior to the internet, as Eichhorn has convincingly argued, photocopied materials, including flyers and leaflets circulating on noticeboards and in bags, functioned as a form of proto-social media; this information is now shared digitally online.

46 Agit-Prop! at Brooklyn Museum, 11 December 2015 – 7 August 2016

47 Siona Wilson, *Art Labor, Sex Politics*, University of Minnesota Press, Minneapolis, 2015, p 159

48 Tara Burk, writing about 1980s AIDS activism, points out that '[t]his art/ history of resistance is part of a groundswell of collaborative art and activist practices in New York City that seized public display opportunities opened by the city's derelict buildings from the early 1970s through the 1990s'. 'Radical Distribution: AIDS Cultural Activism in New York City, 1986–1992', *Space and Culture*, vol 18, no 4, 2015, pp 436–449, p 439.

signifies its importance to the group.) The very presence of graffiti in a community can be 'figured by the establishment as a violent attack on the social fabric', yet as Murphy and O' Driscoll point out, its signification tends to depend on the social positioning of the viewer.[49] A hole has been cut out of the photographed building, and another photograph of a busy kitchen scene layered beneath it, revealing the hidden domestic labour of a woman and children taking place within its walls. A banner pasted across the top redundantly asks: 'Who's still holding the baby?'.

As previously contended, the Hackney Flashers display at the 1979 Hayward exhibition was not universally well received. Art critic Brian Sewell reportedly suggested that 'it belonged in a village hall'.[50] This icy assessment did not unduly bother the Flashers; in part, I think, because it is not wholly inaccurate. Created for the alternative display spaces that existed, or were proactively seized, in 1970s London, the noticeboards of *Who's Holding the Baby?* initially depended upon civic engagement, discussion and collective organising. The joke is really on the dated critic for failing to recognise Western contemporary art's imminent expansion into the realm of the social, an impulse that was primarily directed by feminist collectives and artists, including the sociological work of the Hackney Flashers.

Conclusion

Sarah Schulman's passionate account of urban change in downtown New York introduced the concept of cultural and intellectual gentrification to a broad audience.[51] This 'gentrification of the mind' is characterised by banalisation, increased conservativism, intensive consumerism, and the replacement of diversity with a suffocating homogeneity. As these homogenising impulses began to creep into urban planning with greater alacrity, the Hackney Flashers countered by revealing how various forces (a paucity of childcare resources, poor housing provision, a lack of mental health services) were functioning to reinforce the marginality and isolation of working-class mothers and their families. The fact that this agitprop project has powerfully resurfaced into institutional contexts – into the collection of a national museum in Madrid, and exhibitions in New York and London – is promising.[52] At a time when leading accounts of art activism (such as those printed in the popular forum e-flux), say nothing on the topic of feminism, it is clear that a materialist analysis foregrounding social reproduction is required to counteract this tendency.[53] Such an analysis demonstrates that the social relations between parents and their nannies, between mothers and fathers and families, between all those that cook, clean and care for us (whether paid or unpaid), are fundamental to sustaining not only urban life but capitalism itself.

The Hackney Flashers' work marks a prescient engagement with the decline of welfare – both in practice and ideologically. Today, we are in a further period of reorganisation (even disintegration) of those apparatuses of support, as London undergoes a process of 'social cleansing' orchestrated through housing. However, these transformations have attracted wider attention due to the expanded manifestation of de-classing processes, which are clawing in greater numbers of the lower

49 Murphy and O' Driscoll, *Space and Culture*, op cit, p 332

50 'Birdsong meets the Hackney Flashers', blog interview, 11 August 2015: https://birdsong.london/birdsong-meets-the-hackney-flashers/, accessed 13 March 2017

51 Sarah Schulman, *Gentrification of the Mind: Witness to a Lost Imagination*, University of California Press, Berkeley, 2012

52 Stills Centre for Photography (Edinburgh) recently pulled another of Jo Spence's collaborative projects out of storage. The Polysnappers' 'Family, Fantasy and Photography' (1981) covers comparable terrain to that of the Hackney Flashers although it has much greater focus on the role of media representation in ideologically shaping family life and social relations. See Victoria Horne, 'Exhibition Review', *This Is Tomorrow*, http://thisistomorrow.info/articles/jo-spence-1, accessed 10 October 2016.

53 See Boris Groys, 'On art Activism', *e-flux journal* 56, June 2014. An exception to this is the international feminist art journal *n.paradoxa*'s special issue on 'Art Activism', vol 23, January 2009.

middle classes (those historical gentrifiers and 'young urban professionals' or 'yuppies') who are in turn struggling to remain in a city that has been flooded with domestic and overseas investment. It is hoped that the historical details of visual ephemera, activism, agitprop, collective organising and public space can inform us of strategies for inventing pockets of resistance within city space. If the 1970s negotiated the remains of deindustrialisation in cities and the introduction of neoliberal forms of social and economic organising, we are currently in the throes of a later developmental stage of hyper-flexibility gathered under the misnomer 'sharing economy'.[54] How to insist on understanding housing, property and care, not as commodities but as basic needs and sources of pleasure, is once again the key directive for the future.

54 Alex Hern, 'Why the Term "Sharing Economy" Needs to Die', *The Guardian*, 5 October 2015, available at https://www.theguardian.com/technology/2015/oct/05/why-the-term-sharing-economy-needs-to-die, accessed 7 September 2016

Third Text, 2017
Vol. 31, No. 1, 79–95, https://doi.org/10.1080/09528822.2017.1364548

'To Think the Home in Terms of the Factory'

Social Reproduction, Postproduction and Home Movies in Godard and Miéville

Elisa Adami and Alex Fletcher

[R]econfiguring our image of society as an immense circuit of domestic plantations and assembly lines where the production of workers is articulated on a daily and generational basis.[1]

In an article written for the French newspaper *Libération*, Jean-Luc Godard described his latest film, *Numéro deux* (Number Two, 1975), made in collaboration with his partner, the film-maker Anne-Marie Miéville, as an attempt to 'think the home in terms of the factory'.[2] Drawing on theories of social reproduction, this article examines how this metaphor plays itself out within *Numéro deux*, as well as Godard and Miéville's film-making practice more broadly, especially the production methods that they developed in the 1970s. In particular, it focuses on how their use of video and their foregrounding of the space of film *post*production serves to challenge traditional notions of film production, editing and authorship – briefly examining the editing room as a historically gendered place of work. We conclude by reading Godard and Miéville's television works, particularly their strategy of amateurisation and their investment in the domestic, in relation to the category of the 'home movie'. The place of the home and their practice of small-scale film production, it is argued, represents an attempt to explore an alternative mode of production to the one that the metaphor of the factory typically designates.

Numéro deux focuses on the domestic life of three generations of a working-class family living in a social housing apartment somewhere (outside 'the city') in France. The film is composed of discrete fragments

1 Silvia Federici, 'The Reproduction of Labour Power in the Global Economy and the Unfinished Feminist Revolution', in *Revolution at Point Zero: Housework, Reproduction, and Feminist Struggle*, PM Press, Brooklyn, New York, 2012, p 96

2 Jean-Luc Godard, 'Penser la maison en termes d'usine' ('To Think the Home in Terms of the Factory'), *Libération*, 15 September 1975, in *Jean-Luc Godard par Jean-Luc Godard*, Volume 1, Alain Bergala, ed, Cahiers du cinéma, Paris, 1998, pp 380–382

This article was originally published with errors. This version has been amended. Please see Erratum (http://dx.doi.org/10.1080/09528822.2017.1393186).

in which the different members of the family are presented and observed in their everyday activities and kinship, with a detached, quasi-naturalistic gaze. As Robert Stam describes it, the film discards 'narrative drama… in favour of the close scrutiny of the everyday', representing 'a kind of ultimate banalization and proletarianization of what is conceivable as a cinematic subject'.[3] Yet, as Harun Farocki notes, its relentless focus on the 'ordinary' does not result in 'a conceptual minimalism, but rather an explosion of meaning'; we begin to see 'that even the most routine household activities and bodily functions are semantically dense'.[4] The matter-of-fact title of the film similarly signifies multiple determinations. On the one hand, it refers to its subject matter, woman – recalling Simone de Beauvoir's 1949 *The Second Sex* – and the recurring theme of anality and excrement; on the other, it refers to its formal and technological features. Shot on video, and then reshot in 35mm film while the images played on video monitors, two monitors can often be seen playing simultaneously within a single frame, as well as the images within monitors being split in two through superimposition. Doubling also appears in the oppositions that populate the film, such as film/television, sound/image, political/pornographic, factory/landscape, man/woman. Responding to her own question of whether the film is political or pornographic, Sandrine, the mother, asks 'Why is it either/or? It can be both sometimes,' affirming the film's drive to undo binary oppositions for a more complicated account of relation and difference.[5] Furthermore, events repeat themselves, or 'happen partially', deferred for a later syntagmatic moment.[6] As Sandrine at one point comments, people always say 'Once upon a time' when they could as well say 'Twice upon a time.'

Godard's remark that *Numéro deux* is an attempt 'to think the home in terms of the factory' introduces, for Michael Witt, a key notion in the film: that of 'seeing as' – to 'project a in terms of b' – which is the 'premise of all metaphor'.[7] Metaphorical sense is produced through a violation of a term's ordinary usage, which allows a new meaning to emerge. By bringing 'two things together', as Anne Carson notes, we see their 'incongruence' and 'also a new congruence, meanwhile continuing to recognize the previous incongruence through the new congruence'.[8] Metaphors, puns, and double entendres appear throughout *Numéro deux*, such as in the intertitles, which are continuously transformed letter-by-letter – this is what the subtitle of the film, *Essais Titres* (Test Titles), presumably refers to. The principle metaphor is that of the factory, which has a range of applications in the film, and is initially brought out in Godard's opening monologue in his editing studio. He comments that the room, with its machines which need money from a producer in order to be put to work, is a kind of factory, and that he occupies both the role of a boss and a worker. His body too is a factory, a notion which appears later in relation to Sandrine and Pierre, her husband. Like a factory worker, their bodies go on strike: constipation, in the case of Sandrine, and impotence, in the case of Pierre. The house, Sandrine's site of work, becomes a factory in which mechanical failures accumulate: the toilet gets blocked and the washing machine breaks down. Marriage, as Stam adds, is seen as a 'co-production' and making love, Sandrine tells Pierre, is often a job. 'Childbearing is *repro*-duction,' Stam continues, 'while films are made by mechanical – and television programs by electronic – reproduction'.[9]

3 Robert Stam, *Reflexivity in Film and Literature: From Don Quixote to Jean-Luc Godard*, Columbia University Press, New York, 1992, pp 222–223

4 Kaja Silverman and Harun Farocki, *Speaking about Godard*, New York University Press, New York, 1998, p 141. There is a discernible affinity here in subject matter – if not in style – with another film released the same year: Chantal Akerman's *Jeanne Dielman, 23 Quai du Commerce, 1080 Bruxelles*, 1975.

5 Ibid, p 146

6 Stam, *Reflexivity in Film and Literature*, op cit, p 230

7 Michael Witt, 'On Communication: The Work of Anne-Marie Miéville and Jean-Luc Godard as "Sonimage" from 1973 to 1979', dissertation, University of Bath, 1998, p 180

8 Anne Carson, *Eros the Bittersweet: An Essay*, Princeton University Press, Princeton, New Jersey, 1986, p 73

9 Stam, *Reflexivity in Film and Literature*, op cit, p 223. For a reading of the prominence of machines and bodies in terms of Deleuze and Guattari's notion of 'desiring machines', taken from their 1972 book *Anti-Oedipus*, see Douglas Morrey, *Jean-Luc Godard*, Manchester University Press, Manchester, 2005.

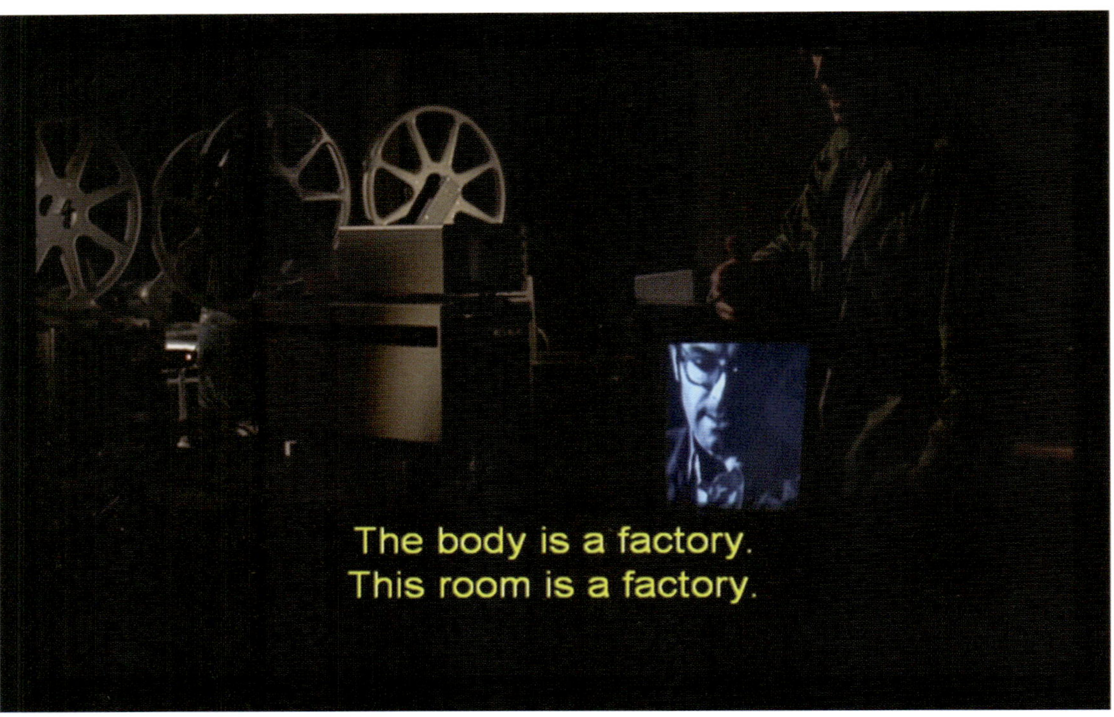

Jean-Luc Godard and Anne-Marie Miéville, *Numéro deux* (Number Two), 35mm and video, © 1975 Gaumont/Société Nouvelle de Cinématographie

In the same monologue Godard describes his interest in the operation of punning: a pun, he says, is 'a word that slides on a thing' and 'shows short-circuits' and 'interference'. Or as Carson defines it, in a pun you 'perceive homophony and at the same time see the semantic space that separates the two words. Sameness is projected onto difference in a kind of stereoscopy.'[10] Metaphorical production is played out audio-visually in *Numéro deux*, as a method for projecting ways of *seeing* and *hearing* connections between spheres and spaces usually perceived as separate. As Witt argues, however, this projection is not one-way, but 'bi-directional', setting the 'heterogeneous material with which it comes into contact' in tension with it and challenging the 'assumptions of each as premise'.[11] This metaphorical mixing of modes, or what Paul de Man refers to as catachresis, consequently disrupts any epistemological notions of representation not disfigured by rhetorical tropes.[12] This is particularly significant for the problem of sexual difference in *Numéro deux*. As Constance Penley contends, 'conceptions of bodies and sexes are necessarily metaphorical, that is, always seen in terms of something else'.[13] There is, she writes, no 'non-metaphorical representation' of the sexual difference, or the body, which results not from 'biology', but 'the subject's positioning in language and culture'.[14] Godard's monologue on the leitmotifs of work and production is followed by an intertitle: REPRODUCTION. We then cut to two video screens: on the right, a football match, and on the left, a cramped household scene with grandparents, father and child. As David Sterrit puts it, reproduction 'has obviously taken place in this

10 Carson, *Eros the Bittersweet*, op cit, p 34

11 Witt, 'On Communication', op cit, p 178

12 Paul de Man, 'The Epistemology of Metaphor', *Critical Inquiry*, vol 5, no 1, autumn 1978, p 13, p 22

13 Constance Penley, 'Les Enfants de la Patrie', *Camera Obscura*, 8–10, autumn 1982, p 50. In Butlerian terms, gender is the cultural interpretation of sex, which becomes naturalised and made to appear as if biological. See Judith Butler, *Gender Trouble: Feminism and the Subversion of Identity*, Routledge, London and New York, 1990.

14 Ibid, p 50

family – that is how families are made!'[15] Reproduction now establishes itself as one of the film's subjects.

Social Reproduction

For Laura Mulvey, *Numéro deux* is Godard's 'most thorough and self-conscious attempt to depict the problem of sexuality under capitalism', and marks 'a crucial shift in terms of Godard's presentation of sexuality' more generally, in that the problem of sexuality is no longer '*wholly* signified by a woman' – male sexuality is investigated not only as that which 'turns woman into an image of its desire', but is also posited as 'the repression of homosexuality'.[16] As she argues, with the exception of Godard and Jean-Pierre Gorin's *Tout va bien* (Everything is Fine, 1972) – their last completed feature, working under the name of the Dziga Vertov Group – previous attempts to portray women often tended to confine their concerns to the sexual or marital, excluding them from the economic, except in terms of 'managing' consumption – for example, Godard's 1966 film *Deux ou trois choses que je sais d'elle* (Two or Three Things I Know about Her).[17] In Godard and Gorin's *British Sounds* (1969), for instance, the spaces of the factory and the home remain discrete, with their own separate discourses: over images of a noisy car factory, the voice reads lines from *The Communist Manifesto* and in the silent interior of a suburban house, in which a naked woman moves from room to room, we hear lines from a feminist essay by Sheila Rowbotham.[18] What is elided here, as Mulvey contends, is

> the evident fact that the contrast with labour in factory production would, in the home, be domestic labour, that of wife and mother as producer and reproducer of labour-power, with the all-too strident noises that accompany it.[19]

It was notably with Marxist feminists in Italy in the 1970s, rather than within the Anglophone or French contexts, that social reproduction emerged as a key concept for grasping certain forms of gendered domination in their historical specificity under capitalism.[20] Whereas *Operaismo* (Workerism) argued that more and more activities that were once considered extra-economic had become subsumed by what they termed the 'social factory', thinkers such as Leopoldina Fortunati, Mariarosa Dalla Costa and Silvia Federici revealed the central role of the home and the unpaid labour performed by women in producing and reproducing workers, or their labour power.[21] As Federici recounts,

> to us, it was immediately clear that the circuit of capitalist production, and the 'social factory' it produced, began and was centred above all in the kitchen, the bedroom, the home – insofar as these were the centres for the production of labour-power.[22]

In the transition from feudalism to capitalism, as Federici outlines in *Caliban and the Witch*, 'a new patriarchal order was constructed',

---

15 David Sterritt, *The Films of Jean-Luc Godard: Seeing the Invisible*, Cambridge University Press, Cambridge, 1999, pp 137–138

16 Laura Mulvey, 'Images of Woman, Images of Sexuality', in Colin MacCabe, ed, *Godard: Images, Sounds, Politics*, BFI, London, 1980, p 95, pp 97–98

17 Ibid, p 94

18 We could contrast this with a scene in *Numéro deux* in which the character of the grandmother performs housework in silence, while her voice-over reads passages from Germaine Greer's 1970 book *The Female Eunuch*. Her silence is in marked contrast with the strident noises that populate the rest of the film, serving as an emblem of her marginality, particularly in relation to the talkative grandfather, with his numerous stories.

19 Mulvey, 'Images of Woman, Images of Sexuality', op cit, p 87

20 See Endnotes, 'The Logic of Gender', *Endnotes 3*, September, 2013, p 57

21 The term 'social factory' came out of Italian Marxism in the early 1960s, particularly the work of Raniero Panzieri and Mario Tronti, in the journal *Quaderni Rossi*. In the early 1970s Mariarosa Dalla Costa and Selma James founded the International Wages for Housework Campaign – connected to the group *Lotta Femminista* – who developed a critique of *Operaismo* based on the *political* demand that women's work should be acknowledged through a wage.

22 Federici, 'Introduction', *Revolution At Point Zero*, op cit, pp 7–8

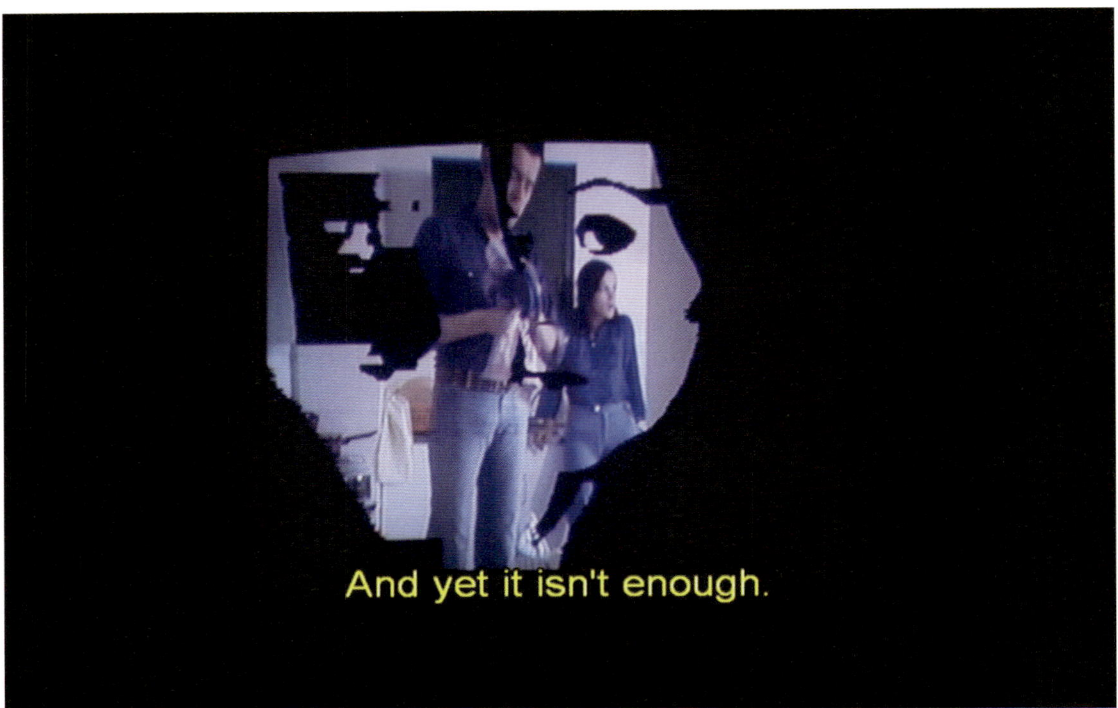

Jean-Luc Godard and Anne-Marie Miéville, *Numéro deux* (Number Two), 35mm and video, © 1975 Gaumont/Société Nouvelle de Cinématographie

categorising women as a type of natural commons, 'as their work was defined as a natural resource, laying outside the sphere of market relations'.[23] This naturalisation of, what Silverman terms, 'the so-called "separate spheres" of man's and woman's labour', is exemplified in a scene in which Pierre explains to his daughter, Vanessa, why he finds it 'impossible' to help Sandrine with the washing. For her, he says, it's 'automatic'; 'It's the factory for her. For me, it's home.'[24]

In a later scene, we see Pierre assisting Sandrine with the dishes, while she explains her reasons for leaving a briefly held job, going on to enumerate her obligations as housewife and mother. 'There's too much… yet not enough', she concludes, recognising the social limits and constraints put upon her. We then cut to a shot containing two monitors: the left portrays the grandmother cleaning the floor and the right Sandrine performing fellatio – 'women's work', as Silverman notes.[25] In a voice-over, Sandrine describes her labour in terms of producing at a loss, asking 'Who was profiting?,' answering her own question with 'not him… someone behind', and then 'something between us', which she names 'work'. Sandrine generates the metaphor for producing at a loss in order to understand her own peculiar form of production, housework (and sex work), in which her products are used rather than exchanged, and therefore not directly visible.[26] In *The Arcane of Reproduction* from 1981, Fortunati attempted to show how this elusive activity of 'indirectly waged reproductive work' constitutes a disavowed necessity for capitalist value production, which is nonetheless 'posited as "natural" production', *appearing*, as she says, 'as the creation of *non-value*' (emphasis in the

23 Silvia Federici, *Caliban and the Witch: Women, the Body and Primitive Accumulation*, Autonomedia, Brooklyn, 2004, p 97. The book develops on research began in the mid-1970s in collaboration with Fortunati and was published in Italy in 1984 under the title *Il Grande Calibano*.

24 Silverman and Farocki, *Speaking about Godard*, op cit, p 162. Pierre's 'psychic intractability' is linked to male desire; 'not wanting to see her dirty panties', as he puts it.

25 Ibid, p 164

26 Ibid. As Dave Beech explains, insofar 'as workers appear as use values to capitalists, mothers can be said to produce use values'. Dave Beech, *Art and Value: Art's Economic Exceptionalism in Classical, Neoclassical and Marxist Economics*, Brill, Boston, 2015, pp 323–324.

Jean-Luc Godard and Anne-Marie Miéville, *Numéro deux* (Number Two), 35mm and video, © 1975 Gaumont/Société Nouvelle de Cinématographie

27 Leopoldina Fortunati, *The Arcane of Reproduction: Housework, Prostitution, Labor and Capital*, Hilary Creek, trans, Autonomedia, Brooklyn, New York, 1995, p 69, p 8. For an excellent exposition of the book, see Maya Gonzales, 'The Gendered Circuit: Reading *The Arcane of Reproduction*', *Viewpoint Magazine* 3, 2013, https://viewpointmag.com/2013/09/28/the-gendered-circuit-reading-the-arcane-of-reproduction/, accessed 7 June 2017

28 Ibid, p 8

29 As Beech argues, the 'deconstruction' of Marx's 'distinction between productive and unproductive labour cannot be achieved by claiming that certain practices are productive of something'. Marx's distinction 'refers exclusively to the production of profit'. Beech, *Art and Value*, op cit, p 324.

30 Endnotes, 'The Logic of Gender', op cit, p 62

31 Jason W Moore, *Capitalism and the Web of Life: Ecology and the Accumulation of Capital*, Verso, London and New York, 2015, p 2, p 54

original).[27] Despite the 'seeming separation' of production and reproduction, or 'value/non-value', this appearance, for Fortunati, is based on their 'indissoluble connection', which is not simply ideological, but structural.[28] That is, under capitalism (or the value form), we structurally and practically perform this separation between value/non-value, or productive and unproductive labour.[29] While some Autonomist Marxist feminists argue that 'every activity which reproduces labour-power produces value', it is therefore more precise to say, as Endnotes do, that 'for labour-power to have a value, some of these activities have to be cut off or dissociated from the sphere of value production'.[30] Or as Jason W Moore puts it, we are 'captive to capitalism's either/or organization of reality': 'Value does not work unless most *work* is not valued.'[31]

For Fortunati, 'the sexual division of labour' takes a spatial form in the place of the home, 'seen' as 'a "mode of production" in itself', 'a non-capitalist "island" existing in the heart of capital'.[32] A more generic idea of nature as a place lying outside the social transpires in a recurring formula in *Numéro deux*, initially spoken by the children near the beginning of the film. 'There was a landscape, and we put a factory in it', Nicholas, the boy, states, to which Vanessa responds 'There was a factory, and we put a landscape around it' – a variation of this statement occurs in relation to whether the children think their parents are a factory or a landscape. One way to make sense of Vanessa's enigmatic retort is to read it together with Henri Lefebvre's *The Production of Space* (1974).[33] For Lefebvre, space is not a neutral medium, which capital occupies through the site of the factory, for instance; space is what capital produces, reproduces and transforms. Forms of production and patterns of consumption shape *social* space as well as organise what appears as

Jean-Luc Godard and Anne-Marie Miéville, *Numéro deux* (Number Two), 35mm and video, © 1975 Gaumont/Société Nouvelle de Cinématographie

32 Fortunati, *The Arcane of Reproduction*, op cit, p 13, p 8. For the distinction between 'spheres' and 'space', see Endnotes, 'The Logic of Gender', op cit, p 57.

33 Henri Lefebvre, *The Production of Space*, Donald Nicholson-Smith, trans, Blackwell, Oxford, 1991

34 For a Lefebvrian account of the way landscape photography is transformed by spatial abstraction, see John Roberts, *Photography and Its Violations*, Columbia University Press, New York, 2014, pp 120–145.

35 Doreen Massey, *Space, Place and Gender*, Polity, Cambridge, 1994, pp 183–184

36 Lefebvre, *The Production of Space*, op cit, p 309. Lefebvre, in the same passage, refers to this as a process of 'metaphorization', whereby 'the image of the woman supplants the woman herself'.

37 Massey, *Space, Place and Gender*, op cit, p 179

38 Ibid, p 180

non-social – from the island of the home to the rural landscape.[34] Pierre seems to convey this idea in an aphoristic remark: 'In fact, there isn't one factory and one landscape. The two are one.' As Doreen Massey notes, many readers are blind to a central argument that Lefebvre makes concerning 'space's gendering and its implicit but forceful sexuality'.[35] Lefebvre defines spatial abstraction in capitalist modernity as a type of 'castration': 'Over abstract space reigns phallic solitude and the self-destruction of desire.'[36] The most evident aspects of this 'joint control of spatiality and identity', for Massey, is the distinction between public and private, particularly the *spatial separation* of home and workplace' (emphasis added).[37] The construction of 'home' as 'a woman's place' is, therefore, one example in which space is articulated through the 'mutual accommodation' of capitalism and patriarchy.[38] Correspondingly, the notion of the 'limits of women's mobility' is framed, in *Numéro deux*, as a 'rigid division between inside and outside', with the camera echoing Sandrine's 'imprisonment' by 'never moving outside the confines of the flat' – the apartment is glimpsed only once from the exterior, at a distance, in a monitor near the beginning of the film, functioning as a counter-shot to a monitor with the children on the balcony.[39] The division of interior/exterior as one of sexual difference is manifested in a repeated scene shot from the balcony of the apartment, in which successive shots of Pierre leaving for and returning from work are superimposed over an image of Sandrine lying asleep in bed.[40] In Mulvey's interpretation, the

Jean-Luc Godard and Anne-Marie Miéville, *Numéro deux* (Number Two), 35mm and video, © 1975 Gaumont/Société Nouvelle de Cinématographie

39 Mulvey, 'Images of Woman, Images of Sexuality', op cit, p 96. The apartment and consumer goods it contains, as Mulvey notes, recalls the postwar development of capitalism documented in previous films by Godard, in which it 'stood for *embourgeoisement*' but now stands for 'the basic subsistence of working-class life'. Ibid, p 95.

40 In another scene, we also see Sandrine returning from a failed job search and encountering a woman campaigner whom she declines to engage with.

41 Mulvey, 'Images of Woman, Images of Sexuality', op cit, pp 95–96

42 Amie Siegel, 'Factories and the Factory', in Tom Conley and T Jefferson Kline, eds, *A Companion to Jean-Luc Godard*, John Wiley and Sons, Malden, Massachusetts, 2014, p 355

43 Silverman and Farocki, *Speaking about Godard*, op cit, p 142. In his 2002 essay 'Cross Influence/Soft Montage', Farocki described his point of departure for *Interface* (1995), his first installation using double projection, as deriving from

bed evokes a space more intimate yet more confined, the cosiness of the home inside the prison block, but at the same time takes us back to essential associations between woman and sexuality.[41]

In an attempt to portray the complex entanglement of economic, social and spatial relations, *Numéro deux* constructs a series of *spatial* montage techniques – the aforementioned doubling of video monitors and the layering of images within the single screen. As Amie Siegel writes, the film '*enacts* the housing block' in which it is set, 'placing individual scenes as simultaneous architecture within the frame', with the shots or tableaux mirroring the 'communal and isolated, connected and distant' relations of the building, as well as the 'apart and together' experience of 'familial proximity'.[42] Farocki characterises the use of this doubling as 'soft montage', since 'what is at issue is a general relatedness, rather than a strict opposition or equation'. The film, he argues, 'does not predetermine how the two images are to be connected; we must build up the associations ourselves in an ongoing way as the film unfolds'.[43] To borrow Yvonne Rainer's phrase, the film proceeds by a logic of 'accretion'.[44] By accreting a series of audio-visual fragments, Godard and Miéville compel us to consider what Lefebvre termed the 'ambiguous continuity' between spheres and spaces that appear as separate, as well as the divergence that is revealed in such moments of connection.[45] Moreover, as Fortunati, Massey and others remind us, the film indicates how these spheres are articulated with, and constitute articulations of, gender. For Mulvey, a central question raised by *Numéro deux* is the possibility of representing or narrating the dynamic processes and abstract relations that overdetermine our

Numéro deux. See Antje Ehmann and Kodwo Eshun, eds, *Harun Farocki: Against What? Against Whom?*, Koenig Books, London, 2009, p 72.

44 This phrase is borrowed from an intertitle appearing in her 1974 film, *Film about a Woman Who…*, which reads 'An emotional accretion in 48 steps'. For the script, see *The Films of Yvonne Rainer*, Indiana University Press, Bloomington, 1989, p 82.

45 Lefebvre, *The Production of Space*, op cit, p 87

46 Mulvey, 'Images of Woman, Images of Sexuality', op cit, p 100

47 Louis Althusser, 'Cremonini, Painter of the Abstract', *Lenin and Philosophy and Other Essays*, Ben Brewster, trans, Monthly Review Press, New York and London, 1971, p 237. For an account of the influence of Althusser on Godard and Miéville see Witt, 'On Communication', op cit, pp 21–29.

48 For an extensive theoretical exploration of the (im)possibilities of 'representing' capital in contemporary art and popular culture, see Alberto Toscano and Jeff Kinkle, *Cartographies of the Absolute*, Zero Books, Winchester, 2015.

49 Althusser, 'Cremonini, Painter of the Abstract', op cit, p 237. State functionaries, like all individuals, for Althusser, on a significantly simplified reading, are merely the '*Träger*', 'supports', or 'bearers', of the system. See Louis Althusser and Étienne Balibar, *Reading Capital*, Ben Brewster, trans, Verso, London, 1970.

50 Music is mostly used to intimate the psychic interior space and feelings of individual family members, and it is sometimes faded in and out, in an often discordant, non-diegetic manner, or is heard through Pierre's circulating pair of headphones which family members secretly borrow.

51 Mulvey, 'Images of Woman, Images of Sexuality', op cit, p 101

52 Colin MacCabe, 'Godard since '68', in *Godard: Images, Sounds, Politics*, op cit, p 23

everyday lives.[46] The fact that the factory is never *seen* in the film, and that the monitors are mostly framed by a disproportionately large void of empty black space, suggests what Louis Althusser in a 1966 essay terms 'the *determinate absence* which governs' and '*informs*' our 'concrete', lived relations (emphasis in original).[47] This absence is not simply 'off-screen' – the factory from which Pierre returns every evening – but the impersonal and intangible relations of what Sandrine refers to as 'the State', and then, 'the social system'.[48] As Althusser argues, the system '*as a structure*', 'can never be depicted by its presence, *in person*, positively, in relief'; we can merely 'paint' the 'visible connexions' of its 'traces and effects' (emphasis in original).[49] Music in the film becomes another alternative to the failure of vision, for experiencing, or hearing, what both the grandfather and Sandrine term, 'to see the unbelievable', which Sandrine defines as 'what you don't see'.[50] The question, then, is not merely 'how those relations are caught in the image', as Mulvey asks, but how they emerge in the connections *between* images, as well as in text, sound, music and voice-over.[51] It is the sphere of postproduction, and the place of the editing room in particular, where such connections occur and to which we now turn.

Postproduction

Numéro deux is the first work to be realised by Godard and Miéville with their production company Sonimage (discussed below). Made a year after *Ici et ailleurs* (Here and Elsewhere, 1976) was completed but a year before that film was released, what unites these and subsequent projects by the two film-makers is an experimental use of video technology and 'the dual emphasis on subjectivity and production'.[52] Although Godard had experimented with video prior to his collaboration with Miéville, *Ici et ailleurs* marks a significant step in their sustained exploration of the medium.[53] Video, as Witt observes, offered a technical means for 'conducting comparative visual research', since it allowed the 'fluid, quasi-musical passage to and fro between different moments', 'that is more difficult and time-consuming to achieve in 35mm'.[54] The idea of doubling the image in *Numéro deux*, Farocki infers, must have came to Godard and Miéville from working with video editing technology, which 'is usually done while sitting in front of two monitors', so that the editor 'becomes accustomed to thinking of two images at the same time, rather than sequentially'.[55] As both Witt and Farocki highlight, video offered Godard and Miéville the possibility of *formally* actualising the metaphoric processes articulated in *Numéro deux*, in the guise of a comparative audio-visual thinking, or what Witt refers to as 'videographic thinking'.[56] Video is not employed mechanically 'as a tool for processing and connecting images and sounds', but is rather treated as an instrument of thought, 'presenting the process and effects of the comparison' for further reflection.[57]

Commenting on *Ici et ailleurs*, Gilles Deleuze identifies the primary place of the 'interstice' in the associational logic of the film, with the

Jean-Luc Godard and Anne Marie Miéville, *Soft and Hard (Soft Talk on a Hard Subject between Two Friends)*, video, © 1985 Gaumont

53 Michael Witt, *Jean-Luc Godard, Cinema Historian*, Indiana University Press, Bloomington, 2013, p 45. This exploration, as the book details. can be seen as a series of experimental investigations leading up to Godard's cinema history series *Histoire(s) du cinéma* (1988–1998).

54 Ibid, p 54

55 Silverman and Farocki, *Speaking about Godard*, op cit, p 142

56 Witt, *Jean-Luc Godard, Cinema Historian*, op cit, p 52

57 Ibid, pp 52–53. As Witt adds, a 'simple technique' used as 'a tool for visual thinking' was 'videographic superimposition', which allowed for 'the creation of composite images through montage *within* the frame'. This technique is especially present in Godard and Miéville's film *Comment ça va?* (How is it going?) (1978). Ibid, p 53.

58 Gilles Deleuze, *Cinema 2: The Time Image*, Hugh Tomlinson and Robert Galeta, trans, Athlone, London, 1989, p 180

emphasis on 'difference' providing a space for 'resemblance to be graded'.[58] Quoting the film, Deleuze states that it ceases to be 'an uninterrupted chain of images each one the slave of the next', and instead becomes 'the method of BETWEEN' – between 'two actions... two affections... two visual images... two sound images'. This mode of linkage is construed by Deleuze as 'the method of AND', 'this and then that'. Indeed, this primacy of the 'and' (*et*) appears in *Ici et ailleurs* in the form of images, figured, for instance, as expanding electronic text on a screen or a sculptural model lit from different angles. Deleuze latches on to the grammatical form of the conjunction AND in order to emphasise the disjunctive aspect that is retained in the film's method of joining, or synthesis.[59] Jacques Rancière, in discussing Godard's *Histoire(s) du cinéma*, which is nonetheless applicable, refers to this 'sentence-image' grammar as the method of parataxis.[60] As a poetic form, parataxis describes a fragmentary mode of transition, which undermines subordination to hypotactic logic; signaled, for example, by the use of conjunctions such as 'therefore'.[61] Akin to Farocki's notion of 'soft montage', parataxis gives an integrity or self-sufficiency to compositional elements while leaving their connection open for the reader or viewer. The conjunction in the film's title refers to the 'here' of France, which is put in relation to the 'elsewhere' of Palestine. The film developed out of an uncompleted film project by the Dziga Vertov Group entitled *Jusqu'à la victoire* (Until Victory), which documented, in a propagandistic and triumphant manner, the future return of the Palestinians to their homeland. Four years later, *Ici et ailleurs*

59 This is akin to what, elsewhere, Deleuze terms a 'disjunctive synthesis'. See Gilles Deleuze, *The Logic of Sense*, Mark Lester and Charles Stivale, trans, Athlone, London, 1990.

60 Jacques Rancière, *The Future of the Image*, Gregory Elliott, trans, Verso, London and New York, 2007, pp 43–51

61 For a philosophical account of parataxis, see Theodor W Adorno, 'Parataxis', in *Notes to Literature*, Volume Two, Shierry Weber Nicholsen, trans, Columbia University Press, New York, 1992, pp 109–149.

62 Witt, 'On and Under Communication', in *A Companion to Jean-Luc Godard*, op cit, p 320

63 In an early article from 1956 entitled 'Montage, my fine care', Godard argues that invention and 'improvisation takes place in front of the moviola just as much as it does on the set'. See Jean Narboni and Tom Milne, eds, *Godard on Godard*, Da Capo Press, New York and London, 1972, p 40. For an excellent account of editing in Godard and its connection to thought, see Volker Pantenburg, *Farocki/Godard: Film as Theory*, Michael Turnbull, trans, Amsterdam University Press, Amsterdam, 2015.

64 For a similar argument, although primarily focusing on digital postproduction, and connecting it to debates around immaterial labour, see Hito Steyerl 'Cut! Reproduction and Recombination', in *The Wretched of the Screen*, e-flux journal, New York and Sternberg Press, Berlin, pp 176–190.

65 Timothy Barnard, *Découpage*, Caboose, Montreal, 2014, pp 15–16. Barnard argues that 'the term editor only really took hold amongst cutters with the founding of the Society of Motion Picture Editors in 1937, when they adopted it in the hope of parlaying the lofty term into higher pay'.

66 Ibid, p 15. Famous women film editors working in Hollywood in the early days of cinema include Anne Bauchens, Margaret Booth, Dorothy Spencer and Barbara MacLean.

67 As the credits of *Man with a Movie Camera* express, the

reworks the ten hours of rushes shot in Lebanon, Syria and Jordan, scrutinising and deconstructing the footage and the film's ambitions. Working with video technology in postproduction, Godard and Miéville carefully endeavour to recover the *voices* captured in the images that had been drowned in the impulsive superimposition of the film-makers (this is figured especially in the technique of video superimposition in the film). Miéville recounts that she and Godard spent every day for a year and a half organising and editing the material.[62] Images of the elsewhere of Palestine are set in tension with the here of France, via the domestic family setting in which the television set becomes key for how individuals receive and consume such images. Postproduction in *Ici et allieurs*, as in their subsequent works, becomes a central space for self-interrogating and reflecting on their production methods.[63]

In his opening monologue in *Numéro deux*, Godard implicitly puts into dialogue the home and the editing studio, two spaces typically seen as separate from production proper, by thinking both in terms of the factory. Although not explicitly stated, we could argue that the separation of the reproductive labour of the home from that of the factory is approximated in the conception of editing as a minor and structurally distinct role in *film* production. Indeed, as the history of editing attests, postproduction has not only been conceived as something temporally secondary to production, but as something second-class.[64] Historically, as Timothy Barnard notes, editors were conceived as 'lowly cutters', and their work, therefore, has seen 'near invisibility in film history'.[65] Moreover, as Barnard writes, this work was often performed by women, since 'cutting was one of the few jobs in the classical film industry deemed menial and insignificant enough to be entrusted to a woman', whose main role was 'to parcel out the images in accordance with the shooting script'.[66] Even in the Soviet film industry of the 1920s, where editing was perceived not only as hack-work but also as an art, we can see the gendering of this practice as well as the privileging of production, most famously embodied in the title of Dziga Vertov's *Man with a Movie Camera* (1929).[67] As Barnard quips, 'Vertov's masterpiece was not called "Man with a Moviola", after all.'[68] That the person who was sitting at the editing table was a woman, Vertov's partner and collaborator Yelizaveta Svilova, is telling. Another pioneer of Soviet film editing, and the inventor, as Jay Leyda argues, of what came to be known as the 'compilation film', was Esfir Shub.[69] Shub's mastering of montage came out of her experience gained while working at the state film production body Goskino (later Sovkino), where she worked as an editor, in charge of titling and re-editing imported foreign films for domestic distribution, rendering these films 'suitable' for Soviet audiences. In her first film, *The Fall of the Romanov Dynasty* (1927), Shub uses pre-existing film footage, such as newsreels of official parades and Romanov home movies, to critically reflect on historical events leading up to the Russian revolution. Shub's commitment to intentionally minimising her authorial presence, in which evaluation and interpretation are articulated through a more subtle building up of the whole, comes across in the only credit in the film and factory-like hierarchy goes: 'Author-supervisor experimenter: Dziga Vertov', 'Chief Operator: Mikhail Kaufman', 'Assistant Editor: E Svilova'. For an account of the work and art of editing and re-editing in Soviet film culture in the 1920s see Yuri Tsivian, 'The Wise and Wicked Game: Re-editing and Soviet Film Culture of the 1920s', *Film History*, vol 8, no 3, 1996, pp 327–343.

68 Barnard, *Découpage*, op cit, p 16

69 See Jay Leyda, *Films Beget Films*, Hill and Wang, New York, 1971; Esther Leslie, 'Art, Documentary and the Essay Film', *Radical Philosophy* 192, July/August 2015, pp 7–14

70 Leyda, *Films Beget Films*, op cit, p 25

71 Martin Stollery, 'Eisenstein, Shub and the Gender of the Author as Producer', *Film History*, vol 14, no 1, 2002, p 96. Shub's investment in editing, as Stollery points out, appears more a creative resort than a voluntary choice, in the face of a gender-based exclusion from pursuing film directing.

72 Silverman, 'The Author as Receiver', *October* 96, 2001 p 27. Walter Benjamin, 'The Author as Producer', in *Understanding Brecht*, Anna Bostock, trans, Verso, London, 1973, pp 85–103. For an example of 1970s Brechtian film theory see *Screen*, and in particular, vol 15, no 2, summer 1974.

73 Silverman, 'The Author as Receiver', op cit, pp 20–21

74 Witt, 'On Communication', op cit, p 7. The fact that Miéville's role is often obscured by critics who commonly conflate their co-productions with the proper name of Jean-Luc Godard, as well as failing to recognise the centrality of her work and influence, often as a co-writer and co-editor, on his other 'singularly authored' features, is emblematic of traditional as well as gendered preconceptions of authorship as already discussed (Gorin often also suffered the same fate). See Jerry White, *Two Bicycles: The Work of Jean-Luc Godard and Anne-Marie Miéville*, Wilfrid Laurier University Press, Waterloo, Ontario, 2013.

film's poster: 'Work by E. I. Shub'.[70] As Martin Stollery contends, 'it is historically significant that it was a woman who pioneered' a genre 'based upon a repudiation of established notions of authorship'.[71]

In the 1960s and 1970s, political film-makers and critics drew on Walter Benjamin's Brechtian notion of 'The Author as Producer' in order to align their art 'with work rather than inspiration or creation', relegating 'the artist to the status of a labourer' and allowing 'for a more collective… notion of the conditions under which an artwork comes to be'.[72] Although typically associated with the idea of the director-centred approach of the *auteur*, connected with the journal *Cahiers du cinema*, Godard could be said, even in his earliest films, as Silverman contends, 'to be working toward authorial divestiture'.[73] This deconstruction of the author clearly took a much more 'sustained and self-conscious' form during his Dziga Vertov Group period. Formed in 1968 – the year of the publication of Roland Barthes's 'Death of the Author' – the quasi-anonymous group constituted, as Witt puts it, a 'concrete demonstration of the Structuralist challenge to authorship', which continued with Godard's collaboration with Miéville.[74] For Silverman, *Numéro deux* 'represents an even more concerted attempt at authorial divestiture' in the way that the film is *produced* with not only Miéville but also the actors.[75] As she writes, the categories 'direction' and 'writing' are replaced with the 'much more labour-significant "production", which is credited not to one, but four names'.[76] As the credits, recited by Sandrine, state: *Numéro deux* is 'a film produced by A.-M. Miéville and J.-L. Godard, with S. Battistella, P. Oudry and Others'. In a scene towards the end of the film, Godard, slumped over a recording console, listens to Sandrine, whose voice has come to take on a meta-critical function, challenging the male director as an originator of discourse. 'The heroic creator', as Farocki comments, has 'become a simple conductor of prerecorded music', or what Silverman terms the author as *receiver*.[77] In this last segment, abandoning her character-role, Sandrine the actress argues that 'letting others tell you news about yourself is a crime', and, pointing to the presumption of film-makers to speak not only for their subjects, but also their audience, continues: 'We go to the movies. We buy a ticket. We sell our role as producers in exchange.' Here instead Sandrine speaks for herself, articulating her position as woman and worker.[78]

Conclusion: Home Movies

In a 1973 interview published in *Cinéma Pratique*, Godard remarked 'that the real "political" film' that he would like to make would be 'a home movie' because, for him, it is a mode of film-making that represents 'the popular base of cinema'.[79] Although the films that followed this pronouncement, such as *Numéro deux*, are not home movies in the strict sense – which are, or used to be, as Godard says, made to be shown to other family members (such as the Romanov home movies

75 Silverman, 'The Author as Receiver', op cit, p 21

76 Silverman and Farocki, *Speaking about Godard*, op cit, p 145

77 Ibid, p 169

78 This question of speaking for others is discussed by Godard in an interview from 1972, concerning *Tout va Bien*. In it, he questions workers' documentaries that think they can 'listen directly' to people who 'have been denied a voice for so long' and film-makers who think they 'can be of use to them with no problem'. We can see a parallel with such filmic concerns in the debates around the method and purpose of a 'workers' inquiry' that took place in Italian Marxism in the 1960s and 1970s, particularly those who argued that it needed to be a workers' *self*-inquiry. See Asad Haider and Salar Mohandesi, 'Workers' Inquiry: A Genealogy', *Viewpoint Magazine* 3, 2013: https://viewpointmag.com/2013/09/27/workers-inquiry-a-genealogy/, accessed 7 June 2017.

79 Quoted in MacCabe, 'Godard Since '68', op cit, p 23

80 The Internet and digital sharing culture, and online platforms such as YouTube, have clearly radically transformed the idea of a home movie, and amateur film more generally, being confined to a future audience consisting of *only* family and friends.

81 White, in a slightly odd yet nonetheless intriguing comparison, connects the idea of the home movie in Godard and Miéville with that of Stan Brakhage. Both, as he points out, moved to the countryside (Brakhage, in the US, to the Rocky Mountains) in order to practice small-scale production, and both shared a preoccupation with the domestic. White, *Two Bicycles*, op cit, p 31.

82 MacCabe, 'Godard since '68', op cit, p 23

83 Witt, 'On and Under Communication', op cit, p 319

84 Silverman and Farocki, *Speaking about Godard*, op cit, p 142

85 Michael Renov, 'Video Confessions', in *The Subject*

that Shub appropriated for her film) – the genre category is nonetheless useful for thinking about the work and production methods that Godard and Miéville went on to pursue.[80] Soon after this statement was made, Godard and Miéville left Paris and established their company, Sonimage: an experimental studio-laboratory in Grenoble, in the French Alps, moving it to Rolle, in Switzerland, in 1977.[81] The initial idea behind this move, as MacCabe writes, 'was to work against the whole process of economic, political and cultural centralization' embodied, for Godard, in the city of Paris.[82] Godard's antagonistic relation to the overly centralised film industry is manifested in his monologue in *Numéro deux* when he claims that his studio, away from the city, 'is a factory', but one that is different from the others such as Fox, Metro, Mosfilm and other big multinational companies. 'We have taken power,' he quips.

The process of 'decentralisation', combined with the use of video technology, made it possible for Godard and Miéville 'to work collaboratively with small production teams'.[83] As Farocki says, the intimacy and physically confined nature of a film like *Numéro deux* would have been difficult to achieve in 35mm, a technology that 'usually requires a large crew'.[84] Employing video meant that they 'only needed a crew of three', resulting in a lack of invasiveness that Farocki deems 'very close to a home movie'. What is distinctive about video in comparison to its home movie antecedents, such as 16mm and 8mm film, is not its handicraft format, but rather the fact that the 'independent video-maker or home consumer has been relieved of certain mediating contingencies – material, temporal – that separate shooting from viewing'.[85] The 'immediacy' of video, as Witt observes, significantly 'democratized the filmmaking process' for Godard in that it 'facilitated dialogue, and helped to dissolve the divisions and hierarchies between the various technical roles'.[86] A contributing factor is the fact that the 'video image can not only be viewed by the entire crew as it is recorded, but can also be immediately reviewed and subjected to collective discussion', which 'resulted in significantly different and generally much smoother working relations' in making *Numéro deux*.[87]

Godard's employment of video and his conception of the home movie as representing a democratic or popular form of film-making can be seen to converge with the notion of 'deskilling' in twentieth-century art history and the numerous artistic endeavours to eliminate ideas of 'competence', based on a normative criteria of artistic skill, from the 'horizon of both artistic production and aesthetic evaluation'.[88] To identify with the home movie is to identify with the amateur in order to challenge both the hierarchy of artistic skill and the limited catalogue of subjects deemed legitimate for art-making.[89] Home movies could be said to be the 'popular base of cinema' in the way in which, as John Roberts shows in discussing the relationship of popular forms of photography to art, its 'deflationary logic… hides a genuine democratizing impulse'; 'an impulse that continually reconfigures itself in art and culture as a return of the repressed'.[90] This 'strategy', of what Witt calls 'deprofessionalization and amateaurization', can be seen in Godard and Miéville's first television series, *Six fois Deux (Sur et sous la communication)* (Six Times Two [On and

of Documentary, University of Minnesota Press, Minneapolis, 2004, p 198

86 Witt, 'On and Under Communication', op cit, p 325

87 Ibid, p 325

88 See Hal Foster et al, eds, *Art since 1900: Modernism, Antimodernism, Postmodernism*, Thames & Hudson, London, 2011, p 531. For an art theoretical account of the concept of deskilling, see John Roberts, *The Intangibilities of Form: Skill and Deskilling in Art After the Readymade*, Verso, London and New York, 2007. Whereas deskilling in twentieth-century art history typically meant the displacement of artisanal forms of craft labour by technological forms of production and reproduction, in Godard's case, deskilling designates the adoption of low-cost technologies and small-scale modes of production, more akin to 'artisanal' ideas of working, as a strategy to de-professionalise and democratise the highly professionalised, factory-like, production methods of the large film studios.

89 As White points out, Brakhage too aligned himself with the amateur in his 1972 essay titled 'In Defense of Amateur'. For Brakhage, 'any art of the cinema must inevitably arise from the amateur, "home-movie" making medium'. Stan Brakhage, *Brakhage Scrapbook*, Robert A Haller, ed, Documentext, New Paltz, New York, 1982, p 168.

90 John Roberts, *Photography and Its Violations*, Columbia University Press, New York, 2014, p 88. As Roberts notes, the photographic snapshot, akin to the home movie, reclaims the domestic and the contingent and reinvests photography 'with a nonprofessional ethos borrowed from Conceptual art and (to a lesser extent) workers' photography of the 1930s'. Ibid, p 77.

91 Witt, 'On and Under Communication', op cit, p 330

92 Margaret Ganahl and R S Hamilton, 'One Plus One: A Look at *Six Fois Deux*',

Under Communication], 1976).[91] The series consists of six pairs of episodes, around fifty minutes in length, that were broadcast on French television on consecutive Sunday evenings. It generally features long and unstructured interviews with various people, mostly unknown, as well as experimental visual essays, using devices such as a video pen to write electronically over images or empty screen, much like writing on a blackboard.[92] Godard and Miéville refer to this process in one episode as wanting 'to show what a television screen is': a 'surface on which things are written', which they seek to deconstruct.[93] The episodes 'provoke speculation' about the way in which 'professional' television production influences 'the way we see the world and our position in it'. As Margaret Ganahl says, it 'enacts its analysis of the process of communication and offers us a distinctly different form of television'.[94] Again, television is compared with the factory, in order to denaturalise its shaping and transmission of information and the experimental method casts in relief the rigid conventions and codes of television, which are made to seem strange and unfamiliar.[95] The professional/amateur binary also appears at the level of content, for instance, in episode 3b, which is composed of an interview with Marcel, an amateur film-maker, sat at his editing table. Earning his living at a watch factory, where we see him perform similarly minute labours, Marcel insists that he would never want to be paid for his hobby, which he does purely for pleasure.[96]

As Witt argues, Sonimage's attempt to work in the medium of television came out of a recognition of the profound changes brought about in mass media and the effects this had on distribution and consumption.[97] Godard refers to television as a 'family affair', in that the spectator of television, unlike the isolated cinema-goer, is the unit of family.[98] In Sonimage's second television series, *France tour détour deux enfants* (France Tour Detour Two Children, 1979), questions around television, the family and French society more generally, are explored through two children: Camille and Arnaud. Loosely inspired by a nineteenth-century school primer, the twelve-part series analyses how television has taken the place of the primer as *the* form of mass communication. Like television, as Penley says, the children are 'programmed': 'The interrogation of the children's lives in the interviews ceaselessly points to the serialization, the regulated flow and repetition of their domestic, school and leisure schedules.'[99] The emphasis on the control of space and time, as well as the comparisons of school with the prison, show the clear influence of Michel Foucault's *Discipline and Punish* (1975). The 'many puns on copying and reproduction' invoke, as Penley observes, Foucault's 'motif of the body as a recording surface', with the children figuring as what Foucault calls 'Docile Bodies' shaped by their 'various institutional settings'.[100] The series evidences the way that questions of social reproduction are entangled and imbricated with the state – or what Althusser called 'ideological state apparatuses' such as the school, in preparing potential, and docile, labour power.[101] We also witness the work that the state deems remunerable in the two scenes where the children are asked whether their mothers are paid for their work and, upon receiving a 'no', are asked why not? At stake in the series as a whole, as Penley notes, is

Camera Obscura, 8–10, autumn 1982, p 93

93 Ibid, p 94

94 Ibid, p 89

95 Ibid, p 330

96 For an interesting reading of that episode, as well as the series more generally, see Gilles Deleuze, 'On "Sur et sous la communication": Three Questions about "Six Fois Deux"', in Raymond Bellour with Mary Lea Bandy, eds, *Jean-Luc Godard: Son + Image, 1974–1991*, Museum of Modern Art, New York, 1992, p 84.

97 Witt, 'On and Under Communication', op cit, p 326

98 Constance Penley, 'Les Enfants de la Patrie', p 34

99 Ibid, p 34

100 Ibid, p 35

101 Althusser's renowned short text, 'Ideology and Ideological State Apparatuses', was published in 1970. The essay was in fact an extract from a much longer book to do with the reproduction of capitalism as a whole, only recently published in English. See Althusser, *On the Reproduction of Capitalism*, G M Goshgarian, trans, Verso, London and New York, 2014.

102 Penley, 'Les Enfants de la Patrie', op cit, p 53, p 41. Rather than being shown as a prime-time series, as Penley notes, it was in fact slotted into the late Friday night art cinema spot on France's second channel in March and April, 1980. Ibid, p 40.

103 Ibid, p 53

104 Nicole Brenez, 'The Forms of the Question', Jann Matlock, trans, in Michael Temple, James S Williams and Michael Witt. eds, *For Ever Godard*, Black Dog Publishing, London, 2004, pp 162–63

105 Penley, 'Les Enfants de la Patrie', op cit, p 51

106 Witt, 'On and Under Communication', op cit, p 325

107 Ibid, p 325

108 A notable comparison in Germany would be the work

Sonimage's desire to engage with television in order 'to change the programming': its 'economics, distribution, themes, temporalities, forms of address and viewers'.[102] Most of all, she writes, they 'would like to make "local" television (television's version of home movies), programs that we would make to show others, telling them about our lives and work'.[103] This desire is captured in a two-minute film that Godard and Miéville made for French TV in 1977. In it, we see Miéville's adolescent daughter, distractedly watching television (supposedly broadcasting a popular song by Patrick Juvet, *Faut pas rêver* [Do not dream]), while Miéville off-screen asks her about her day. The scene cuts to a scrolling electronic text, which states: 'When the left takes power, will television still have so little relation to people.'[104]

'Decentralizaton, local autonomy, personal and community production' are the politics proposed by Sonimage.[105] Low-cost technologies such as video meant that Sonimage had 'control over the whole production process', from 'filming and editing to postproduction'.[106] Video gave them 'a high degree of economic and creative autonomy', allowing them to work in the Sonimage laboratory-workshop more in the manner of an artist in a studio, which would be difficult in the mainstream film industry.[107] The move into television, however, was part of a larger historical shift, which saw decreasing opportunities for radical and experimental film within the institution of cinema. Yet TV was also embraced for its potential to reach a far greater audience and as a key arena of the public sphere that necessitated engagement rather than being left to the enemy. Sonimage's work therefore pre-empts a larger history of avant-garde film-makers producing for television.[108] In Britain, it was the conception of Channel 4 in the early 1980s, and The Independent Film and Video Department in particular, that fostered such work.[109] It is with a film made for Channel 4 in 1985, *Soft and Hard (Soft Talk on a Hard Subject Between Two Friends)*, that, as Catherine Grant argues, Godard and Miéville come closest to reprising the idea of a home movie.[110] In it, the camera is turned on themselves, performing their daily routines in domestic and rural settings in a sometimes slapstick, sometimes serious, fashion. It features the couple on their sofa discussing questions of communication, television and art, as well as their joint and separate work, and their everyday life.[111] The 'factory' is again invoked in a scene in which we see Miéville at the editing table.

The space of the home and the small-scale production we see in *Soft and Hard*, and Sonimage's work more generally, should be construed not as one of retreat from the reaches of the 'social factory' into bourgeois notions of the artist as secluded individual, for instance, but as a place where alternative modes of production and ways of working collaboratively can be tested and explored. As Volker Pantenburg recently speculated, in relation to the proliferation of various film-making couples that appeared in the 1970s, perhaps this follows the logic that the couple is the smallest collective unit.[112] Most crucially, as Witt contends, the work of Sonimage was 'an attempt to live out a working practice in which the division of labour and of the sexes were dissolved'; and, like Marcel, the amateur film-maker, a bid to find 'pleasure in one's own work', not by selling our role as producers in exchange, as Sandrine says in *Numéro deux*, but by practising a different type of exchange: 'to love work, and work at love'.[113]

of Alexander Kluge, whose move into television was formalised in 1988, with the establishment of his company, DCTP. See Stuart Liebman, 'On New German Cinema, Art, Enlightenment, and the Public Sphere: An Interview with Alexander Kluge', *October* 46, autumn 1988, p 29. In recent years, as Maria Lind and Hito Steyerl note, due to the increasing privatisation of media and cuts in public funding, experimental film and documentary 'has again been increasingly pushed into the art field' (Farocki would be a key example). Maria Lind and Hito Steyerl, 'Introduction: Reconsidering the Documentary and Contemporary Art', in *The Greenroom: Reconsidering the Documentary and Contemporary Art #1*, Sternberg Press, Berlin, and CSS Bard, Annandale-on-Hudson, New York, 2008, p 14.

109 As Rod Stoneman recounts, the overall context of this period involved the movement of people associated with *Screen*, the BFI and the London Film-makers Co-op, into Channel 4's The Independent Film and Video Department. This, in part, was a consequence of the drying up of funding for experimental film from bodies such as the BFI and Arts Council England. See Rod Stoneman, 'Sins of Commission', *Screen*, vol 33, no 2, summer 1992, pp 127–144. See also Laura Mulvey and Jamie Sexton, eds, *Experimental British Television*, Manchester University Press, Manchester, 2007.

110 Catherine Grant, 'Home-movies: The Curious Cinematic Collaboration of Anne-Marie Miéville and Jean-Luc Godard', in *For Ever Godard*, op cit, p 111. *Soft and Hard* was commissioned by MacCabe for Channel 4 in order to raise funding for Godard and Miéville's *Je vous salue, Marie* (Hail Mary, 1985), which they needed money to finish. MacCabe, *Godard: A Portrait of the Artist at 70*, Bloomsbury, London, 2003, p 292.

111 Ibid, p 111

112 As Pantenburg observed, there is a film history of the working couple that remains to be written. The most

notable examples from the 1970s include: Jean-Marie Straub and Danièle Huillet, Laura Mulvey and Peter Wollen, Valie Export and Peter Weibel. These remarks are taken from an unpublished paper, 'The Third Avant-garde: Laura Mulvey, Peter Wollen, and the Theory Film' presented at the Whitechapel Gallery, Saturday 14 May 2016, for the Mulvey and Wollen retrospective 'Beyond the Scorched Earth of Counter-Cinema'.

113 Witt, 'On Communication', op cit, p 10

THIRD TEXT

CRITICAL PERSPECTIVES ON CONTEMPORARY ART AND CULTURE

Announcing our forthcoming special issue, marking the 70th year anniversary of South Asian independence and Partition, and the 30th year anniversary of Third Text

To Draw the Line: Partitions, Dissonance, Art –
A Case for South Asia

Numbers 145–146, volume 30, Issue 2/3, March/May 2017

Guest Edited by Alice Correia and Natasha Eaton

http://www.thirdtext.org
article downloads and subscriptions:
http://www.tandfonline.com/pricing/journal/ctte20
subscribe to Third Text table of contents alerting services:
http://www.informaworld.com/alerting
subscribe to eUpdates and e-newsletter:
http://www.tandf.co.uk/journals/eupdates.asp
Sales of single issues and Third Text Publications titles:
http://www.centralbooks.com/

GIRL
GANG

Third Text, 2017
Vol. 31, No. 1, 97–116, https://doi.org/10.1080/09528822.2017.1366410

Domestic Unrest

Social Reproduction and the Temporalities of Struggle in Lizzie Borden's *Born in Flames*

Beth Capper

Where does the *impossible domestic* fit into the general strike?
Saidiya Hartman[1]

Economic management cannot win the battle that rages in the realm of social reproduction. Here management encounters forms of what we will call planning that resist its every effort to impose a compulsion of scarcity through seizing the means of social reproduction.
Stefano Harney and Fred Moten[2]

Still from Lizzie Borden, *Born in Flames*, 1983, (detail), 35mm, courtesy of First Run Features, television broadcast condemning the actions of the Women's Army

1 Saidiya Hartman, 'The Belly of the World: A Note on Black Women's Labors', *Souls: A Critical Journal of Black Politics, Culture, and Society*, vol 18, no 2, 2016, pp 166–173, p 171, emphasis in the original

2 Stefano Harney and Fred Moten, *The Undercommons: Fugitive Planning and Black Study*, Minor Compositions, Brooklyn, New York, 2013, p 81

3 Angela Mitropoulos, *Contract and Contagion: From Biopolitics to Oikonomia*, Minor Compositions, Brooklyn, New York, 2013

'For the first time in our history we'll provide women with wages for housework.' These words are uttered by the President of the United States in a televised address to the nation in Lizzie Borden's speculative fiction film *Born in Flames* (1983), seconds before the broadcast is interrupted by a collective of militant feminists with guns who call themselves the Women's Army. This mass-mediated announcement marks a pivotal moment in the film where state power and feminist politics conjoin in the ultimate domestic address – and via television, the ultimate domestic medium. The President's call provides an 'oikopolitical' gesture, to borrow a term from political theorist Angela Mitropoulos, which sutures the financial health and wealth of the familial household to the wellbeing of the nation.[3] In the film's broader diegesis, it is a moment that serves to condense many of the political antagonisms that *Born in Flames* dramatises throughout, one that pits a narrowly defined white feminism against an anti-racist and coalitional feminism invested in the collective destruction of capitalism, patriarchy and imperialism in all of their multiple machinations and forms. By condensing these antagonisms under the sign of 'the domestic' the film underscores the constitutive exclusion of women of colour, and black women in particular, from 'domestic' imaginaries of home, family and the (US) nation, even as these women simultaneously provide the labour necessary for the maintenance of such imaginaries. At the same time, *Born in Flames* reminds us that before, beyond and against 'the domestic' lie the subversive powers of feminist community.

Within the film's oppositional logic, 'wages for housework' is positioned as the hallmark of just such a white feminist politics, one that (perhaps unwittingly) colludes with the state's attempts to de-escalate the organising efforts of the Women's Army against the maldistributions of labour and welfare by answering such demands with the allocation of a reformist provision.[4] It is against this understanding of social reproduction installed under the sign of wages for housework that the film indexes another exploration of social reproduction as a significantly wider terrain of contestation, one that encompasses various, often overlapping, responses to structural abandonment, the rise of the prison industrial complex, welfare austerity and multiple forms of waged and unwaged reproductive work. This terrain is better understood, following Fulvia Serra, as a process rather than a sphere:

> … more than a container with fixed boundaries (a sphere)… [social reproduction] should be considered a process, a continuously changing one, which expands and contracts both in response to its own internal dynamics, and under the pressure of the continuous attempts at enclosing it on the part of the capitalist machine.[5]

Bringing this antagonistic and dual character of social reproduction to the fore, *Born in Flames* represents social reproduction as work done both for and against the state and capitalism by foregrounding the work of collective childcare, community planning, and the creation of autonomous social programmes and initiatives. *Born in Flames* is thus a film about the work involved in (re)producing and sustaining community that, as Miranda Joseph has brilliantly underscored, is often obscured in the fetishisation and romance of community.[6]

Indeed, if *Born in Flames* can be distilled into one clear political lesson, it is that community and collectivity do not come easily. Set in the aftermath of an ostensibly peaceful social democratic revolution in the United States, *Born in Flames* explores the structural antagonisms that persist in the aftermath of 'revolution' both within the left and among feminist groups, and much of the film's ninety minutes are spent engaging and staging disagreement among women as to what form feminist movement might encompass. As a media text that reflects upon, and participates in, the political debates within and between feminisms of the 1970s – a time when the charge of 'reformism' against the Wages for Housework (WfH) movement was a common refrain – *Born in Flames*'s representation of the movement is unsurprising. Recent reassessments of the parameters, goals and theoretical-practical analyses of the WfH movement, however, have increasingly challenged such diagnoses of reformist or bourgeois impulses, urging the need for a reactivation of the perspectives generated by WfH in our contemporary moment. In the US context, Kathi Weeks has called upon us to imagine 'how the wages for housework movement might be deployed to confront the present and reimagine

4 Throughout this article, I capitalise 'Wages for Housework' only when referring to the proper name of the political and intellectual movement.

5 Fulvia Serra, 'Reproducing the Struggle: A New Feminist Perspective on the Concept of Social Reproduction', *Viewpoint Magazine* 5, 2015, https://www.viewpointmag.com/2015/10/31/reproducing-the-struggle-a-new-feminist-perspective-on-the-concept-of-social-reproduction/, accessed 1 August 2016

6 Miranda Joseph, *Against the Romance of Community*, University of Minnesota Press, Minneapolis, 2002

Still from Lizzie Borden, *Born in Flames*, 1983, 35 mm, courtesy of First Run Features, President Metzger addresses the nation on the implementation of the wages for housework program its possible futures'.[7] When situated in relation to this renewed uptake, *Born in Flames*'s depiction of wages for housework might then strike us as the residue of feminist debates anachronistic to present concerns, out of time with the reclamation of a feminist perspective that is only now being fully felt and understood.

Against such an appraisal, I will suggest that *Born in Flames* has much to contribute both to reassessments of WfH and to an understanding of the contemporary embrace of social reproduction as a central political category and pivotal terrain of struggle. This contribution emerges at once through and *against* the film's explicit naming of wages for housework, and can be located instead in its invitation to reflect upon the ways in which (feminist) communities and collectivities reproduce themselves as well as the racial divisions of work and reproduction that endure as part of this process. By rearticulating the politics of feminist collectivity as a division of labour that persists *among* women, *Born in Flames* recalibrates processes of social reproduction that have often been obscured in the contemporary circulation of WfH. These are processes, however, that I will show were addressed and interrogated by significant activist-intellectuals within the international WfH movement. Thus, even as *Born in Flames* forwards an analysis of social reproduction resonant with that of WfH, the film remains unable to articulate this analysis under WfH's sign. Nevertheless, *Born in Flames* critically recasts the problematic of social reproduction by unearthing how the administration of racialised and gendered relations of coercion, violence and labour discipline endemic to state-capitalist forms have been reproduced within oppositional, and specifically feminist, collective projects.[8]

Born in Flames's stagings of division among feminists at the scene of social reproduction would seem to fall away in the film's final image of feminist 'terrorism' against the state-run media, when the Women's Army blows up a television tower at the top of the World Trade Center. By leaving the audience with this incendiary fantasy of queer-feminist coalition and solidarity, *Born in Flames* ostensibly supplants dissensus with collective unity. Yet to read such a progressive temporal structure into *Born in Flames* is surely to miss the film's challenge to linear narratives of social transformation. As Stephen Dillon has argued, *Born in Flames* juxtaposes two opposing narratives of social transformation: the state's narrative that the War of Liberation signalled a radical rupture with former structures of political domination; and the standpoint of the Women's Army, who emphasise the racial and sexual divisions ongoing before and after the revolution. Dillon refers to these two opposing temporalities as *Born in Flames*'s 'temporality of violence', revealing the accumulations of state violence that occasion the eruption of anti-state violence at the film's culmination.[9] To Dillon's insights, I want to add that the film offers differential 'temporalities of struggle', where the War of Liberation is posed not only against the revolutionary counter-violence of the Women's Army, but also against the ongoing work of planning, survival and social support that both enables, and is a constitutive component of, the film's depiction of feminist revolution. With this in mind, how might we understand this final scene of revolutionary violence in relation to the duration of everyday struggle that, as Neferti Tadiar has argued,

7 Kathi Weeks, *The Problem with Work: Feminism, Marxism, Antiwork Politics, and Postwork Imaginaries*, Duke University Press, Durham, North Carolina, 2011, p 117. Following Weeks, I highlight the difference between wages for housework as a perspective that transforms the very terms of political analysis and the demand for wages for housework as one demand among others. For more on this distinction, see Silvia Federici with Nicole Cox, 'Counterplanning from the Kitchen (1975)', in *Revolution at Point Zero: Housework, Reproduction, and Feminist Struggle*, PM Press, Brooklyn, New York, 2012, pp 28–41, p 30.

8 This concern is anticipated by Borden in an earlier exploration of dissensus among feminists. Her rarely viewed debut *Regrouping* (1976) initially started out as a collectively produced feminist documentary about a women's group, but culminated with the group unravelling and picketing the film's short run of public screenings. The resulting film is a fascinating meditation on the deconstitution of feminist collectivity as well as the coercions, erasures and dynamics of labour and power that can underpin the demand for solidarity.

9 Stephen Dillon, '"It's here, it's that time": Race, Queer Futurity, and the Temporality of Violence in *Born in Flames*', *Women & Performance: A Journal of Feminist Theory*, vol 23, no 1, 2013, pp 38–51

has a tendency to fall away in narratives of revolution?[10] How might attending to the work of social reproduction that undergirds the film's dramatisations of political organisation reorientate our reading of *Born in Flames*'s narrative of feminist revolution? And how might *Born in Flames*'s engagement with the question of whose socially reproductive work undergirds and sustains feminist coalitional movements pressure and advance contemporary conversations about coalition, solidarity and (black) autonomous struggle?

To answer these questions, I turn to the film's multiple, sometimes competing, figurations of housework and the domestic. I highlight glimpses of a black domestic that appear within the film, where this domestic designates at once a labouring figure (a domestic *worker*) and a space from which to struggle. This other domestic imagination supports and exceeds the film's representation of feminist revolutionary coalition, as well as negates the (white) familial household and its spatial separation of public and private. These glimpses, I argue, provoke another image of the domestic, in contrast to the one advanced by the President and refused by the Women's Army.

In this article, I track the film's entangled articulations of social reproduction, the racialised and gendered work of community, and the domestic as an internally differentiated site of struggle in order to advance two related arguments. First, I explore how *Born in Flames* dissects the process of reproducing and maintaining feminist collectivity and, in so doing, dramatises the social reproduction of feminist coalition. *Born in Flames* illuminates how sustaining feminist community depends upon an uneven distribution of work enacted primarily by its black female characters, and therefore strains to articulate the overlapping but non-identical relationship between multiracial feminist coalition and the autonomy of black feminist struggle. Second, I situate *Born in Flames*'s engagement with social reproduction in relation to pamphlets and speeches produced by Black Women for Wages for Housework (BWfWfH) that reconfigure conceptions of 'housework' and the 'domestic' beyond the domains of the nuclear family and the household. These writings theorise domestic labour's constitutive entanglements with racial slavery and develop a theory of 'housework' that contends with racialised divisions of labour (*between* women) not easily subsumed within the analysis of the sexual division of labour that has dominated the contemporary reception of the WfH campaign. I put the film into conversation with these texts not in order to suggest that *Born in Flames*'s own representation of the WfH perspective fails to achieve historical accuracy. Rather, by reading *Born in Flames* through the lens of this activist and intellectual archive, I aim to unpack the film's previously overlooked politics of black feminist social reproduction and, in so doing, illuminate the divisions of reproductive labour that enable and interrupt multiple visions of feminist community.

(Un)Working Feminist Community

The few critics who wrote about *Born in Flames* upon its 1983 release addressed the film as an exploration of the multiplicity of differences (in terms of class, race, gender and sexuality) between women as

10 Neferti X M Tadiar, *Things Fall Away: Philippine Historical Experience and the Makings of Globalization*, Duke University Press, Durham, North Carolina, 2009

social subjects. This is understandable given that much of the film pivots upon the productive tension between antagonism among women of different racial and class backgrounds, on the one hand, and coalitional struggle across difference, on the other. The film follows several women with different relationships to the Women's Army and the question of feminist revolution. The founder of the Women's Army and the film's central protagonist is black queer radical Adelaide Norris. Influenced by arguments from her mentor Zella Wiley (played by the civil rights lawyer Florynce Kennedy) she advances the necessity of armed struggle against the state. The 'feminist' opposition to the Women's Army is led by three white women who work for the state's newspaper, *The Socialist Youth Review*. These women criticise Norris and the Women's Army for what they (mis)-perceive as the group's gendered 'separatism' from the putatively universalist aspirations of state socialism. Meanwhile, the hosts of two underground radio stations, Honey from Radio Phoenix and Isabel from Radio Ragazza, hold opposing positions on the Women's Army; Honey is supportive, Isabel is hesitant. However, by the end of the film, the two stations come together as Phoenix-Ragazza Radio when the Army mobilises to attack the state-run media.

Born in Flames's exploration of the politics of feminist coalition is mirrored in the film's formal strategies. One prominent montage features a scene of female workers in a chicken factory followed in succession with images of an infant bottle-feeding, a nurse laying out surgical instruments onto a table, a hand sliding a condom onto a penis, and a woman packing groceries. Here, *Born in Flames* brings 'productive' labour into formal proximity with service work, sex work, caring labour and domestic work, and shows how racial and sexual divisions organise labour across these sites. In so doing, the film stresses the potential for collective alliances among women over shared, though distinct, conditions of low-wage and unwaged labour. Across the film's composition, Borden also sought to reject the conventions of classical cinematic narrative, drawing instead on broadcast media such as radio and television both as inspiration for the film's aesthetic codes and as critical fodder within its diegesis. Borden notes how television, a form whose textual system relies on the production of continuity through the discontinuity of discrete segments, significantly influenced her editing process: 'I tried to make the editing function as much like commercials as possible.'[11] The heterogeneous yet unified structuration of the televisual corresponds well to the thematic of coalitional unity through difference.

The film's coalitional politics is indebted to 1970s US black feminist theory and activism. Media historian Lucas Hilderbrand highlights how the film's premise echoes the Combahee River Collective's 1977 'A Black Feminist Statement', which outlines the impoverishment of a socialist revolution that is not also an anti-racist and feminist revolution.[12] In 'A Black Feminist Statement' the freedom of black women from systems of oppression provides the condition for the broader social and political liberation for all people.[13] In *Born in Flames*, however, the Statement's invitation for a collective response to black women's oppression is turned on its head, and black women are unevenly burdened with the task of destroying the structures that simultaneously target and exclude them

11 Anne Friedberg, 'An Interview with Filmmaker Lizzie Borden', *Women & Performance: A Journal of Feminist Theory*, vol 1, no 2, 1984, pp 37–45, p 43. For a consideration of television's dialectic of continuity and discontinuity, see Jane Feuer, 'The Concept of "Live" Television: Ontology as Ideology', E Ann Kaplan, *Regarding Television: Critical Approaches – An Anthology*, University Publications of America, Frederick, Maryland, 1983, pp 12–22.

12 Lucas Hilderbrand, 'In the Heat of the Moment: Notes on the Past, Present, and Future of *Born in Flames*', *Women & Performance: A Journal of Feminist Theory*, vol 23, no 1, 2013, p 8

13 Combahee River Collective, 'A Black Feminist Statement', in Cherríe Moraga and Gloria Anzaldúa, eds, *This Bridge Called My Back: Writings by Radical Women of Color*, Kitchen Table Women of Color Press, Latham, New York, 1981, pp 210–219

Still from Lizzie Borden, *Born in Flames*, 1983, 35 mm, courtesy of First Run Features, Honey and her friend argue about the Women's Army

on behalf of the liberation of all. *Born in Flames* thus emphasises how the production and maintenance of coalitional feminist struggle against the state and towards the liberation of all women depends upon the *hard work* of black women. The film's attention to black women's work within and for a broad-based multiracial feminist coalition registers an ambivalence surrounding the coalitional form as the grounds from which to realise black feminist freedom.

The emphasis on black women's work for feminist coalition and community is clearest in the film's depiction of Norris. Norris undertakes much of the work of convincing the film's other central characters that anti-state violence is necessary and overdue. Moreover, while disagreement and dissensus are celebrated in the film as a vital aspect of the process of political organisation, many of Norris's interactions evidence the inability of the film's white characters to understand the disproportionate state violence experienced by black women and women of colour *as violence*. The state's discourse of revolution and white feminist articulations of progress in the film are secured through the necessary invisibility of this violence, which includes the quotidian violences of structural unemployment and the assault on black women's welfare rights that undergird the reproduction of the white social order and its feminist apparatus.

Norris's efforts are met with varying responses, from the ambivalence of her white lesbian co-organiser in the Woman's Army who tells Norris that is it going to be 'a difficult task to get all the women to think along that same line because the reality of having to deal with taking up arms is really heavy', to the charges of counter-revolutionary activity levelled at the Women's Army from the female editors of *The Socialist Youth Review*. In one conversation with these editors, Norris tries (and fails) to convince them of the uninterrupted duration of state violence against black women and other women of colour, both before and after the 'War of Liberation'. Invested in a progressive temporal narrative of 'women's liberation', the editors tell Norris that 'things are so much better than they were before'. In response, Norris exhorts:

> Better now? You know, the way my mother brought us up, there were eight of us, and she took care of us doing domestic work, all by herself… And daycare, hmmm, we took care of ourselves. No one took care of us. And there are plenty of women nowadays living in that same manner.

On a descriptive register, Norris's response reveals how the experience and the temporality of liberal progress is secured through an invisible infrastructure of gendered black labour. Linking the privatisation and commodification of racialised reproductive labour to the exigencies that incited her childhood work for her family ('we took care of ourselves') and that continue to drive her political movement work ('there are plenty of women nowadays living in that same manner'), Norris implicitly bridges a connection between her mother's domestic work and her own socially reproductive work with the Women's Army. On a performative register, however, at the same time as Norris enunciates

Still from Lizzie Borden, *Born in Flames*, 1983, 35 mm, courtesy of First Run Features, television broadcast condemning the actions of the Women's Army

14 Cineaste Magazine, 'Lizzie Borden: Labor Relations', in Gary Crowdus and Dan Georgakas, eds, *The Cineaste Interviews 2: Filmmakers on the Art and Politics of the Cinema*, Lake View Press, Chicago, 2002, p 32

15 Friedberg, 'An Interview with Filmmaker Lizzie Borden', op cit, p 38

16 For example, Borden told Friedberg: 'The problem with much of the critical material on the film is that it assumes a white middle-class reading public for articles written about a film that they assume has only a white middle-class audience. I'm very confused about the discomfort that reviewers feel.' Friedberg, 'An Interview with Filmmaker Lizzie Borden', ibid, p 38.

17 Ibid, p 38

18 Dillon, 'It's here, it's that time', op cit, p 48

19 Ibid, p 48; Jared Sexton, 'People-of-Color-Blindness: Notes on the Afterlife of Slavery', *Social Text*, vol 28, no 2, p 103, pp 31–56, p 48. Sexton's argument here is foreshadowed by the Combahee River Collective's insight that 'If black women were free, it would mean that everyone else would have to be free since our freedom would necessitate the destruction of all systems of oppression.' See Combahee River Collective, 'A Black Feminist Statement', op cit, p 215.

the politics of social reproduction as the impetus and the terrain of her struggle, she also *enacts* the communicative labour necessary for unworking the editor's racist agnosia to further – that is, to re-*work* – the coalitional goals of the Women's Army.

The critical reception of *Born in Flames*, marked by an anxious misrecognition of the critique of white bourgeois feminism as black women's primary aspiration, is further indicative of the relationship that the film narratively explores between coalition and a politics of black feminist liberation. Despite Borden's assertion that *Born in Flames* was a film 'about black women' addressed to multiple audiences, critics assumed that *Born in Flames* was primarily targeted at a white (feminist) audience.[14] In an interview with Borden in 1984, Anne Friedberg reads *Born in Flames* as a film that 'demands a certain discomfort from the audience' and that 'forces the viewer to confront his or her own political position(s)... in terms of class and race politics',[15] thereby implicitly centring the position of the white film spectator. In this reading, black women have actorly value within the film only insofar as they perform and produce a fantasy of feminist coalition that proves both instructional and cathartic for white (feminist) audiences. Borden rejects Friedberg's reading, stressing that she did not conceive the film as privileging the inscription of a white female spectator. However, the sense of audience discomfort that Friedberg describes was a common reaction to the film.[16] Moreover, when Borden discusses her experience of working with black female actors, she equally reproduces the pedagogical function of black actors for her own process as a white film-maker, suggesting that the 'whole process of getting over whatever discomfort I might have felt as a white filmmaker working with black women... was exorcized by the process of making the film.'[17]

It is therefore particularly telling that, in the film's field of diegetic action, the production of feminist solidarity, ultimately depends upon Norris's death rather than the reproductive work that she undertakes on behalf of feminist coalition throughout the film. Norris is murdered while incarcerated for transporting weapons for the Women's Army, although the state claims her death is a suicide. Norris's murder is put to narrative and political work, serving as the galvanising event that halts all feminist antagonisms, with each faction coming together in collective unity. In his treatment, Dillon argues that the fact that Norris's death pushes the film's narrative towards insurgency shows how anti-blackness is revealed as 'the truth of the [faux] revolutionary state', one that ultimately impels the Women's Army towards a truly revolutionary form of anti-state violence.[18] Here, Dillon builds upon Jared Sexton's claim that

> black existence... indicates the (repressed) truth of the political and economic system. That is to say, the whole range of positions within the racial formation is most fully understood from this vantage point.[19]

For Dillon, then, following Sexton, Norris's death is the moment where the socialist state unveils itself as structurally anti-black, illuminating the impossibility of 'liberation' while black people remain unfree.

Sexton's argument, however, equally supports an alternative reading of the significance of Norris's death in the film, where her murder is further evidence of the inability of feminist coalition to fully acknowledge both the centrality of anti-black violence and its quotidian nature. In his article, Sexton powerfully contends that the horizon of black freedom might be at odds with (indeed, may be directly negated by) a politics of multiracial coalition, particularly one that fails to recognise 'significant differences of structural position born of discrepant histories between blacks and their political allies, actual or potential'.[20] Observing that a *metaphorics* of racial slavery and black suffering has long been activated as the enabling allegorical grammar for a range of a progressive political movements, even when such movements have failed to address racial slavery and black suffering themselves, Sexton underscores how spectacular scenes of suffering serve to 'obscure and to naturalise' anti-black terror.[21] In *Born in Flames*, a similar dynamic is apparent in the spectacular and 'eventful' violence of Norris's death and the ongoing violence of her life. In one scene after Norris's death, the editors of *The Socialist Youth Review*, now in support of the Women's Army, debate whether or not to print an image of Norris's dead body. While they are critical of sensationalising her death, they suggest that 'we could use those images to mobilise the women'. This scene follows shortly after the film's own deployment of the image of Norris's death and can be read as a form of meta-textual commentary on the ways in which Norris's murder functions instrumentally within the film's diegesis on behalf of feminist solidarity. The spectacle of (Norris's) death, which draws the Women's Army further towards armed struggle, is framed within the film against the quotidian violence that Norris exhaustively belabours in her debates with other (non-black) women and that she actively works against. It is telling, for example, that the newspaper editors only join the Women's Army after Norris's death rather than after their meeting with Norris where she outlines the terms of black women's demands and struggles. Yet while *Born in Flames* strains against the spectacularisation of black suffering by treating the deployment of Norris's murder self-consciously, it nevertheless makes black women available to violent death as the engine that motors its own narrative and political movement. Such a deployment of black death as spectacle mirrors the expenditure of, and trade in, black bodies by state power.[22] Where Dillon reads the centrality of black freedom to the film's imagination of feminist coalition, I read the exhaustion of black women, literally to death, in order for coalitional politics to live and flourish.

Impossible Domestics

The (in)visibility of racially gendered labour that structures the narrative legibility of 'revolution' forms the crucible of *Born in Flames*'s competing temporalities of struggle, and it is the figure of Norris whose life, death and labour most centrally brings the opposition of 'revolution' and 'social reproduction' to a crisis. Norris's work for the Women's Army is best understood as being akin to what film theorist Kara Keeling has

20 Ibid, Sexton, 'People-of-Color-Blindness', pp 47–48

21 Ibid, p 34. On the power of the 'terrible spectacle' to dissimulate the quotidian operations of anti-black violence, see also Saidiya Hartman, *Scenes of Subjection: Terror, Slavery, and Self-Making in Nineteenth-Century America*, Oxford University Press, Oxford and New York, 1997; and Jared Sexton and Steve Martinot, 'The Avant-Garde of White Supremacy', *Social Identities*, vol 9, no 2, 2003, pp 169–181.

22 See Deborah McDowell, 'Viewing the Remains: A Polemic on Death, Spectacle, and the [Black] Family', in Marianne Hirsch, *The Familial Gaze*, University Press of New England, Hanover and London, 1999, pp 153–177.

described as a form of affective labour that 'produces social networks and forms of community'.[23] This labour enables, but also holds the power to disrupt, the production of cinematic common sense, which names the ways in which political discourse operates to exclude particular bodies, groups and actions from regimes of intelligibility. According to Keeling, however, there is not simply one common sense but rather multiple common senses that 'harbor viable alternatives to white bourgeoisie North American common sense', even as these alternatives may also render 'otherwise' ways of knowing unavailable.[24]

Within the dominant logics of *Born in Flames*'s 'revolutionary' common sense, Norris only garners value at the moment of her death, marking her as both a martyr and a militant. This logic negates Norris's work in imagining and building alternative infrastructures of social reproduction, pitting revolutionary violence and martyrdom against the work of maintenance and care. This common-sense notion is offered in the film by Isabel, the host of Radio Ragazza, who refuses to believe that the Women's Army are responsible for anti-street-violence activism performed by a group of militant women on bicycles. Setting up an opposition between militancy and social reproduction, Isabel tells her friends:

> It couldn't have been the Women's Army!... They are a service to the community: they deal with childcare, daycare centres, and stuff like that... they're not aggressive enough, they're not terrorists.

Strikingly, Isabel fails to recognise that the street bicycle gang is itself a social programme, emerging as a grass-roots response to sexual violence and harassment meant both to replace and oppose the policing and criminalising apparatus of the state.

While *Born in Flames* at times traffics in a discourse that revalorises death and/as militancy by negating the labour of care, this inscription of revolution's temporal compass is interrupted throughout the film, however fleetingly, by a counter-politics and a counter-temporality instantiated through Norris's life and her efforts to survive and create resources that enable the survival of others. Attending to these fleeting moments in the film's depiction of Norris opens an imagination of black feminist social reproduction that references the multiple sites, institutional locations and collective forms of care that black women create and navigate in order to secure their own social reproduction, as opposed to a narrower conception of domestic work oriented around the physical, sexual and emotional labours of family life and matrimony. Throughout, *Born in Flames* directly references many of the policies that have foreclosed black women's access to the nuclear family and its state-sponsored privileges, including the workfare programme, which forced women to work off welfare grants, and the Full Employment and Balanced Growth Act of 1976, which, as the film emphasises in a news report, mandated that 'male heads of families' would be guaranteed jobs over non-married women, queer women, and women (and men) whose subjection to processes of sexual racialisation marked them outside the normative prescriptions of the heteronormative family-form.[25] The film impresses

23 Kara Keeling, *The Witch's Flight: The Cinematic, the Black Femme, and the Image of Common Sense*, Duke University Press, Durham, North Carolina, 2007, p 147

24 Ibid, p 21

25 For an account of the impact of the 1976 Full Employment Act on black women, see Marisa Chappell, 'Demanding a New Family Wage: Feminist Consensus in the 1970s Full Employment Campaign', in Stephanie Gilmore, ed, *Feminist Coalitions: Historical Perspectives on Second-Wave Feminism in the United States*, University of Illinois Press, Urbana and Chicago, 2008, pp 252–284. See also 'Every Mother Is a Working Mother', *Safire: Black Women for Wages for Housework (USA)*, vol 1, no 1, 1977, pp 1–2.

the need for black women to create alternative forms of social reproduction to combat the regulatory mechanisms and austerity logics of the state, such as in one of the film's earliest scenes where, in a nod to the Black Panther Party's breakfast programmes, a group of black women gather around a kitchen table to discuss the difficulty of sustaining a community centre run by the Army that offers free childcare.

Yet even as the film's most explicit polemic belabours the point that historical machinations and contemporary policies have assaulted – indeed, rendered unavailable – 'the domestic' as a site for black women's social reproduction, it is simultaneously the case that many of the glimpses we see of Norris's life and of the daily lives of other black women are structured through the *mise-en-scène* of domestic interiors, where the work of self-care and the work of revolutionary planning take place synchronously. In this regard, *Born in Flames* establishes the household as a base of organisation for the Women's Army throughout the film's duration such that kitchens, living rooms and bedrooms serve as the location for planning meetings and debates over revolutionary tactics. The importance of the household as a site of resistance is also indicated by the state's surveillance of domestic spaces and the formal mirroring of this violent intrusion through the film's camerawork. *Born in Flames* moves rapidly between alternating modes of spectatorial identification, at times establishing house meetings as covert visual spaces in which the audience participates as an accomplice to the Women's Army, at other times occupying the perspective of the state by employing a technique that Thomas Y Levin has called 'surveillant narration', in which the camera's gaze comes to resemble the gaze of closed-circuit television.[26] In these domestic meetings, social reproduction and anti-state 'terrorism' are placed side by side as necessary components for bringing forth the abolition of the state. These scenes of planning re-signify the house away from its associations with the nuclear family and towards a vision of *collective housekeeping* where the 'hidden abode' of the household provides cover for radical struggle.[27] This rendering of a black domestic imagination interrupts dominant logics of the domestic as a white bourgeois space, as well as narratives (such as Daniel Patrick Moynihan's infamous 1965 report on the pathology of the 'Negro' family) that uphold the nuclear family unit as the crucible of black uplift. Indeed, the black feminist social spaces perceptible in the film bolster Moynihan's worst fears of a domestic unit organised according to the 'wayward reproductions' of militant black feminist community.[28]

Historian Christina Hanhardt notes that *Born in Flames* dramatises the political work of 'processing' and likens the experience of watching the film to participating in an organising meeting:

In *Born in Flames* women are mostly talking, debating, and making plans. For anyone who has been to such a meeting, you likely have experienced that moment when, four hours in, you realise that this might go on forever and that there really will be no future.[29]

Though Hanhardt humorously emphasises the drawn-out duration of planning *for* the revolution, I want to linger on her evocative suggestion

26 Thomas Y Levin, 'Rhetoric of the Temporal Index: Surveillant Narration and the Cinema of "Real Time"', in Thomas Y Levin, Peter Weibel and Ursula Frohne, eds, *CTRL-[SPACE]*, The MIT Press, Cambridge, Massachusetts, 2002, pp 578–593

27 Kiran Garcha's illuminating analysis of the role of the home as a base of operations for the Black Panther Party is in line with my argument here. See Kiran Garcha, 'Bringing the Vanguard Home: Revisiting the Black Panther Party's Sites of Class Struggle', *Viewpoint Magazine* 5, 2015, https://viewpointmag.com/2015/10/31/bringing-the-vanguard-home-revisiting-the-black-panther-partys-sites-of-class-struggle/, accessed 2 August 2016.

28 Alys Eve Weinbaum argues that such 'wayward reproductions' produce crises within 'the dominant racial and gender order'. See *Wayward Reproductions: Genealogies of Race and Nation in Transatlantic Modern Thought*, Duke University Press, Durham, North Carolina, 2004, p 14.

29 Christina Hanhardt, 'LAUREL and Harvey: Screening Militant Gay Liberalism and Feminist Radicalism circa 1980', *Women & Performance: A Journal of Feminist Theory*, vol 23, no 1, 2013, pp 17–37, p 32

Still from Lizzie Borden, *Born in Flames*, 1983, 35 mm, courtesy of First Run Features, a household meeting

that such planning often feels as if 'there really will be no future' and the complication of revolution's temporal orientation that this suggestion announces. In *Born in Flames*'s scenes of counterplanning from the kitchen we witness the radically present instantiation of a future that is otherwise than the drive towards 'revolution', where those forms of life figured in the black domestic at once enable and exceed revolution as *telos*. This imagination of (counter)planning is closer to what Stefano Harney and Fred Moten elucidate in the epigraph to this article as 'seizing the means of social reproduction'. Contrasting their articulation of planning with both state-socialist practices of planning and with the state management of populations that they herald under the banner of 'policy', Harney and Moten argue that planning takes place in the socially reproductive 'realm' where the means of struggle are constantly being invented:

> In the undercommons of the socially reproductive realm the means, which is to say the planners, are still part of the plan. And the plan is to invent the means in a common experiment launched from any kitchen, any back porch, any basement, any hall, any park bench, any improvised party, every night.[30]

What Harney and Moten describe as modes of living through and beyond 'the evidence of mass incapacity'[31] that is everywhere present (and impressed through the *mise-en-scène* of *Born in Flames*) gives confirmation to a black domestic, an impossibility within the optics of the state and its metrics of policy, that is constantly taking shape. In *Born in Flames*, such efforts to seize the *means* of reproduction inaugurate another meeting of black women where a different temporality and practice of social life is reproduced. This domestic imagination is necessarily discontinuous from the formal meetings that Hanhardt mentions and can instead be discovered in a poetics of fleeting moments where black women are engaged in daily acts of collective self-care, self-reproduction, and friendship – such as brushing teeth, studying, watching television, playing basketball, talking, laughing, arguing and dancing – that do not advance the film's narrative and where social reproduction is not fully instrumentalised for the (re)production of the state or the Women's Army. Nevertheless, such ephemeral moments form a crucial infrastructure that inhabits at once the tense of the 'now' and that persists as an unincorporable remainder. These moments evidence another time of social reproduction, one that drags against the forward thrust of the filmic narrative and that exceeds its scenes of organising, planning and protest, and its propulsive musical score.[32]

In one sequence midway through the film, the editors of *The Socialist Youth Review* serve as talking heads on a TV debate show centred on the infantile 'gratuitous desire for excitement' espoused by the Women's Army. This televisual sequence is interspersed with a montage of women handing out flyers and organising on the streets against sexual violence, signalling that which necessarily falls away from the televisual logics of visibility. The contradiction established by this disjuncture between image and the televisual voice-over is then cut by the introduction of a third temporal configuration, one that speaks neither the

30 Harney and Moten, *The Undercommons*, op cit, p 74

31 Ibid, p 73

32 For a compelling account of the relation between the film's score and its musical cacophony of female voices embroiled in debate, see Frances Morgan, 'Trapped and Free', *Sight and Sound*, vol 24, no 3, February 2014, p 61.

language of freedom's fulfilment nor of ongoing injustice. Consisting of only two shots – a shot/reverse shot of Zella Wiley and Norris exchanging an intimate glance in which it is unclear whether the background noise is diegetic or extra-diegetic (are the women watching TV or not?) – the encounter between the two women stalls the accumulation of tightly interwoven but discontinuous sequences that elsewhere govern the film's coalitional imaginary. This longing look between Wiley and Norris encodes an image of black feminist collective autonomy revealed as the otherwise invisible condition of the film's political drama but that is nevertheless in surplus to the film's narrativising claims.

Emotional Housework

The expanded and revisionary black domestic that appears in *Born in Flames* cannot be fully incorporated into the film's narrative field of feminist coalitional struggle. Yet this appearance is still only a productive potential within the film, one that exists in conflict with – and is at times disappeared by – *Born in Flames*'s own (re)production of cinematic common sense. I thus want to return again to *Born in Flames*'s enunciation of wages for housework as the antithesis of black feminist struggle in order to interrogate how the film's critique of the domestic partakes in the reification of this demand and the insurgent possibilities held within. At stake in my analysis of *Born in Flames*'s claim that WfH did not, and could not, account for the specificity of black women's domestic struggles are the ways in which the repetition of (feminist) narratives about feminist movements operate to make unavailable robust intellectual, activist and social genealogies. As such, I turn to the theory of social reproduction promulgated by Black Women for Wages for Housework (BWfWfH) co-founders Margaret Prescod and Wilmette Brown. BWfWfH was a committee within the WfH movement that took inspiration from black women's organised struggles for welfare rights in and after the 1960s. Again, my argument is not that the film does not achieve historical fidelity in its representations of the WfH movement, but rather that its discursive economy of social reproduction and revolutionary action adheres to a common sense that at times obscures black feminist demands for an autonomous domestic vision.

In her pamphlet, *Black Women: Bringing It All Back Home* (1981), Prescod proposes 'housework' as a capacious analytic that draws together heterogenous yet structurally consonant forms of labour and self-reproduction that black women perform on a daily basis across remunerated and unremunerated locations. Prescod moves from a discussion of the emotional labour involved in working as a domestic for white families to the work of managing everyday racial violence at school, in each instance activating 'housework' as a privileged theoretical frame. In one passage, for example, Prescod describes a racist encounter at school in the following mode:

I remember in high school in New York I had a teacher who in front of the class used to call me 'swamp woman' because I was from the West Indies... That's a lot of housework, coming home after a day of that kind of harassment and knowing you had to get yourself together to go out the next day and deal with that stuff all over again. That's a lot of housework.[33]

33 Margaret Prescod, *Black Women: Bringing It All Back Home*, Falling Wall Press, Bristol, 1981, pp 27–28

Prescod apprehends a racially administered double-shift that she labours to perform between school and home; the emotional housework of negotiating her teacher's harassment is doubled by the work of self-reproduction and rejuvenation she must then undertake at home in order to manage the repetitions of tomorrow's harassment. Providing a framework to understand emotional housework that pivots away from its neat delineation within the hetero-domestic dynamic and the sexual division of labour, Prescod attunes us to the processes of gendered racialisation that disperse the boundaries of the 'house' while rendering invisible the intricacies of its constitutive labours.

In light of this political analysis, BWfWfH called for black women's autonomy within the WfH campaign, even as intellectual treatises such as Prescod's challenged the broader campaign to recalibrate the parameters of reproductive labour by centring black women's relation to housework and the domestic. In a 1976 speech delivered at 'the first international conference on lesbians and the wages for housework movement', Brown contoured a racialised *division of labor* between Black women and white women' through which white women have been granted protections and power over black women. She continues:

> It is Black women who work as maids for white women and not the other way around. We are the Whores. We are the illegitimate mothers. Because of this we organise autonomously from white women. We organise on the basis of the particular conditions of our lives as Black women... and we organise autonomously to struggle for wages for housework.[34]

Brown installs racial blackness as a site of critical rupture and of possibility. Pinpointing the sexual division of reproduction as irreducibly and asymmetrically cut by the exigencies of race, she fundamentally transposes the terrain of 'housework' to the field of (re)productive relations *between* women. Brown's assertion of black women's necessary autonomy from white women is thus based on an acknowledgment of the forms of power – incisively articulated in terms of labour – that *constitute* the structural relation between black women and white women, and the dangers of black women's interests being subsumed under the sign of an undifferentiated category of 'woman' as well as its privileged civic institution, the household. However, Brown is careful to distinguish between autonomous struggle and separatism: 'it is important for Black people to distinguish between autonomy, which means organising independently... and separatism, which describes white people in and of themselves as the enemy'. Whereas separatism rejects a priori the possibility of coalitional struggle and solidarity, autonomy, for Brown, 'can be the basis for Black and white people organising together' but only once black women have collectively defined their needs and interests and once the articulation of these collective interests forms a central infrastructure of coalitional movement.[35]

Although Prescod and Brown broadly shared with white women in WfH a knowledge of domestic labour's wayward, even insurrectionary, potentials, they also disclose the unthought labours through which the house and the housewife (the negative foundation of Brown's 'Whore') cohere.[36] Whereas Silvia Federici and Nicole Cox in their

34 Wilmette Brown, 'The Autonomy of Black Lesbian Women', speech delivered at Toward a Strategy for the Lesbian Movement Conference, Toronto, Ontario, 24 July 1976, p 5, emphasis mine, http://www.wagesforhouseworkny.com, accessed 15 July 2016

35 Wilmette Brown (with Foreword by Janice Owens and Introduction by Juliet Yelverton), *Black Women and the Peace Movement*, Falling Wall Press, Bristol, 1983, p 68

36 On the plantation and the slave ship as the negative conditions of the US domestic imaginary and its gendered logics, see Hortense Spillers, 'Mama's Baby, Papa's Maybe: An American Grammar Book', *Diacritics*, vol 17, no 2, 1987, pp 65–81, p 72.

37 Federici with Cox,
'Counterplanning from the
Kitchen', op cit, pp 28–41

38 Prescod, *Black Women*, op
cit, p 15. In a gesture
reminiscent of Angela Y
Davis's field-defining
'Reflections on the Black
Women's Role in the
Community of Slaves', *The
Black Scholar*, vol 13, no 4,
1971, pp 2–15, Prescod
argues for the fundamental
importance of black
women's housework not
only for but also *against* the
slave regime.

39 The definitive account of
reproductive labour and
reproductive violence as
constitutive features of
chattel slavery is provided
by historian Jennifer
Morgan's *Laboring
Women: Reproduction and
Gender in New World
Slavery*, University of
Pennsylvania Press,
Philadelphia, 2004. The
analytic capacities of
'labour' to describe
slavery's administration of
gendered and sexualised
terror, however, remains an
open question within the
fields of black and black
feminist studies. In *Scenes
of Subjection*, for example,
Saidiya Hartman, develops
the analytic of 'fungibility'
in contradistinction to that
of 'exploitation' to
elaborate the slave regime's
intricate conscription of
violence, and in 'The Belly
of the World', p 168, she
further exacts that 'the
category of labor
insufficiently accounts for
slavery as a mode of power,
domination and
production.'

40 Saidiya Hartman, 'The
Belly of the World', op cit,
p 171

1975 'Counterplanning from the Kitchen' assert the domestic as an insurgent site of contradiction precisely because it is immanent to capitalist social relations,[37] Prescod and Brown suggest that the generalisation of the domestic as a figure of gendered struggle is premised on a fundamental misrecognition of the ways in which the material production of the (white, national) domestic has been secured through the simultaneous exclusion of black women and the expropriation of their labour. While for many white women in the WfH movement, then, domestic space was a given field to be struggled both within and against, for BWfWfH 'the domestic' might be more properly understood as an incisive site of *im-possibility*. This *im-possible* domestic is clearly rendered in Prescod's imaginative historiography, where the reproductive labour (sexual and otherwise) endured by enslaved women is articulated in relation to the contemporary situation of black women's domestic organising. Black women are named in her text as the primary site of contradiction and the agency of destruction within the plantation system and its progeny. She writes:

> we can see within the housework of the Black woman in the time of slavery two things were going on: the utilisation of that woman to reproduce the master and his family, and at the same time that woman making a struggle against that work, to destroy that work.[38]

Pressing against the limits of the rubric of 'labour' to encounter fully the terrors of chattel slavery, its historical surrogates and their constitutively gendered character, the retooled sign of 'housework' opens an account of the quotidian violations that consolidate the 'domestic' and that signal *the means* of its most decisive point of breakdown.[39] Black women thus figure as the corrosive element within *this* domestic scene, given their absolute centrality to its material engendering and their history of expulsion from its protections, and hence emerge in Prescod's text as the primary agency for the realisation of the domestic *otherwise*.

The question that remains, and that should give us pause, is that of the incalculable work of this other domestic vision, its conditions of appearance and the differential modes of collectivity through which and to which such work is harnessed. In this vein, Saidiya Hartman has recently written of the black domestic as an impossible domestic, a figure whose

> freedom struggle remains opaque, untranslatable into the lexicon of the political. She provides so much, yet rarely does she thrive. It seems that her role has been fixed and that her role is as a provider of care, which is the very mode of her exploitation and indifferent use by the world, a world blind to her gifts, her intellect, her talents.[40]

In *Born in Flames*, this opacity of black domesticity and black women's domestic labours alternately *enables* and *intercedes* the film's vision of feminist coalitional struggle, at times rendered invisible again so as to resolve the contradictions of the racialised division of reproductive labour, but elsewhere surfacing as a surplus that directs the viewer to the possible future of another social reproduction enacted in the present. This other social reproduction is that which falls away from the cinematic narrativisation of feminist class struggle. As the film ambivalently registers the often deadly conditions of translation through which black women's labours and the social reproductions they support become legible in dominant idioms of domesticity and political revolution, we occasionally catch a glimpse of a black domestic that lies elsewhere, beyond and before 'revolution', where the planners and their planning go on, and on.

The author would like to thank Angela Dimitrakaki, Kirsten Lloyd, the anonymous reviewers, and Michael Litwack for their generative feedback.

Free People's
Medical Clinic
Saturday , September 20th, 2014
12-6pm Affordable Health Care Act
Navigation & HIV Screenings
12:30-1:45pm Afrocentering -
Pilates with Aimee Cox
1-3:30pm Walk-in Nurses Hour
with Shaquana Barham
2-6pm Well Women Care with
Ancient Song Doula Services
2:30-4pm Black Folk Dance
4-8pm Massage Therapy
4:30-8pm Walk-in Community Acupuncture
Performances throughout the day

Third Text, 2017
Vol. 31, No. 1, 117–132, https://doi.org/10.1080/09528822.2017.1364920

'Usefulness' in Contemporary Art and Politics

Larne Abse Gogarty

Simone Leigh, *Free People's Medical Clinic*, 2014, photo by Shulamit Seidler-Feller, courtesy Creative Time

1 For a critical history of accelerationism through the twentieth century, see Benjamin Noys, *Malign Velocities: Accelerationism and Capitalism*, Zero Books, Winchester, 2014.

2 One useful example in understanding this distinction comes from Charles Tolman who suggests that alienation will only be countered by transforming the relations of production, whereas environmental damage could be addressed through the forces of production. Yet, as Tolman stresses, 'Environmental problems… will remain unsolved not because capitalism is incapable of developing the necessary forces of production, but because its priorities, its *relations*, will necessarily stifle such developments.' (Emphasis added.) See Charles Tolman, 'Karl Marx, Alienation, and the Mastery of Nature', in Bob Jessop and Russell Wheatley, eds, *Karl Marx's*

Recent discourse on socially engaged art, or social practice, has increasingly emphasised usefulness, as exemplified by Cuban artist Tania Bruguera's establishment of the Asociación de Arte Útil in 2011, which has since developed partnerships with major art institutions such as the Queens Museum, the Van Abbemuseum and the Middlesbrough Institute of Modern Art (mima). Beyond the Asociación and Bruguera's practice, the notion of usefulness has permeated the field of social practice more broadly, with 'use value' frequently posed as an undisputed moral good, and a category that might be wrested from its socio-economic relation to exchange value within capitalism. In this article, I analyse Arte Útil's affirmation of usefulness and 'use values' in relation to Marxist, post-Marxist and feminist theories of social reproduction, also drawing in issues of race and migration. The central question is this: how can we understand the aesthetic and political stakes of artworks that strive to be 'useful' through performing tasks associated with social reproduction that have historically taken place in the home or via the welfare state?

I begin by plotting how I view the evolution of usefulness as a prized characteristic in recent social practice through discussing exhibitions and the affiliation of institutions to the notion of Arte Útil, particularly focusing on mima. After outlining these developments, I address how 'usefulness' relates to the dialectic struck up between art and life within the avant-garde, stressing that 'life' needs to be thought alongside labour power and social reproduction as historically contingent categories. Next, I examine how the affirmation of 'use' relates to broader discussions on the left. In particular, I address recent philosophical-political strategies including accelerationism that,[1] like Arte Útil, frequently place too much stock in the forces rather than the relations of production within capitalism.[2] As I will stress, 'forces of production' arguments that

Social and Political Thought, London and New York, 1999, p 25.

push technocratic solutions as the path towards social change are too frequently marked by an over-investment in the virtues of being realistic, rational and indeed useful. I write this at the tail end of 2016, when the supposedly improbable (at least in the white, liberal imagination) happened on both sides of the Atlantic in the shape of Brexit and the election of Donald Trump. If there is anything this moment should tell us, it is that the centre ground – the so-called realistic and the rational – has failed and seemingly has nothing to offer us or our worst enemies. Rather than sink into nihilism or attempt to produce a left populism that cynically seeks to capture this moment through promoting a nostalgic nationalism, we need a movement and art that are full of expressive feeling, material and emotional solidarity, as well as an unrelenting refusal to acquiesce or become useful to our enemies in any way.

Arte Útil

Bruguera's establishment of the Asociación de Arte Útil in 2011 follows on from her earlier practice, which she had categorised under the title 'Arte de Conducta' (usually translated as 'Behaviour Art'), a term that sought to distance performance from spectacle and instead to foreground the social.[3] One of the most notable instances of Arte de Conducta was Bruguera's establishment of the *Cátedra Arte de Conducta* (Behaviour Art Department). Conceived in 1998, and executed between 2002 and 2009, this project was essentially a school for Arte de Conducta, forming a key gestation point for the later development of 'Arte Útil' (Useful Art) as an association which artists and institutions can declare affinities with. Such affinities are guided by an eight-point programme that projects must meet if they are to be deemed useful, with this also informing the curatorial strategy of exhibitions such as the 'Museum of Arte Útil', held at the Van Abbemuseum in Eindhoven (2013–2014). The eight criteria for Arte Útil are as follows:

To be useful, a project must:

1 Propose new uses for art within society
2 Challenge the field within which it operates (civic, legislative, pedagogical, scientific, economic, etc)
3 Be 'timing specific', responding to current urgencies
4 Be implemented and function in real situations
5 Replace authors with initiators and spectators with users
6 Have practical, beneficial outcomes for its users
7 Pursue sustainability while adapting to changing conditions
8 Re-establish aesthetics as a system of transformation.[4]

Bruguera's *Immigrant Movement International* (IMI) project is a key work within the development of Arte Útil and was included in the Van Abbemuseum exhibition. IMI is described as an 'artist-initiated socio-political movement' that focuses on the political representation and support of migrants; the project was funded by the Queens Museum and Creative Time, and initially based out of a community space in Corona, Queens.[5] Also included in the Van Abbemuseum exhibition were projects by an international selection of artists and activists including WochenKlausur,

3 Francesca di Nardo, 'Arte de Conducta', *Janus*, vol 1, no 22, January 2007, p 81

4 See the Arte Útil website http://www.arte-util.org/about/colophon/, accessed 18 July 2016.

5 See Tania Bruguera's website: http://www.taniabruguera.com/cms/486-0-Immigrant+Movement+International.htmm, accessed 18 July 2016.

View of participants at Arte Util Summit 2016 in the atrium at mima, 2016, image: courtesy mima

Women on Waves, the 'Rolling Jubilee' movement and Theaster Gates. This work was grouped under various headings, such as 'Reforming Capital', 'Legislative Change' and 'Space Hijack', that denoted the different political and aesthetic strategies on display within the exhibition.

The category of Arte Útil – and the notion of usefulness expressed in the eight-point programme that guided the exhibition – serves to form a broad church of artists and artworks that cohere loosely around some broad principles that emphasise the importance of results that can be seen and perhaps even measured, as indicated by the notion of 'practical, beneficial outcomes'. Other aspects are more speculative, such as the desire to '(r)e-establish aesthetics as a system of transformation', meaning that Arte Útil as a genre tends to straddle the poles of utilitarianism and utopianism.

Alongside the Van Abbemuseum, Creative Time and the Queens Museum, mima presents one of the clearest institutional allegiances to Arte Útil, following its recent rebranding. Describing itself as a 'useful museum, a civic institution that promotes art as a tool for social change',[6] mima's affiliation with Arte Útil was prompted by the move of Alastair Hudson into the role of Director in October 2014; Hudson also happens to be the co-director, along with Bruguera, of the Asociación de Arte Útil, whose summit was held at mima in July 2016.[7]

Within mima's programming, they have established the 'Office of Useful Art' as well as the Arte Útil archive, both of which contribute to informing the development of 'crowd sourced' exhibitions such as

6 See 'About' section on mima website http://www. visitmima.com/about/, accessed 18 July 2016.

7 Prior to taking on this role, Hudson had been the Deputy Director of Grizedale Arts in the Lake District, which has long been renowned as a key centre for community art and socially engaged practice in the UK.

8 Alastair Hudson interview by Axisweb, 'What Is Art for? Part One – The Use Value of Art', https://vimeo.com/134189412, accessed 18 July 2016

9 In *The German Ideology*, Marx and Engels famously wrote: 'In communist society, where nobody has one exclusive sphere of activity but each can become accomplished in any branch he wishes, society regulates the general production and thus makes it possible for me to do one thing today and another tomorrow, to hunt in the morning, fish in the afternoon, rear cattle in the evening, criticise after dinner, just as I have a mind, without ever becoming hunter, fisherman, herdsman or critic.' See Karl Marx and Friedrich Engels, *The German Ideology: Part One* [1845], C J Arthur, ed, International Publishers, New York, 2004, p 53.

10 Alastair Hudson interview by Axisweb, 'What Is Art for? Part Two – The Museum 3.0', available at https://vimeo.com/134770141, accessed 18 July 2016

11 Ibid

12 Ibid

'Localism' (October 2015 to February 2016). Other recent exhibitions have responded to the closure of the local Redcar Steelworks and forthcoming aspects of the programme include more traditional shows by artists including Winifred Nicholson and Jane and Louise Wilson. Overall, mima strives to stand as a 'useful museum', and in what follows I detail their strategic plan as guided by the principles of Arte Útil, drawing primarily on a series of interviews with Hudson. In particular, I am interested in the histories that Hudson invokes through his notion of the 'museum 3.0' and how these inform his conception of use value.

Fundamentally, mima seeks to break with the history of the modernist art gallery, which Hudson associates with what he calls a Kantian model of autonomy that has affected not only the category of art, but also how art institutions are structured in terms of staffing.[8] Whereas major galleries like Tate in the UK keep clear divisions between the various arms of the institution (press, development, education, curating), mima seeks to integrate the various departments that make up the museum. To paraphrase Marx and Engels, mima aims to *regulate general production* and thus make its staff capable of doing one thing today, and another tomorrow – to write a press release in the morning, run education programmes after lunch, curate an exhibition in the afternoon, meet with private donors in the evening – without ever becoming press officer, curator, development officer, educator.[9] The idea of melding different departments emerges from the desire to make 'social development' the main goal; meaning that the institution would not have education programmes geared towards contextualising exhibitions, but rather that the entire activity of the museum would revolve around its social programmes.

This guides Hudson's dream of the 'museum 3.0' becoming a 'civic building', comparable to the library, swimming pool, school or town hall.[10] The main agenda here is to demonstrate how art can apply to everyday life, with Hudson's inspiration drawn from the history of art *before* modernism, where the relationship between art and day-to-day life was apparently more intimate, via 'ritual', the church and design, and thus, in his view, more 'useful'. In the present, mima wants to rekindle this intimacy through 'reprogramming' the museum so that art supports what Hudson calls the 'human programme', rather than the reverse, which he views as the dominant model within contemporary art. By 'human programme', Hudson means all those aspects of the art institutions that usually play a supporting role, including the café, the shop, the education programme or the community programme. Hudson then expands on this ambition of reversing the usual dynamic between the 'human programme' and art by describing how mima hopes to transform their relationship to the state, or 'superstructure', as he puts it. Here, the state is understood in terms of its provision of services that contribute to social reproduction such as housing, healthcare, schools and education, and as he explains, mima aims to take on a supporting role within these sectors, with this providing the key to how art can really 'make a difference'.[11] By playing a more directly supporting role within such sectors, Hudson suggests that this might overcome the old paternalistic model of the art institution that affirms the experience of visiting as a process of self-improvement for the poor.[12] In addition, he suggests that by becoming more 'useful' and 'making a difference', the age-old problem

13 Alastair Hudson interview by Axisweb, 'What Is Art for? Part Three – Everything Is a Project', https://vimeo.com/134770141, accessed 18 July 2016

14 Alastair Hudson interview by Axisweb, 'What Is Art for? Part One – The Use Value of Art', op cit

15 Alastair Hudson interview by Axisweb, 'What Is Art for? Part Two – The Museum 3.0', op cit

16 Ibid

17 Paul R La Monica, 'Google to Buy YouTube for $1.65 Billion', *CNN Money*, 9 October 2006, http://money.cnn.com/2006/10/09/technology/googleyoutube_deal/index.htm?cnn=yes, accessed 19 July 2016

18 Earlier in 2016, after reaching a back-tax deal with the Conservative government, critics from the Labour Party and elsewhere claimed that the deal was not enough as Google had on average paid only 2.77 per cent on their profits over the previous decade, compared to the standard 20 per cent corporation tax on profits. See Daniel Boffey and Jill Treanor, 'Google £130m UK back-tax deal lambasted as "derisory" by expert', *The Observer*, 23 January 2016, https://www.theguardian.com/technology/2016/jan/23/google-uk-back-tax-deal-lambasted-as-derisory, accessed 18 July 2016.

19 Hudson interview by Axisweb, 'What Is Art for? Part Two – The Museum 3.0', op cit. I am not completely sure what 'institutes' specifically Hudson is referring to but would associate this kind of organisation with Settlement Houses, although the context there is in the United States. For a brief history of settlement houses see Mina Carson, 'Settlement House Movement', in Wilma

of debating 'what is art' might be over. Through this active dissolution of art's (pretence of) autonomy, it will become less a designation of certain objects, material properties, or processes, and instead could stand as an 'ecology' that simply means undertaking all sorts of activities 'artfully'. As such, Hudson affirmatively cites the more 'everyday' understanding of the 'art of cooking' or the 'art of gardening' as the model to strive towards in reintegrating art with everyday life at mima.[13]

As well as drawing on what Hudson describes as an earlier 'symbiosis between, craft, design and architecture and social activity', he also cites the model of 'usership' common in digital culture as inspiring the museum 3.0.[14] He gives YouTube as an example of the relevance of digital cultures to mima, stating that 'the value of YouTube is not created by YouTube – it's created by how it's used… the usership creates the value and the meaning of YouTube',[15] Hudson draws a parallel between this and mima's ambitions, suggesting that he wants the 'value of the museum' to be created by its users, from the children who come for workshops, to gallery-goers, university researchers, the staff, café visitors and even the drug user in the toilets on the top floor.[16]

The issues that arise from Hudson's desire to use the art institution to support the state, as well as his affirmation of YouTube as a model for mima, are evidence of a blind spot with regards to property relations and the inherently exclusionary notion of citizenship. Firstly, in Hudson's suggestion that the 'museum 3.0' might make a difference by supporting the state, or 'superstructure', as he calls it, by mentioning only healthcare, schools and education there has been a parcelling out of the 'good' side of the state, from a traditional social democratic viewpoint. Presumably, mima is not interested in supporting police, prisons or borders guards, all of which exist to guarantee a citizenship that is fundamentally connected to racialisation and property ownership. This parcelling out is then replicated in Hudson's understanding of use value, as exemplified in his affirmation of YouTube. While YouTube users may provide the majority of the content, it is Google that, since 2006, when it was purchased for $1.6 billion in stock, owns the company.[17] The value apparently produced by its users and affirmed by Hudson as a model he wishes to emulate is capitalised on by Google, a firm now notorious for tax evasion that therefore fails to contribute to maintaining those aspects of the state that underpin Hudson's very idea of usefulness.[18]

Of course, such shortcomings within Hudson's conception of the 'useful museum' demonstrate the systematic nature of the processes which mima is, understandably, hoping to disrupt. In emphasising use value as a quantifiable good, Hudson says that this idea goes back to the 'old idea of the institute, which is the early nineteenth-century incarnation… the DNA of the current art gallery and museum system' where art, science, socialising and provision of basic services would take place in one setting.[19] In seeking to revivify that model, Hudson suggests that the collection of mima could be used to teach people to make products that they could then sell in the shop, or that mima might provide clothing, food and shelter. These proposals reach their endgame in Hudson's speculation as to whether people should in fact be paid to visit the museum, arguing that 'in a way, that would be an ultimate demonstration of use

Mankiller et al, eds, *The Reader's Companion to U.S. Women's History*, Houghton Mifflin Company, Boston and New York, 1998.

value'.[20] Notwithstanding the contradiction between viewing the 'institute' as the DNA of the current system and simultaneously viewing it as rooted in a Kantian model, I am wary of the idea that the 'institute' is rooted in a model where members have paid in to receive services and 'know what they get' out of that institution, and that this underpins the affirmation of 'use value'.[21] How much does this model – paying in to receive services that are expected, or in fact being paid to visit – travel beyond the paternalism implicitly criticised by Hudson? Do these ideas not suggest that one form of paternalism (art as a civilising process) has simply been supplanted with another, one which assumes that poor people are not interested in art unless it fulfils a basic level of social reproduction? Going back to the organisation of the museum, this impoverished quality can also be seen as permeating the plan to amalgamate different departments in the institution. When viewed in relation to consistent cuts to the arts, how does fulfilling multiple roles not signal overwork while wages continue to fall, rather than the destruction of the division of labour?

mima's ambitions, like those of Arte Útil as a movement, are caught between the utopian and the utilitarian, with art representing the possibility of a utopian transformation, but only once it is rid of its autonomy – all those characteristics which permit it to be somehow 'outside' the everyday. To elaborate further, I want to take up this issue of utopianism and utilitarianism in relation to the history of the avant-garde and its concern with the category of 'life'.

Life and the Avant-Garde

20 Ibid

21 Alastair Hudson interview by Axisweb, 'What Is Art for? Part Three – Everything Is a Project', op cit

22 Claire Bishop, 'The Social Turn: Collaboration and Its Discontents', *Artforum*, vol 44, no 6, February 2006, pp 178–183. Bishop later developed the relationship between the avant-garde and social practice in her book *Artificial Hells: Participatory Art and the Politics of Spectatorship*, Verso, London, 2012.

23 Stewart Martin, 'Artistic Communism – A Sketch', *Third Text* 99, vol 23, no 4, July 2009, pp 481–494

24 Evan Mauro, 'The Death and Life of the Avant-Garde: Or, Modernism and Biopolitics', *Mediations: Journal of the Marxist Literary Group*, vol 26, nos 1–2, autumn 2012 – Spring 2013, p 135

25 Ibid

The poles of utopianism and utilitarianism fuel the continuation of comparisons between social practice and the avant-garde, which have proliferated since at least the early 2000s, despite the apparent novelty of the category of Arte Útil. In Claire Bishop's often-cited 2006 essay 'The Social Turn: Collaboration and Its Discontents', she noted that the 'mixed panorama of socially collaborative work arguably forms what avant-garde we have today' with such claims permeating much of the discussion on social practice to one degree or another.[22] For Stewart Martin, the comparison with the avant-garde underpins his criticisms. As he suggests, the attempt to produce an identity between life and art will not necessarily produce social transformation, as 'life' needs to be understood within the context of capitalist life – as a subsumption of life by capital.[23]

Similar arguments to Martin are also put forth by Evan Mauro, who argues, in his corrective to Peter Bürger's classic text *Theory of the Avant-Garde* (1984), that the category of 'life' is inextricably tied to social reproduction. Mauro reads this through Michel Foucault's notion of biopolitics, developing a series of historical correspondences.[24] He begins with nineteenth-century population management and the expansion of the nation-state as a biopolitical solution to 'bourgeois liberalism, whose very remoteness from "life" was precisely the complaint of the historical avant-gardes'.[25] Moving beyond the 'historical avant-gardes' as characterised by Bürger, Mauro writes:

> After the midcentury realization of biopolitical state forms, but before the subsequent institutional critiques of the Keynesian regulation of social life,

and the ways these critiques were repurposed by a resurgent neoliberalism to scale back the institutional security of 'life' under the midcentury nation-state in favor of greater flexibility, precarity, and self-management – these, and not only the logic of commodification, make up the 'politics' against which the avant-garde needs to be defined.[26]

In stressing that the 'life' side of the avant-garde dialectic must be viewed as correspondent with social reproduction, Mauro offers a corrective to Bürger's argument, which views the decline of the 'historical' avant-garde as primarily related to the gradual institutionalisation and commodification of its artworks.[27] If we stay with Mauro's focus on 'life', it becomes clear that the majority of artworks contained under the banner of Arte Útil are situated as 'useful' for their provision of tasks associated with aspects of social reproduction that are necessary to life. As Hudson notes, healthcare, housing and education form areas into which mima might intervene. Childcare is also mentioned, as is the 'art of cooking'; all activities that fall under the banner of social reproduction as a category that denotes the reproduction of labour power, generationally and through maintenance. This aspect of Arte Útil forms its most significant link to the avant-garde, while the emphasis on usefulness marks its comparative weakness against the desire for a sublation of the categories of art and life. In order to qualify this further and address Arte Útil's biopolitical implications, let us turn to an artwork that directly sought to intervene into the crisis of social reproduction.

WochenKlausur are an Austrian collective that were featured prominently in the 'Museum of Arte Útil' at the Van Abbemuseum. Here, staying in a British context, their project to create a Women-led Workers' Cooperative in Drumchapel, Glasgow is notable. As WochenKlausur's website explains, entrepreneurs have left Drumchapel since the late 1970s and the area is one with a level of high unemployment that has now, over three generations, become entrenched.[28] This led WochenKlausur to encourage a group of unemployed women to form a co-operative, which subsequently decided to address the health problems that affected many in the area as a result of poor diet. WochenKlausur and the group they facilitated opened a pop-up shop selling 'meal bags' which contained fresh fruit and vegetables and simple recipes to encourage healthy cooking. The project also sought to provide employability training and skills development for these women, in business planning, marketing and accounting. In this project, there are two stages of dealing with faltering social reproduction. The women engaged by WochenKlausur were not working and were facing barriers, and the project they produced was centred on encouraging 'better' levels of social reproduction within a relatively impoverished neighbourhood. Overall, WochenKlausur worked with a population viewed as a 'burden' by the British state – the unemployed – at a time when government schemes including Mandatory Work Activity and the Community Action Programme required claimants to take up work placements in order to continue receiving benefits. The project thus tended to cohere with, rather than confront, the paternalism of the state and capitalism as a mode of production, within which – as Michael Denning writes – 'the only thing worse than being exploited is not being exploited'.[29]

Within Arte Útil, Bruguera writes that 'failure is not a possibility. If the project fails, it is not Arte Útil.'[30] Through this, Bruguera implies

26 Mauro, 'The Death and Life of the Avant-Garde, op cit, pp 135–136

27 Peter Bürger, *The Theory of the Avant-Garde*, Michael Shaw, trans, Manchester University Press, Manchester, 1984

28 See the description of the project on WochenKlausur's website http://www.wochenklausur.at/projekt.php?lang=en&id=41, accessed 18 July 2016.

29 Michael Denning, 'Wageless Life', *New Left Review* 66, November/December 2010, pp 79–97. Here p 79. The quote is attributed to British economist Joan Robinson.

30 Tania Bruguera, 'Reflexions on Useful Art', November 2012, http://www.taniabruguera.com/cms/592-0-Reflexions+on+Arte+til+Useful+Art.htm, accessed 11 July 2016

31 Alex Kershaw interview with Tania Bruguera, 'Immigrant Movement International: Five Years and Counting', *Field: A Journal of Socially Engaged Art Criticism* 1, Spring 2015, p 20, available at http://field-journal.com/issue-1/bruguera, accessed 18 July 2016

32 Karl Marx, *Capital: A Critique of Political Economy, Volume 1*, Ben Fowkes, trans, Penguin Books, London, 1990, pp 272–273

33 Frank B Wilderson III, 'The Prison Slave as Hegemony's (Silent) Scandal', in Joy James, ed, *Warfare in the American Homeland: Policing and Prison in a Penal Democracy*, Duke University Press, Durham, North Carolina, 2007, p 23

34 Notably, one precedent to the 1981 Nationality Act's racialised relinquishing of *jus soli* can be observed in the British government's pre-emancipation exclusion of slaves born in their American colonies from birthright citizenship. For a discussion of *jus soli* and the 1981 Nationality Act, see Ian Baucom, *Out of Place: Englishness, Empire, and the Locations of Identity*, Princeton University Press, Princeton, 1999. For a more recent discussion of citizenship and race in Britain, see Imogen Tyler, *Revolting Subjects: Social Abjection and Resistance in Neoliberal Britain*, Zed Books, London, 2013.

35 Carole Pateman, 'The Patriarchal Welfare State', in Amy Gutmann, *Democracy and the Welfare State*, Princeton University Press, Princeton, 1988, p 235

that the stakes are higher and the possibility of experimentation is lower, despite the desires for Arte Útil and institutions like mima to prioritise aesthetics as a system of transformation. Within Arte Útil institutions and projects, artists are explicitly positioned as providing services that enable the reproduction of individuals. The reason Arte Útil 'cannot fail' is because the state and capital have already decided that the people Arte Útil seek to engage are irrelevant. The women of Drumchapel that WochenKlausur worked with were essentially being encouraged to make themselves less disposable in the eyes of the state and capital – along lines that conform to extremely violent and normative notions of usefulness.

What then are the politics of affirming the affective, reproductive and 'useful' dimensions of social practice today as its aesthetic and political link to the avant-garde? If these aspects have tended to cohere with – *rather than confront* – state and capital, how does this connect with Bruguera's statement that 'when the work is properly done, the artist also expands their own spectrum as a citizen and as a person',[31] as well as Hudson's affirmation of mima as a 'civic institution'?

Useful Citizens

Citizenship within bourgeois society is founded in property ownership and work, and those apparently 'not working' in the eyes of the state have long been compelled to become productive through a variety of means, including the Victorian workhouse, contemporary workfare initiatives and the use of prison labour. Through such measures, the capitalist state has produced differential levels of citizenship, dependent on one's access, as Marx describes, to the double freedom that comes with wage labour (free to sell one's labour, and free of any other commodity to sell).[32] Women have historically lacked full citizenship alongside migrants, prisoners, people of colour and the totally dispossessed. In the United States, we might mention how police violence and the prison system continues the structural anti-blackness founded by slavery as a means to void full or even partial citizenship; for Frank Wilderson 'black citizenship and black civic obligation are oxymorons'.[33] Or, in the UK, we might refer to the removal of *jus soli* (birth right citizenship) from the 1981 Nationality Act, rendering many people who had grown up in the country with migrant parents suddenly precarious. The Act also radically racialised the possibilities of obtaining citizenship for those born in former British colonies by asking residents of the Commonwealth to prove they had British ancestry, meaning that those who would qualify were far likelier to be white.[34]

These limits of citizenship are also mapped onto dispossession more broadly; as Carole Pateman stresses, 'poverty-stricken individuals are not, and, unless the outcome of participation in the market is offset in some way, cannot be, full citizens'.[35] As such, the moral basis of the welfare state partly lies in its ability to 'offset' the market and provide resources for incorporation into citizenship for those who are not working, or whose work is unrecognised as work for reasons of racism, impoverishment, criminalisation and patriarchy. This 'offsetting' is essential because mass unemployment is a permanent feature of capitalist economies, and the state must therefore form a means to produce, as David Harvey writes, a 'structured coherence' in tandem with wage labour.[36] This idea of 'structured coherence', and the process of incorporation and expulsion from citizenship via the state, links to social reproduction and usefulness, and reveals some of the problems in affirming these categories as emancipatory or radical, especially where they are simply offsetting or minimising damage.

Moreover, the dynamic between citizenship and work is founded upon the continued differentiation between forms of 'real work' deserving of citizenship and other activity not recognised as legitimately incorporated into wage labour, such as the work done by undocumented migrants and prisoners, traditionally female-gendered activity and slave labour. This dichotomy between work and non-work has a *moral* (and thus an ethical) function, and feminists, abolitionists, activists and artists have long sought to trouble and attack this dynamic. Aspects of current social practice continue in this vein, with mima's calls for people to be paid to visit the museum undoubtedly stemming for a well-intended desire to challenge the way that different forms of activity are valued as work and non-work. However, like the recent growth in calls for a Universal Basic Income (UBI), this fails to recognise the foundational issue of private property as the cornerstone of capitalism, as well as the ever-present, frequently violent regulation of who counts as a citizen within various state formations. These two central limits also permeate the discourse and politics of accelerationism, which has taken up the call for UBI.

As two key proponents of accelerationism, Nick Srnicek and Alex Williams, note, three factors are needed to make UBI meaningful.[37] It must provide enough money to live on, be given out unconditionally, and it must supplement rather than replace the welfare state. The first and third elements of this argument relate to the requirements UBI must fulfil if it is not to support increased marketisation.[38] The second point, around unconditional access, draws us further into the issues arising from Arte Útil's emphasis on citizenship. I consider the primary risk and limit of UBI to be its potential coherence with rising anti-immigrant rhetoric and policies across popular discourse and the media, and with governmental policy and legislation. While Srnicek and Williams's caveat that UBI would have to be universally accessible by immigrants and prisoners seeks, thankfully, to counter this prospect, I find their faith in that possibility difficult to share in the present moment, and indicative of accelerationism and Arte Útil's comparable failure to adequately consider and respond to the ways that their central emphasis on citizenship and technology have been drawn into the very heart of right-wing discourse and politics.[39]

We can see that calls for UBI from the accelerationist camp align with Hudson's ideas, particularly those that suggest payment for visiting the museum, as well as his affirmation of 'usership'. The limits of these arguments lie in their quality as 'forces of production' solutions that fail to address the relations of production. Along the same conceptual lines, 'use value' cannot be affirmed as a weapon against value in the present because it is only made coherent through its relation to exchange value. Just as how UBI – in our present moment – would be taken up in tandem with a further enshrining of discriminatory forms of citizenship

36 David Harvey, *The Urban Experience*, Baltimore: The John Hopkins University Press, 1989, p 145

37 Srnicek and Williams authored the '#Accelerate Manifesto for an Accelerationist Politics', 2013, but have since stated that they avoid the term accelerationism because of the 'miasma of competing understandings that has arisen around the concept'. However, they also explain that they have not abandoned its principles as they understand them. Nick Srnicek and Alex Williams, *Inventing the Future: Postcapitalism and a World without Work*, Verso, London, 2015. See chapter 1, footnote 54.

38 See the chapter 'Post-work Imaginaries' in Srnicek and Williams, *Inventing the Future*, op cit.

39 This is especially pressing now with regards to accelerationism's shared intellectual heritage with the so-called 'alt-right' and 'neo-reactionary' movement, with Nick Land standing as the central figure. See Benjamin Noys, 'Futures of Accelerationism', talk given at FASTER/SLOWER/FUTURE: The Road to Post-Capitalism, Kaaitheater, Brussels, Belgium 22–23 October, 2016, https://www.academia.edu/29295882/Futures_of_Accelerationism, accessed 28 November 2016.

via providing an income that was guaranteed for some while utterly inaccessible for others, we must critically consider how and why certain patterns of behaviour and activity are registered as useful in the present. Use is not a neutral or straightforwardly 'good' category but one that is shaped by history, in the same way that the determination of the value of labour power, unlike other commodities, 'contains a historical and moral element'.[40] The 'historical and moral element' that partly determines the value of labour power precisely signals the whole arena of social reproduction, and that which is affirmed because of its usefulness by Arte Útil.

For Srnicek and Williams, social reproduction could be transformed and made more efficient through a 'forces of production' solution. As they write, 'assistive technologies and affective computing are… making inroads in automating some of the highly personal and embarrassing care work that might be better suited to impersonal robots'.[41] Now this automation might work happily in some situations, but it is also very easy to imagine the automation of care as related to diminished numbers of nurses and care workers within the context of an expanded ageing population. As Nina Power writes, the accelerationist drive towards automation is overwhelmingly marked by a 'desire for a lack of dependency',[42] with the affirmation of robotic care work encapsulating this. The 'useful' dimensions of such a robot are clear, but the quality of the relations through which that use is manifested are never guaranteed, in the same way that a knife may be used to cut bread or stab someone, to put it crudely. The material object is useful in both situations but there is no positive content to 'use value' as such. As Marx writes, use values become a reality 'only by use or consumption' and the mode, or relations, of use or consumption are variable.[43]

Usefulness, Social Reproduction and Social Practice

In aspects of social practice, we can see the fetishisation of usefulness as emerging from a desire that, like elements of accelerationism, seeks to 'mirror' and thus exceed the workings of state and capital from a supposedly progressive perspective. A recent two-part feature for *e-flux journal* entitled 'The Insurgents' by Nato Thompson, then chief curator of Creative Time, the foremost commissioning organisation within social practice, encapsulates this approach.[44] Thompson describes the 'cultural turn' of the US military during the last Iraq war and how they sought to capture 'hearts and minds' through counter-insurgency efforts that drew on anthropological research, as well as writing by Antonio Gramsci and the radical pedagogue Paulo Freire. As Thompson notes:

> It should come as no surprise that the military, in its effort to gain hearts and minds, found itself in dialogue with the methodologies of its ideological adversaries. A tool is a tool.[45]

Following the military's appropriation of historically leftist thought, Thompson elaborates a series of connections between feminist artist

40 Marx 1990, *Capital*, op cit, p 275

41 Srnicek and Williams, *Inventing the Future*, op cit, p 114

42 Nina Power, 'Decapitalism, Left Scarcity, and the State', *Fillip* 20, autumn, 2015, available online at http://fillip.ca/content/decapitalism-left-scarcity-and-the-state, accessed 25 November, 2016

43 Marx 1990, *Capital*, op cit, p 126

44 See Nato Thompson, 'The Insurgents, Part I: Community-Based Practice as Military Methodology', *e-flux journal* 47, September 2013, available at http://www.e-flux.com/journal/the-insurgents-part-i-community-based-practice-as-military-methodology/, accessed 23 June 2016, and Nato Thompson, 'The Insurgents, Part II: Fighting the Left by Being the Left', *e-flux journal* 49, November 2013, available at http://www.e-flux.com/journal/the-insurgents-part-ii-fighting-the-left-by-being-the-left/, accessed 23 June 2016.

45 Thompson, 'The Insurgents, Part I', op cit.

and social practice forerunner Suzanne Lacy, community organiser Saul Alinsky, the Black Panthers, and the general commanding the US Army in Iraq from 2007 to 2008, David Petraeus, as all 'employing community organizing techniques'.[46] Thompson's comparison between the arts and the military rests on the belief that

> while the ends pursued by these two spheres are radically different, aspects of their means are startlingly similar. Comparing examples according to means and not ends offers a new method for understanding formal approaches to the construction of a public. As the manipulation of culture becomes a major priority across a range of disciplines, it might prove instructive to overlook disciplinary boundaries and simply compare methodologies.[47]

Yet, in suggesting that the cultural and progressive spheres should learn 'new ideas and new methodologies concerning tactics for "getting to know people"' from the military,[48] Thompson entirely delinks strategy from tactics, or forces from relations, in a manner similar to Hudson's affirmation that art should support the superstructure.[49] I view this lack of care as coterminous with the ultimately uncritical attitude towards the category of 'life', with 'life' often posed as boundlessly creative and productive rather than as fundamentally linked to social reproduction. For example, the accelerationists argue that the left must 'reconnect' to its Enlightenment roots – a 'rationalist and universal vision of collective human self-construction' that might 'enable, rather than suppress, a generalised human flourishing'.[50] As Benjamin Noys stresses, such statements are intended to be 'politically motivational', seeking to break the sense of inertia in the face of global capitalism; we can say much the same of Arte Útil and social practice in contrast with the corrupt, exploitative machinations of the mainstream artworld.[51] Yet, whether considering Thompson's 'practical' desire to learn from the military, Hudson's affirmation of 'usership', the 'civic' and the 'superstructure', or the accelerationist's affirmation of Enlightenment rationality, all these arguments seek to discover and harness an excessive, vital force that cannot be fully captured by capital, without considering how those very categories may be taken up in ways that are cogent with existing and emerging forms of violence and exploitation. In this final section, I want to consider more closely how similar difficulties emerge in claims that have been made for the status of women's political agency as tied to social reproduction and how this further opens itself up onto the limits of Arte Útil.

Silvia Federici is one of the most significant voices here through her articulation of an idea of the 'reproductive commons'. As Federici writes, the notion of the commons became important within the alter-globalisation movement, and at the turn away from statist models of socialism, forming a response to the 'new enclosures' of 'neoliberal attempts to subordinate every form of life and knowledge to the logic of the market'.[52] For Federici, urban gardens form a significant element in the processes of commoning since the 1980s in the United States. She associates the development and growth of these with migrants from Africa, the Caribbean and the South of the United States, and asserts that their

46 Thompson, 'The Insurgents, Part II', op cit

47 Ibid

48 Thompson, 'The Insurgents, Part I', op cit

49 Ray Brassier has commented on the problem of delinking strategy and tactics. In reckoning with his intellectual debt to Nick Land after Land's move from a Deleuzian, accelerationist position to a far-right, 'neo-reactionary' political and philosophical position, Brassier states that 'once you dissociate tactics and strategy – the famous distinction between tactics and strategy where strategy is teleological, transcendent, and representational and tactics is immanent and machinic – if you have no strategy, someone with a strategy will soon commandeer your tactics. Someone who knows what they want to realize will start using you.' Ray Brassier, 'Accelerationism', talk at the Accelerationism conference, Goldsmiths University, 14 September 2010, https://moskvax. wordpress.com/2010/09/ 30/accelerationism-ray-brassier/, accessed 1 December 2016.

50 Armen Avanessian, Nick Srnicek and Alex Williams, '#Accelerationism: Remembering the Future', originally published in *Tag Allgemeine Zeitung*, 4 February 2014. English translation available at https://syntheticedifice.files. wordpress.com/2014/02/ srnicek-williams-and-avanessian-2014-remembering-the-future1. pdf, accessed 27 July 2016

51 Benjamin Noys, '"Grey in Grey": Crisis, Critique, Change', *Journal of Critical Globalisation Studies* 4, 2011, p 52

52 Silvia Federici, 'Feminism and the Politics of the Commons in an Era of Primitive Accumulation', in *Revolution at Point Zero*, PM Press/Common

Notions/Autonomedia, New York, pp 138–139

53 Ibid, pp 141–42

54 'Common Ground' emphasises working with food 'as a basic need', and describes its aim in building a co-operative network that brings people closer together. However, all too often these artworld initiatives do not investigate the gendered dimension of 'the commons' that Federici's analysis thankfully made so prominent. Instead, projects such as Common Ground – and I am perhaps being unfair by taking this to stand for a whole tendency – frequently tend to link up with architecture and design firms in order to amp up the 'useful', 'practical' dimension. Too often, these partnerships shift the orientation of the work away from a utopian imaginary and towards the cultivation of shared resources among white, bourgeois urban-dwelling individuals with a hankering for the rural. See the Common Ground website http:// museumarteutil.net/arte-util-and-common-ground-project/, accessed 18 July 2016.

55 Federici, op cit, 'Feminism and the Politics of the Commons in an Era of Primitive Accumulation', p 142

56 Avanessian, Srnicek and Williams, *Inventing the Future*, op cit

57 Federici, 'Feminism and the Politics of the Commons in an Era of Primitive Accumulation', op cit, p 143

58 Ibid, p 147

59 Endnotes, 'The Logic of Gender', *Endnotes* 3, September 2013, p 89, https://endnotes.org.uk/en/ endnotes-the-logic-of-gender, accessed 20 July 2016

60 Ibid

importance lies not only in providing food security for neighbourhood consumption, rather than for commercial purposes, but also in strengthening communities and diversifying cultural practices.[53] Notably, the 'urban garden' has become a frequent feature of Arte Útil, with the 'Common Ground' project associated with the 'Museum of Arte Útil' exhibition at the Van Abbemuseum providing one such example.[54]

Yet Federici also stresses that such attempts at commoning have tended to remain stuck at the grass roots.[55] This is precisely the kind of limit that has prompted criticism from the accelerationist camp, with Avanessian, Srnicek and Williams denigrating 'the fantasy of local, small-scaled solutions to our many crises' and characterising such solutions as 'organic', 'localist' and 'folk politics'.[56] The problem with this view is that it does not recognise the internationalism of the struggles somebody like Federici is championing, or their gendered dimensions. As she writes, 'women are the main force standing in the way of a complete commercialisation of nature', offering examples of resistance primarily from the global south.[57] Despite the force of Federici's argument as a necessary corrective to the accelerationist fantasy of full automation, her valorisation of reproductive labour as incipiently revolutionary has become a sticking point for other feminists. Stressing that 'assigning women the task of commoning/ collectivizing reproduction is not to concede to a naturalistic conception of "femininity"', Federici nevertheless acknowledges that 'many feminists would view this as a '"fate worse than death"'.[58]

In an article entitled 'The Logic of Gender', published in *Endnotes* 3, the authors concede that Federici is right – that they do consider her proposition to be 'worse than death' – going on to state that

> even if we might, in the crisis, have no choice but to self-organise these reproductive activities – and even though, most likely, abject reproduction will in the end mainly be foisted upon women – we must fight against this process which reinforces gender.[59]

The category of the 'abject' in this article extends Julia Kristeva's concept beyond the individual to describe activities that were once waged but are in the process of returning to the unwaged sphere 'because they've become too costly for the state or capital'.[60] Marina Vishmidt and Zöe Sutherland have also criticised Federici for potentially idealising 'subsistence scenarios', thus producing a 'conflation of necessity and desirability, particularity and universality, gendered drudgery in the austerity present and utopian horizons'.[61] These criticisms of subsistence models reverberate with the shortcomings I have outlined in Arte Útil as cohering too closely with the logic of austerity through the impoverished quality of how 'usefulness' is conceptualised in relation to a (hopefully) more utopian horizon. Moreover, as mima, and Arte Útil more broadly, volunteers itself as keen to take on aspects of social reproduction previously provided through the state or employment, does this then produce a very different notion of 'abject art' to the representational strategies we usually associate with this term?[62]

Lise Vogel's stress on the necessity of thinking through the lens of overall social reproduction offers a helpful corrective to the valorisation of reproduction by Federici and the uncritical affirmation of reproductive

Simone Leigh, Waiting Room at the *Free People's Medical Clinic*, 2014, courtesy of Creative Time, photo: Shulamit Seidler-Feller

61 Marina Vishmidt and Zöe Sutherland, 'Social Reproduction Feminism: A Critique', talk at the Social and Political Thought Conference, University of Sussex, 20 June 2015

62 The popularity of Julia Kristeva's theory of abjection for a reading of artworks reached an apex in the mid-1990s, spurred on by the exhibition 'Abject Art: Repulsion and Desire in American Art', Whitney Museum of Art, 1993. See the catalogue Craig Houser, Leslie C Jones et al, eds, Abject Art: Repulsion and Desire in American Art, Whitney Museum of Art, New York, 1993. Hal Foster also gives an account of Cindy Sherman and Kiki Smith's work in terms of the abject as specifically feminine; see Hal Foster, 'Obscene, Abject, Traumatic', October 78, autumn, 1996, pp 106–124. More recently, Hannah Black has discussed the revival of representational strategies associated with abjection in contemporary art, adding a much-needed discussion of race to the picture. See Hannah Black, 'This Is Crap?', Frieze d/e 23, spring 2016, https://frieze.com/article/crap, accessed 1 December 2016.

63 Lise Vogel, Marxism and the Oppression of Women: Toward a Unitary Theory, Rutgers University Press, New Brunswick, 1983, p 158

64 Vogel, Marxism and the Oppression of Women, op cit, p 139

65 Heide Gerstenberger, 'The Political Economy of Capitalist Labor', Viewpoint Magazine 4, special issue 'The State', 2 September 2014, https://viewpointmag.com/2014/09/02/the-political-economy-of-capitalist-labor/, accessed 20 July 2016

66 For details of the project see Rizvana Bradley, 'Going

activities as useful within Arte Útil. Vogel describes the social reproduction of labour power as a system that knits together the active labour force, the industrial reserve army, and that portion of the relative surplus population not incorporated in the industrial reserve army. Vogel stresses that within the history of capitalism, this last category – the surplus population – has sometimes included very few persons, aside from very young children.[63] This is certainly not the case in the present due to the collapse of Fordism and the family wage, alongside the economic restructuring of welfare and the ongoing accumulation of capital through means that are radically severed from the reproduction of the proletariat. Moreover, in thinking about Federici's affirmation of the reproductive commons, it is important to stress Vogel's emphasis on the maintenance and replacement of the totality of labourers having always been achieved in ways other than generational replacement and the reproduction of the male worker by his female spouse, through labour camps, workers dormitories and prisons, all of which are heavily intertwined with violent processes of racialisation managed by the state system, as previously discussed, which is foundational to the exclusions of citizenship.[64] Taking this view allows us to avoid an affirmative, moralising view of social reproduction as such, in a way similar to that already detailed around use value.

Moreover, by paying attention to the question of race and migration as introducing a 'combined and uneven' aspect to social reproduction, we can avoid making a 'moral' argument for a return to what Heide Gerstenberger describes as the 'domesticated capitalism' of Fordism,[65] accelerationism's emphasis on rational 'forces of production' solutions, and Federici's support of what we might call subsistence models, all of which have penetrated the ideological ground of Arte Útil in varying degrees and dimensions. When contemporary artists attempt to reanimate individuals and communities who have otherwise been condemned as disposable – left to not-reproduce themselves – this too often involves, in the present, taking on aspects of social reproduction to 'repurpose' those populations and make them 'useful' along lines that draw tacit support from the state and capital.

I want to end by mentioning a recent social practice project that I see as successfully working against this tendency. Simone Leigh's *Free People's Medical Clinic* (*FPMC*, 2014) was organised through the 'Funk, God, Jazz, and Medicine: Black Radical Brooklyn' project, a collaboration between Creative Time and the Weeksville Heritage Centre (Weeksville, Brooklyn).[66] The Clinic drew on histories including the Black Panther Party's free clinics and the United Order of Tents, a secret society of black nurses founded in 1867 by former slaves Annette M Lane and Harriett R Taylor. The *FPMC* provided well-woman care, doula services, massage, blood pressure screening, HIV testing, counselling, lectures on herbalism, as well as dance workshops based on legendary African American dancer Katherine Dunham's technique, yoga and pilates. The project was situated in the former home of Dr Josephine English, the first black woman to have a gynaecological practice in the state of New York. Leigh's project sought to draw on these legacies as a means to contest racialised healthcare in the United States, a history marked by notorious cases such as the infection of 600 black men with syphilis in the Tuskegee medical study, as well as to address more

Underground: An Interview with Simone Leigh', *Art in America*, 20 August 2015, http://www.artinamericamagazine.com/news-features/interviews/going-underground-an-interview-with-simone-leigh/, accessed 27 November 2016

recent incidents such as the death of forty-nine-year-old African American woman Esmin Elizabeth Green. Green passed away in June 2008 after waiting twenty-four hours in the psychiatric emergency room of Kings County Hospital in Brooklyn.[67]

The case of Green's death directly influenced Leigh's conception of the waiting room in the *Free People's Medical Clinic* as a

> space of impossible memorialization… and a space where aesthetic ideas can get worked out. I am compelled by this idea that the artistic form is as important as the information the form delivers.[68]

As Leigh states, in producing this work, she was clear that she was 'not a public health expert' but an artist who believes that 'the number one killer of black women in the U.S. is *obedience*'.[69] The *Free People's Medical Clinic* sought to revivify past struggles as a rallying call against this obedience, drawing on Afro-centric imaginaries, 'bodily knowledge', and contemporary medical emergencies such as HIV to produce both a quasi-autonomous site from which to gain energy for present struggles as well as a glimpse into how healthcare might be more widely reorganised in a transformed future. In its offensive against 'obedience' and attention to form as well as 'information', the *Free People's Medical Clinic* could not be further away from the 'usefulness' of WochenKlausur, the other project mentioned in this article that centred on health. While WochenKlausur's project tacitly encouraged obedience and compliance with the restructuring of welfare – its usefulness lying in its symbiosis with the world around it – the *Free People's Medical Clinic* contested and asked difficult questions of the surrounding medical infrastructure. As such, the *FPMC* actively contradicts and refuses the logics of the world that produced the necessity for art to step into the arena of social reproduction, and in doing so is marked by an attention to history as well as the kinds of expressive, material and emotional solidarity I called for at the outset of this article.

67 Ibid

68 Ibid

69 Ibid

Third Text, 2017
Vol. 31, No. 1, 133–146, https://doi.org/10.1080/09528822.2017.1364913

Exposed

The Politics of Infrastructure in VALIE EXPORT's *Transparent Space*

Elke Krasny

Kazuko Kurosaki, *Operation Mothership* in *Kubus EXPORT*, May 15, 2010, (detail), photo: Elke Krasny

1 As a young artist EXPORT distanced herself from the Viennese Actionists 'in a mode she called feminist actionism (Feministischer Aktionismus), distinguishing herself from the machismo of the core group'. See Mechtild Widrich, *Performative Monuments: The Rematerialisation of Public Art*, Manchester University Press, Manchester, 2014, p 54.

2 MA 57 – Frauenförderung und Koordination von Frauenangelegenheiten, *Der Transparente Raum*, Magistrat der Stadt Wien, Wien, 2011, back cover of programme brochure.

3 I am thinking here of Cherríe Moraga and Gloria Anzaldúa, eds, *This Bridge Called My Back: Writings by Radical Women of Color*, Persephone Press, London, 1981.

On 16 May 2001 the renowned feminist artist and occasional curator VALIE EXPORT took part in the opening ceremony celebrating the completion of *Transparent Space*, her only public artwork in Vienna. A large room-sized cube made of glass, the work is installed in one of the arches formed by the viaduct of an elevated urban railway. The ambiguity of this piece is underscored by its adoption of three separate names: *Transparenter Raum* (Transparent Space), *Kubus EXPORT* (Cube EXPORT) and *Frauenbrücke* (Women's Bridge). *Kubus EXPORT* alludes to the artist's own name, selected as a 'logo in capital letters' in 1967 in order to resist the system of patrilineage as well as to express her adoption of a radical feminist stance under patriarchal art-world conditions.[1] Today, the artist's brand name is inscribed onto the cube's surface while *Women's Bridge* is relegated to the printed brochure occasioned by the opening ceremony.[2] The latter title evokes the language of second-wave feminism as well as its collective activist spirit, yet the artwork itself leaves open the question as to whether women cross the bridge together, have built the bridge collaboratively, work towards having the bridge named after them, or a necessary combination of all three.[3] Second-wave feminist artists identified the structural inequalities underpinning the gendered distribution of resources in institutional and infrastructural terms as well as the persistent gender bias of artworld visibility and art-historical recognition. *Cube EXPORT* and *Women's Bridge* both make strong references to second-wave struggles and, by extension, to current feminist demands. Yet together they point to contradictions at the heart of the artwork: at once an autonomous piece by a famous artist, active since the 1960s, whose name occupies a 'singular visibility' position *and* an art space to be defined by *the plural*, dedicated to offering a platform that promotes the visibility of many women and feminist artists. Meanwhile, its most commonly used name, *Transparent Space*, both places this artwork in the legacy of Modernist architecture's iconic glass houses and opens up a rich seam of more contemporary reference points, including the imperative of neoliberal capitalism to perform and be visible at all times.

What follows is a materialist feminist analysis that insists on the importance of the conditions of production and reproduction to the gender politics of public art and women's relation to labour under neoliberal capitalism. My account hinges on the work's relationship with the different meanings of the verb 'expose': to expose means to make known, to exhibit, to render visible, to deprive of protection but also to reveal wrongdoing. In going on to explore how *Transparent Space* exposes its own contradictions as they relate to feminism (in particular, to feminists making and curating art), I will examine, firstly, the impact of the dynamics of urban transformation processes in their longitudinal dimension as they radically alter infrastructures and their redistributive (in)justice. Secondly, I will consider the commissioning of public art and neoliberal restructuring austerity measures as they render precarious long-term provisions for use and maintenance as well as for curatorial labour (not always clearly distinguished from artistic labour); and thirdly, I will address the legacies of second-wave feminist art-making alongside current and ongoing practices of feminist art-working. I am particularly interested in feminists' capacity to create self-organised and self-built art spaces and how neoliberal capitalism bears on such practices.

Situating Transparent Space

The postal address of *Transparent Space* is given as Lerchenfelder Gürtel, Stadtbahnbogen 48. The Gürtel is Vienna's outer concentric ring road, a heavily used thoroughfare with three lanes of traffic moving in both directions. EXPORT's glass cube is installed in one of the urban railway arches that form the hollow spaces under the elevated track that runs through the middle of this 'beltway'. The road traces the course of the Linienwall, a military fortification dating from 1704, which consisted of an enormous palisade-reinforced earthen rampart, four metres high and four metres wide. In the eighteenth century, it was politically justified by the Austro-Hungarian Empire as city defence against possible attacks by the Turks or the Kurucs, and the residents of Vienna were duly summoned to provide their labour for free in order to build the structure. The Linienwall was therfore a display of unpaid labour performed by the urban public. Not only did it result in a line of defence against external enemies, it also effectively created a line of internal urban segregation by establishing a fiscal and legal border – at its gates a road toll was charged. This border separated Vienna's historical aristocratic and bourgeois districts occupying the space around the imperial urban core from those areas of the urban hinterland reserved for agricultural production, light manufacturing and housing for the working and

VALIE EXPORT, *Kubus EXPORT*, 2001–, photo: Elke Krasny, 2016

urban poor.[4] Today, its path continues to trace a divide, this time between a middle-class district and one with a high proportion of immigrant, working-class and student populations.

The second half of the nineteenth century witnessed Vienna's transformation into a metropolitan capital marked by significant infrastructural investments in transport and culture (museums, theatres, concert halls and universities) as well as housing; in particular, the construction of four- or five-storey apartment blocks for rent. The Linienwall was demolished in 1894 to make room for the massive masonry viaduct of an elevated railway, the Vienna Metropolitan Railway or Stadtbahn, which was built between 1898 and 1901. Today, the Stadtbahn is integrated into the subway system as metro line U6. An important example of early Art Nouveau, the functional yet decorative station and railway architecture was designed by Otto Wagner while the arches below the tracks created spaces destined for small-scale production and business use.

Fast-forward a hundred years to the mid-1990s and many of the viaduct archways lay fallow while the Gürtel itself had become notorious for heavy traffic, street-level prostitution, high levels of unemployment and poor housing conditions. In planning terminology, it was referred to as a 'problem zone'. Following a successful application to the EU Community Initiative 'URBAN' in 1994, the City of Vienna established the URBAN-Vienna Gürtel Plus framework, which oversaw the establishment of more than sixty different social, cultural, labour market, ecological and business initiatives designed to improve neighbourhoods on the impoverished side of the transportation artery.[5] At the same time, the architect and planner Silja Tillner was commissioned to work on the revitalisation of the Gürtel Boulevard. Through the project 'Gürtel Urbion' she focused on ameliorative interventions that set out to create a more pleasant environment: one that was more conducive to business as well as certain cultural activities. Noting that there were '350 to 400 commercially usable Stadtbahn arches' available and owned by the Viennese Transport Authority, she specifically aimed to encourage 'cultural attractions, in particular for innovative music and ethnic food restaurants', the establishment of 'infrastructure for the youth scene' and 'private initiatives to renovate premises with traditional workshops or grocery stores'.[6] Given that many of the archways were boarded up or occupied by businesses that had obstructed views by constructing walls, in material terms Tillner's key strategy centred on the installation of glass facades. While she maintained that the new frontages 'restore[d] the original transparency', I argue that they transform the voids into display sites, effectively exposing the usages and activities undertaken therein.[7] This constellation of EU funding provision, the co-operation it incentivised between different municipal departments as well as district-level government, and the priorities of Tillner's Urbion project created the conditions that led to EXPORT's commission: a public artwork designated as a progressive cultural space for women and intended to play a part in urban regeneration.

Public Art Politics: Visibility and Transparency

On International Women's Day 1999, Renate Brauner, the then Executive City Councillor for Integration, Women's Issues, Consumer Protec-

4 In their book *Unruly Masses: The Other Side of Fin-de-Siècle Vienna*, Berghahn Books, Oxford, 2008, Wolfgang Maderthaner and Lutz Musner describe the economic, cultural and spatial segregation demarcated by this urban border in the late nineteenth and early twentieth centuries.

5 The guidelines stated that 'URBAN is co-financed by two of the European Community's Structural Funds: the European Regional Development Fund (ERDF) and the European Social Fund (ESF)'. Urban Community Initiative 1994–1999, http://ec.europa.eu/regional_policy/archive/urban2/urban/initiative/src/frame1.htm, accessed 21 July 2016.

6 Silja Tillner, *Wien, Urbion Urban Intervention Gürtel West = Vienna, Urbion Der Stand der Dinge*, Stadtplanung Wien, Magistratsabteilung 18, Vienna, 2000, p 35

7 Ibid, p 36

tion and Personnel, made a public announcement regarding the new focus of City of Vienna Women's Department, Municipal Department 57. 'Making women visible' was central to the forthcoming agenda.[8] In the same year, and as the end of its funding cycle approached, the URBAN-Vienna Gürtel Plus initiative reached out to the Women's Department and together they instigated co-funding for what was described in broad and sweeping terms as a new women's cultural project for the Gürtel regeneration. Following a quick application process, EXPORT's public art project was selected and the Women's Department consulted with architect Silja Tillner to determine its location. Discussions with the artist clarified that she was proposing neither a 'monument in the traditional sense' nor a 'conventional sculpture'.[9] Instead, EXPORT opted to create something altogether more ambiguous: a structure that was at once an autonomous artwork and a designated women's art space.

Before addressing the currency of 'visibility' as used in the parlance of feminist governance deployed by Renate Brauner back in 1999, I want to undertake a more detailed examination of the public art politics expressed by the use of glass in this context. If, on the one hand, EXPORT responds to Tillner's work in the area (by then well underway), she also invokes, in a more general sense, the legacies of modern architecture. Premised on the elimination of ornament as well as an emphasis on volume, simplicity and light, many of Modernism's powerful tropes centred on the technological advances of industrial capitalism, and in particular the use of mass-produced building materials such as steel and, above all, glass. Yet this citation creates a chrono-political tension: EXPORT deploys this Modernist architectural language 'after the fact' in a major European city at the turn of the millennium, a time marked by the rise of post-industrial cognitive capitalism apparently predicated on service and cultural economies. This was a moment when the urban decay of the industrial city met the creative city, when 'state-managed capitalism' was evolving into a perpetual 'neoliberal crisis' and when labour was 'feminised' as women entered global labour markets in large numbers.[10] It was under these conditions that EXPORT's almost imperceptible glass structure became a viewing device: in the absence of a distinct, visually graspable form, one sees *through* the public artwork to instead become a witness to its urban surroundings – the elevated train stop with its day centre for the homeless, the infrastructure for rubbish collection, the pedestrians crossing over the Gürtel to get to the neighbourhood's open food market. A super-sized glass vitrine in public space, the structure's out-of-time references call attention to the radical transformations underway.

The 'making women visible' rallying cry of feminist governance and gender-conscious politics adheres to the cause of promoting women's achievements, but what it often does not register are the criteria used to identify 'success' and 'inclusion'. The implicit understanding that public recognition should follow important contributions across all fields of production – whether politics, business, the arts or education – appears to be rooted in the politics of recognition and visibility that are typical of second-wave women's history writing, with its focus on women's historical achievements and contributions. As Gerda Lerner remarks:

8 Ursula Bauer, 'Introduction', in Magistrat der Stadt Wien Frauenbüro, ed, *Der Transparente Raum*, MA 57, Frauenförderung und Koordinierung von Frauenangelegenheiten, Vienna, 2000, p 10

9 Ibid

10 Nancy Fraser, *Fortunes of Feminism: From State-Managed Capitalism to Neoliberal Crisis*, Verso, London and New York, 2013, p 220

VALIE EXPORT, *Kubus EXPORT,* 2001–, photo: Elke Krasny, 2016

> The first level at which historians, trained in traditional history, approach women's history is by writing the history of 'women worthies' or 'compensatory history'. Who are the women missing from history? Who are the women of achievement and what did they achieve?[11]

For it is clear that those who had already attained visibility around the Gürtel – street-level sex workers, women using public transport, women on their way to purchase fresh fruit and vegetables at the nearby market – were not 'the achievers' targeted by Municipal Department 57's slogan. On the contrary, the urban regeneration scheme to which *Transparent Space* contributed effectively displaced the labour of prostitution and 'sanitised' the area. The 'making visible' ideology taken on board by gender mainstreaming governance relies on exclusionary mechanisms of *selective* visibility, which purposefully ignores the precarious visibility to which marginalised and (often) racialised female bodies are structurally exposed.

Much postcolonial and feminist theory has critically engaged with the politics, ethics, economies and effects of visibility. In 1993, Peggy Phelan noted that there is no easy passage from visibility to power, remarking that: 'If representational visibility equals power, then almost-naked young white women should be running Western culture. The ubiquity of their image, however, has hardly brought them political or economic power.'[12] Yet more troubling perhaps are instances where women's visibility is considered to be precisely the problem; an issue requiring remedial action. This was certainly the case for the sex workers that were treated as a symptom of urban decay along the Gürtel: their status as observable 'public women' effectively rendered them yet more precarious and eventually led to their displacement through the dynamics of urban transformation that entangled the development of *Transparent Space*. Of course, many different disenfranchised and underrepresented groups have, in the past, made effective claims to visibility. Therefore, visibility justice and representational justice have to be meaningfully, and at times painfully, negotiated by public art – and in particular, by feminist public art. As stated by Phelan:

> I am not suggesting that continued invisibility is the 'proper' political agenda for the disenfranchised, but rather that the binary between the power of visibility and the impotency of invisibility is falsifying... there are serious limitations to visual representation as a political goal. Visibility is a trap... it summons surveillance and the law; it provokes voyeurism, fetishism, the colonialist/imperial appetite for possession.[13]

What, then, can feminist public art provide to counteract this 'visibility trap' consciously and productively? How can the visibility issue be pushed beyond the logics of representational hegemony centred on the gendered subject and extended to conditions of production and reproduction? Phelan considered this a matter of some urgency: 'it is imperative that those interested in women as subjects find other ways of thinking about the relation between representation and reproduction'.[14] A see-through monument to transparency, *Transparent Space* provokes an analysis of precisely this relationship, opening up both the wounds of rep-

11 Gerda Lerner, 'Placing Women in History: Definitions and Challenges', *Feminist Studies*, vol 3, nos 1–2, Autumn, 1975, pp 5–14, p 5

12 Peggy Phelan, *Unmarked: The Politics of Performance*, Routledge, London and New York, 1993, p 10

13 Ibid, p 6

14 Ibid, p 11

resentation and the agonies of reproduction. Old as they might seem, representation and reproduction remain key themes in addressing the conditions and problems of visibility, gender and labour in the new millennium. Despite the digital revolution, with its emergent struggles over data-driven transparency and perpetual online visibility, not much has changed in physical and material terms when it comes to the complex entanglements of invisibilised feminised labour and the visibility-recognition trap.

'Labour of Love' Politics: The Conditions Exposed

According to a member of the commissioning team, *Transparent Space* 'was supposed to be an autonomous artwork, yet at the same time… [a] space for other cultural activities'.[15] In physical terms, the transition from autonomous artwork to art space is expressed in the two glass doors: as Mechtild Widrich observed, the cube can be opened at both sides to 'make… the glass body into a passage'.[16] EXPORT's *Transparent Space* is always both – an art work and an art space. On the one hand, this constitutes a significant expression of openness: one can enter the artwork, one can be inside the artwork, one can, if only temporarily, inhabit the artwork. Although the doors usually remain closed, unless an art event is scheduled, the important point is that they *can* be unlocked, that it is possible for visitors to enter the artist's work. More radical still is the apparent abandonment of autonomy indicated by the generous invitation occasionally extended to other artists – specifically, women artists and artists with a feminist and/or queer agenda or aesthetics – to present their own work *inside* EXPORT's artwork. If the cube thereby becomes a support structure, it is, nevertheless, a very demanding and precarious one. Precarity is, after all, demanding; precarious support even more so. *Kubus EXPORT* does not hide this fact – it makes it manifest.

The cube effectively exposes the impossible work conditions driven by the austerity of its skeletal support structure; or, put differently, the very *lack of support* it has to offer. As an art space *Kubus EXPORT* is, to say the least, dysfunctional. It does not provide a working infrastructure; there is no backstage, no storage area, no running water. Moreover, its transparency extends to rendering visible how the labour gifted in response to the offering of the space is performed (mostly) by women and feminist artists who are, at times, allowed to use it. In this unprotected environment there is no escape from visibility, no place to prepare unobserved, no place to hide one's discomfort or one's exhaustion, no place to rehearse without being seen. This dual exposure which invites, and indulges, the public gaze both on individuals and on working conditions is familiar from the legacy of Modernist glass houses such as Mies van der Rohe's iconic Farnsworth House.[17] The woman for whom this home was designed – Edith Farnsworth – wrote:

> I don't keep a garbage can under my sink. Do you know why? Because you can see the whole 'kitchen' from the road on the way in here and the can would spoil the appearance of the whole house… the house is transparent, like an X-ray.[18]

15 Bauer, 'Introduction', op cit, p 11

16 Widrich quotes and translates from EXPORT, 'Der Transparente Raum', in Frauenbüro, op cit, p 138. See Widrich, op cit, p 88.

17 The Farnsworth House was constructed in the US (Plano, Illinois) between 1945 and 1951 and is a National Trust for Historic Preservation site.

18 See Alice T Friedman, *Women and the Making of the Modern House*, Harry N Abrams Inc Publishers, New York, 1998, p 141.

Sophia Hatwagner, Matthew Lenkiewicz und Paran Pour, *Hills n' Valleys*, in Cube EXPORT – The Transparent Space, July 2013, photo: Paran Pour

19 Silvia Federici, *Wages against Housework*, Power of Women Collective and the Falling Wall Press, Bristol, 1975, p 2. At first, the City of Vienna's Municipal Department 57 – Vienna Women's Department (MA 57) was responsible for the care and maintenance of *Transparent Space*. This proved to be a financial burden. In 2011, *Transparent Space* became the responsibility of Municipal Department 21 – District Planning and Land Use (MA 21), which decided to open it to artists interested in making use of it. Even though basic maintenance of the glass walls was provided by the City of Vienna, the better part of caring, cleaning and maintaining had to be performed by the artists. At the time of writing, the future use of *Transparent Space* has not been decided. During a 'Werkgespräch' (public conversation on her work) with the author, EXPORT stated that she was keen for *Transparent Space* to operate independently as an artwork and stressed that the cube should only infrequently and exceptionally be turned into an art space. Werkgespräch, *Kubus EXPORT,* 10 May 2010.

20 For a recent critique of the conditions in which feminist politics is found to intersect with the collectivism of the commons in art, see Angela Dimitrakaki, 'Art and Instituting for a Feminist Common/s: Thoughts on Interventions in the New "New Europe"', in Alenka Gregoric and Suzana Milvska, eds, *Inside Out: Critical Discourses Concerning Institutions*, Museums and Galleries of Ljubljana/City Art Gallery Ljubljana, Ljubljana, 2017, pp 38–49.

21 Most iconic in this legacy of feminist self-support is Judy Chicago and Miriam Schapiro's 1972

Demanding continuous maintenance while offering no place to hide, these homes painfully exposed the domestic worker as well as the performance of her labour. Extending what can be described as this Modernist heritage of performing domesticity to her public artwork, EXPORT's Gürtel initiative can be understood as connecting two sites where women's (mostly) unpaid or low-paid 'labour of love' is accomplished: the home and now a women's and feminist art space.[19]

Read as a critical public art manifesto, *Transparent Space* stresses the gendered injustice of the distribution of public art infrastructure. The City of Vienna Women's Department failed to understand that long-term provisions would have to be made for the artwork's physical maintenance as well as for curatorial programming and the production costs of new artworks for the space. It is women artists and feminist artists who have been expected to overcome this lack of both infrastructure and funding provision with their collective energy, their passion and their desire to show their work in public.[20] *Transparent Space* simultaneously honours and harnesses a longitudinal tradition of women artists' and feminist artists' capacity to self-organise and sustain art spaces and infrastructures that run parallel to hegemonic and androcentric state or privately managed museums and galleries.[21] Moreover, it is only through the mobilisation of this tenacious productive and, crucially, reproductive labour that the artists who were allowed by the City of Vienna to make and show art in EXPORT's artwork effectively transformed it into an art space.

While EXPORT's accounts of her frustrating experiences attempting to secure a suitable museum or gallery venue for her own curatorial endeavours underscore the importance she places on adequate institutional support, her trajectory as an artist demonstrates a profound and sustained engagement with the politics of infrastructure.[22] Her *Body-Configurations* series presents a durational and intimate exploration of public space from this perspective, with one of the first photographs showing EXPORT tightly holding herself while crouched next to a line of rubbish bins. Its title, *Einarmung* (1972), is an invented German word that roughly translates as 'embrace', while its composition relates her young female body to both the physical infrastructure of refuse containers and the maintenance labour of garbage collection on the scale of municipal waste management. In photographic documentation of *Bibliothek 1 (Library 1)* (1982), we see EXPORT again, a decade later, this time with arms spread wide, knees bent and heels raised as she grasps the corner of the Austrian National Library. While we may infer from her gesture that such public infrastructure needs to be upheld and supported, in Foucauldian terms, the library might be understood as a site of control, selection and distribution of hegemonic discourse.[23] With collections dating back to the Habsburg Empire, EXPORT's chosen site of intervention is a legal deposit library, obliged to acquire a copy of every book published in Austria: it represents nation-state logics of knowledge production and collection. The contrast the artist draws between her own body and the institution as she grapples with its walls speaks to a specific configuration of the power relations in play as they take on material, built form.

Given EXPORT's own concerns and experience, then, the lack of infrastructural provision in, and for, *Transparent Space* is particularly

Womanhouse in Los Angeles, realised together with their students from the California Institute of the Arts Feminist Art Program. Self-organised feminist art spaces that successfully endured over time include *A.I.R.* in New York (1972–), or *Intakt, International Action Community of Women Artists* in Vienna (1977–).

22 EXPORT, 'Panel 1', in Elke Krasny, ed, *Women's Museum: Curatorial Politics in Feminism, Education, History, and Art*, Löcker, Vienna, 2010, p 47

23 Though Foucault explicitly addresses libraries in his text 'Of Other Spaces: Utopias and Heterotopias', *Diacritics* 16, spring 1986, pp 22–27, I am referring here to another line of Foucauldian thought which he developed in *Discipline & Punish: The Birth of the Prison*, Penguin Books, London, 1977, with its focus on the disciplinary mechanisms of power regimes underpinning the state.

24 Up until 2014, thirty different artists and collectives showed site-specific new visual work as well as performances.

25 Ukeles had her first full retrospective at Queens Museum in 2017. For an introduction to the exhibition and her work since the 1960s, see Jillian Steinhauer, 'How Mierle Laderman Ukeles Turned Maintenance Work into Art', *Hyperallergic*, 10 February 2017, https://hyperallergic.com/355255/how-mierle-laderman-ukeles-turned-maintenance-work-into-art/, accessed 9 June 2017.

conspicuous. For the artist-participants, the career affirmation that follows professional alignment with such an internationally renowned figure must, apparently, counteract this absence. While initially the cube was only rarely made available for use by other artists, between 2011 and 2014 the City of Vienna District Planning and Land Use Department (MA 21) took charge of the space, issuing an open call for proposals in response to a neighbourhood demand for more cultural activities. Although no curator was appointed, nor any budget made available, a large number of artists applied with convincing projects. In an unusual move, the Department disregarded selection procedures and granted all applicants permission to use the cube.[24] It is, then, clear that the cube can afford a valuable opportunity to artists for creating and showing experimental work to diverse audiences; and, indeed, exciting projects were frequently produced inside its walls including projections, installations and performances. In this sense, the work *does* offer generous support in both aesthetic and spatial terms. To make use of this support, the first step is to open the door, literally. Not an easy thing to do. After obtaining the key one has to crouch down, get the key to turn, physically manoeuvre the unwieldy sliding mechanism. If one needs to use the bathroom, one has to make friends with the neighbours, either the nearby police station or the homeless day shelter, or perhaps a coffee house and ask for permission to use theirs. The artist must also negotiate to ensure that visitors can have access to these borrowed facilities. She must source, transport and keep safe any tools necessary for the installation of her work. If artworks leave traces on the glass walls she has to clean up afterwards. And, of course, the floor must be swept. Even though many of the artworks and performances that have taken place at *Transparent Space* gained aesthetically from exploring the glass cube's site specificity and benefitted from its symbolic capital, EXPORT's work stages the art world's structurally exploitative mechanisms, which remain defining of public art irrespective of the latter's feminist allegiances and commitments. Given this structural condition, the question arises as to how the 'free' use of an authored artwork as collective art space enters the cycle of exchange: does such use lead to the accumulation of cultural capital for the (feminist) author-artist – again, irrespective of any intentions on the latter's part?

Traps of Transparency: Risks of Exposure

The terms of analysis set here necessarily form part of a broader discussion on art and maintenance, pointing back to Mierle Laderman Ukeles's *Manifesto for Maintenance Art, 1969!* and her artistic practice as maintenance art, also connected with the struggles of second-wave feminism.[25] However, aside from the different contexts in which EXPORT produced *Transparent Space* in 2001 and Ukeles performed works such as *Washing/Tracks/Maintenance: Outside* at Wadsworth Atheneum in 1973, their interventions operate on different scales and registers. If EXPORT's work can be described as 'monumental', in the sense that it operates on the scale of the urban where it is fashioned as a sculptural container and possibly as a parody of the Minimalist cube (its reform from 'obstacle' to 'facilitator'), Ukeles's can be described as 'ephemeral', operating on the scale of the museum object and the art institution as an always specific material entity. While Ukeles explicitly speaks of, and performs, hidden, undervalued reproductive labour, EXPORT neither speaks of nor performs the latter. While Ukeles's performance depends upon her bodily labour, EXPORT's own body is dissociated from *Transparent Space* and yet she exposes its dependency on the performance of artistic labour and maintenance labour. While Ukeles offers her artwork as 'support' to the maintenance of (art) institutional space, EXPORT offers a skeletal 'support' structure that introduces into public, urban space the need for, and deficit of, maintenance. While Ukeles addresses the invisibilisation of 'women's work' (her manifesto written soon after she became a mother in a nuclear family context), EXPORT addresses the visibility and transparency trap as a condition of women artists' public presence. Ukeles transformed maintenance into art; EXPORT exposed the fact that art intended to politicise public space requires maintenance, that without cared for supports and infrastructures art-making and the display of art are hardly possible – maybe especially so in cases where such display is based on the appropriation of Modernist experiments with domesticity (Mies).[26]

What I want to suggest therefore, is that *Transparent Space* attends to the larger transitions and structural crises concerning infrastructure, public art and labour: firstly, as mentioned earlier, the shift from industrial to post-industrial production; secondly, the updating of capitalism as neoliberalism; thirdly, and consequently, the adjustment of well-funded state-run art institutions and initiatives to the normalisation of austerity measures. How is feminism co-implicated in these developments? Nancy Fraser has provided us with a most lucid and disturbing analysis of 'feminism as the "new spirit of capitalism"'.[27] She provocatively asks: 'Was it mere coincidence that second-wave feminism and neoliberalism prospered in tandem? Or was there some perverse, subterranean elective affinity between them?'[28] The move from 'redistribution to recognition' diagnosed by Fraser can also be witnessed in the field of public art in its relation to the neoliberal transformation of urban space.[29] On the one hand, state-managed as well as privately commissioned public art became more ambitious, and more spectacular, as it was fully incorporated into urban regeneration schemes; on the other, art institutions such as museums, art spaces and Kunsthalles were forced to cope with funding cuts that impacted particularly heavily on the resources available to cover labour costs. These developments must also be considered in the light of the 'liberated' creativity of what Luc Boltanski and Eve Chiapello call 'connexionist' capitalism, whereby flexible networks are said to replace organisations' vertical hierarchies.[30] Combined, these developments underpin the feminisation of labour witnessed in the art field today. Because of its political commitments, *Transparent Space* articulates these processes in complex ways. It mobilises the priorities of second-wave feminism – such as the motivational 'crack the glass ceiling' imperative and capacities for self-organising – as a 'solution' to the issues engendered by later economic developments. Seen in this light, the artwork and art space become a *diagnostic* device of the conditions of production and reproduction of public art – conditions which are ultimately relevant to both 'feminism' as a non-static social movement and 'art' in a more general sense but equally subject to historical determination.

26 Glass is a key material both in Modern and Postmodern architecture and has therefore captured the interest of critical analysis, effectively leading to a subfield of transparency and surveillance studies, and visibility and invisibility studies in architectural theory. Indicatively, see Henriette Steiner and Kristin Veel, eds, *Invisibility Studies: Surveillance, Transparency and the Hidden in Contemporary Culture*, Peter Lang, Bern, 2015. Although space limitations prevent pursuing this angle here, it must be noted that the connection between in/visibility in architecture and in/visible labour remains largely under-examined.

27 Fraser, *Fortunes of Feminism*, op cit, p 218

28 Ibid

29 Ibid, p 219

30 Ibid, p 220. Fraser refers here to Luc Boltanski and Eve Chiapello, *The New Spirit of Capitalism*, Gregory Elliott, trans, Verso, London, 2005.

By way of concluding remarks, I will relay an encounter that can perhaps be counted as part of *Transparent Space*'s history. Soon after its opening in 2001, the artist Cynthia Schwertsik and I began contemplating a project involving *Transparent Space*. The project remains unrealised and its title is *Women Working at the Gürtel* (*Frauen arbeiten am Gürtel*). The title was intended as both a reference to the displaced street-level sex workers and the reproductive labour required for the maintenance of the cube's glass walls, always in dire need of more effective cleaning to maintain the intended transparency. We envisioned a female, in fact mostly feminist, labour force, a brigade of cleaners armed with the necessary equipment, made up of our invited friends, art workers, architects, curators, intellectuals, theorists, urban researchers, at work for twenty-four hours. Rather than undertake this operation in informal or clandestine terms, it was important to the aims of the project for us to go through formal channels so as to obtain permission: we wanted our performance of labour to become recognised as artwork by those who authorise what appears as artwork in public. We contacted the City of Vienna Women's Department and tried to get in touch with EXPORT via Silvia Eiblmayr, a curator with whom the artist had collaborated closely. Unsurprisingly perhaps, our generous offer was politely declined.[31] We say it would have been love. They may have said to themselves that *Women Working at the Gürtel* would have exposed too much.

31 We did not repeat our offer in 2011, when the Municipal Department 21 – District Planning and Land Use took over and opened the space to self-initiated and self-organised artistic projects. It had seemed important to us to perform a public maintenance and cleaning action when the struggles over care and maintenance were first discussed soon after the opening of *Transparent Space.*

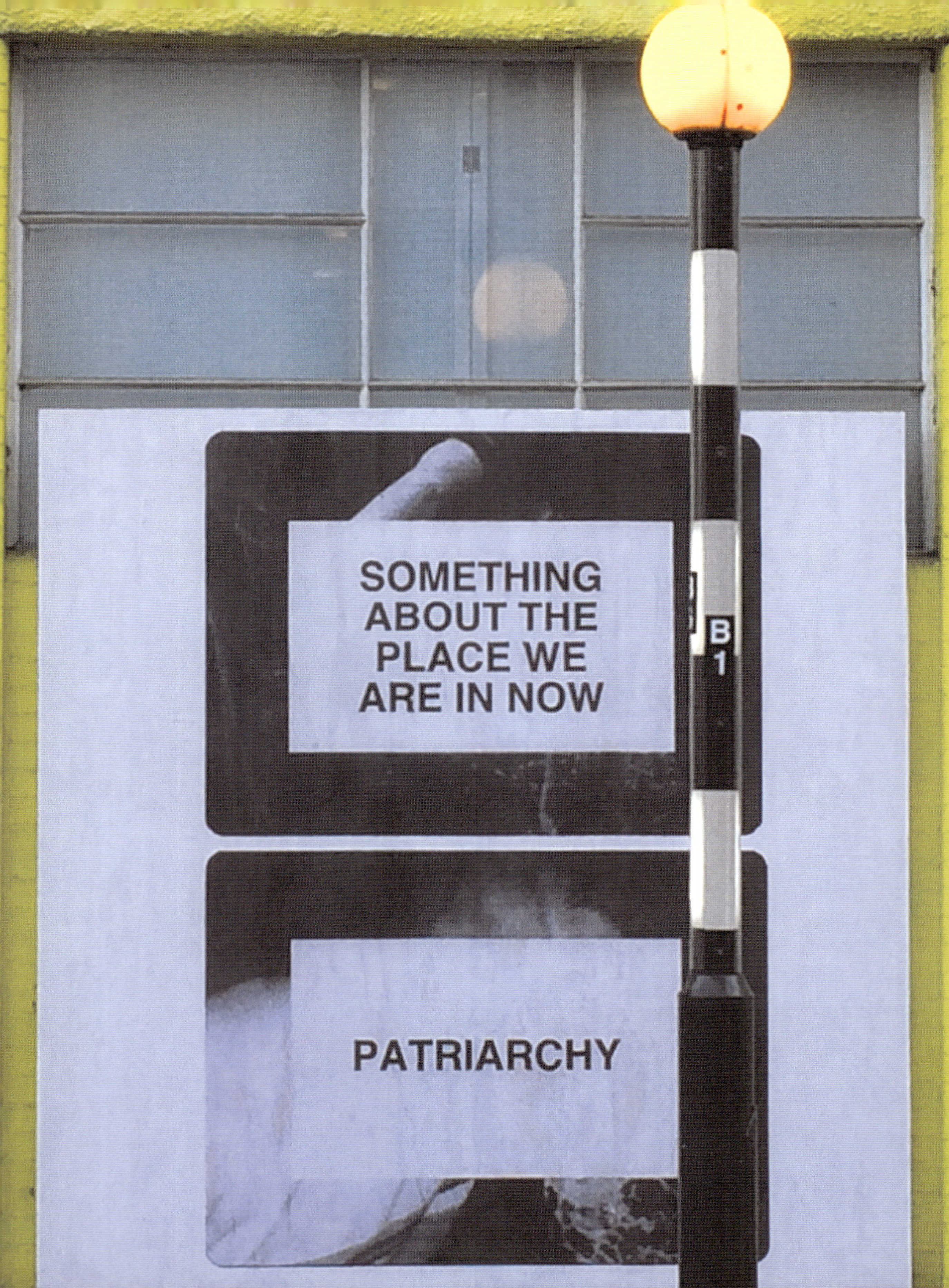

SOMETHING
ABOUT THE
PLACE WE
ARE IN NOW
PATRIARCHY
B
1

Third Text, 2017
Vol. 31, No. 1, 147–168, https://doi.org/10.1080/09528822.2017.1365492

Labours of Love

A Conversation on Art, Gender and Social Reproduction

Danielle Child, Helena Reckitt and Jenny Richards

Introduction: On Loving One's Labour

Following their presentations at the 2016 Association of Art Historians' Annual Conference panel 'Labours of Love, Works of Passion: The Social (Re)production of Art Workers from Industrialisation to Globalisation', panel convenors Angela Dimitrakaki and Kirsten Lloyd invited the authors to contribute to a conversation on reproductive labour in the artworld. The three contributors approach the subject from different perspectives: Danielle is an art historian who adopts a historical materialist approach to thinking about artistic production. A curator and researcher with a long-standing interest in the histories and current relevance of queer and feminist engagements with art, theory and activism, Helena is engaged with how those histories translate and transmit across time, place and context, and recently her research has focused on affective and caring labour within the curatorial and artistic field. Jenny works collaboratively with artists and academics to develop practice-based research projects and public exhibitions that investigate labour and its gendered division. Due to the article's concern with the conditions under which cultural and academic work occurs, the authors felt it was important that they make visible their labour involved in writing this text. The discussion took place over the course of several Skype calls and collective online writing sessions in June and July 2016. The practice-based conversational format felt more appropriate than the traditional monologic approach to academic writing. Rather than presenting research as an individual pursuit, the conversation holds the potential to encourage and reveal its collaborative nature, juxtaposing insights gained from 'theory' and 'practice', and testing them one

Hamish MacPherson,
Breastbeating, 2016, (detail),
commissioned by Manual
Labours, exhibited with *The
Complaining Body* at The
Showroom, London, image
courtesy: the artist and Manual
Labours.

against the other. This format also prompted the authors to delve into all aspects of their lives, including their class backgrounds, familial expectations, and their work experiences in the art, academic and service sectors.

The conversation is presented under four headings, which originated from a set of prompt questions that the authors established. The text begins with each contributor unpacking the term 'labours of love', before expanding into discussions about academic and curatorial work within the neoliberal context and as experienced by the participants. In the second section, the authors consider strategies of resistance to the neoliberal work condition through tactics of unlearning or dis-identification. The third section opens with Silvia Federici's concept of the 'double character of work' (which at once reproduces and valorises us as feminised subjects both for and against our integration into the labour market), sparking a discussion of feminist sociologist Emma Dowling's distinction between value and valorisation. The final section returns to questions of social reproduction and art, drawing upon the feminist critique of Marx, prompted by a consideration of the historical relationships (and divides) between Marxist and feminist art histories.

I What Comes under 'Labours of Love'

Helena Reckitt Starting with our own experiences working in art, culture and education, I'd observe that the idea that people are motivated by love, rather than for material gain, is endemic to the curatorial field that I come out of and the curating master's programme that I teach on. It stems from art's association with the leisured, land- and property-owning classes, in which collecting and working with art were signs of class prestige rather than terrains of labour. Passionate work implies either pleasure or sacrifice, as the rewards are emotional, self-expressive or spiritual, rather than financial. The sacrifices that artists have historically made in their devotion to their art are now expected of everyone who works in the cultural sector. Applicants to the Goldsmiths MFA Curating programme, who are predominantly female and from European, North American and East Asian (but rarely Black British) backgrounds, regularly write of their love for art in vocational terms, and of their education as an investment in the self. 'How can I afford *not* to undertake my MA at the best possible institution, despite the debt I will incur?,' one candidate wrote this year.

Jenny Richards 'A labour of love' was a term I used in 2015 for an artist symposium in Edinburgh.[1] Like the editors of this special issue, I was concerned with the implications of loving one's work and what this means for how we put ourselves to work when love is involved. (And, indeed, what implications does this performance have on our love lives?) The symposium title came from a 1975 essay by the feminist activist and theorist Silvia Federici, 'A Labour of Love',[2] which discusses the cultural conception of housework. In the essay she unpacks the idea that domestic work is not only an unpaid activity performed without question, as it has been naturalised as women's social role, but that it is an activity that, we are taught, must be enjoyed and executed with a smile. To

1 'A Labour of Love', Collective Gallery, Edinburgh, part of *GENERATION: 25 Years of Contemporary Art in Scotland*, 2015. For more information see www.collectivegallery.net/archive/2015-a-labour-of-love, accessed 7 May 2016

2 Silvia Federici, 'Wages Against Housework', Power of Women Collective and Falling Wall Press, New York, 1975

render the labour of the home as a labour of love is a key component to establishing it as a type of activity that escapes categorisation as work, and thus society can continue to undervalue its character.

Danielle Child   The phrase 'labours of love' always struck me as referring to things that you would do unpaid or for enjoyment. Since engaging with a Marxist feminist consideration of the term in relation to artistic practice, it strikes me that 'labours of love' are the things that we (as women) are expected to do in order to keep the capitalist system moving forward (ie housework, reproducing and raising children, taking care of those who rely upon us etc). In terms of my own practice, as an academic and an art historian, research tends to be the thing that I consider a 'labour of love'. Although my contract includes a portion of 'research' hours, it is the thing that would suffer if I only devoted to it the allocated hours or, more realistically, the remaining working hours after teaching and administration.

HR   Perhaps it reflects that unremunerated nature of much of what happens under the banner of research. We, after all, spoke at the annual Association of Art Historians conference 'Labours of Love' panel for no pay or expenses,[3] and are today contributing to a journal article without being paid. Although we agreed to keep a log detailing the hours that we spent working on this text,[4] the fact is that most of the labour that went into our contributions was accrued over many years of reading, writing and practice. The academic system would implode if we demanded payment for the actual hours that we put in.

DC   That's very true, Helena! A lot of academic work is unpaid and yet in the UK we are increasingly exposed to the culture of the Research Excellence Framework (REF) – the system for assessing the quality of research in UK higher education institutions – in which we are expected to produce more outputs which, ultimately, dictate or at least form a narrative for research funding in our institutions.

JR   If the term 'a labour of love' was coined in 1975 to call out the mechanism for the exploitation of social reproduction, today we could add the term 'affective remuneration', which denotes the mass incorporation of this process beyond the realm of social reproduction, in which affect becomes a form of payback. We might not be paid for this article but we can include it in our REF submission (although I can't as I'm not in academia). Considering we all have personal experiences of this deceitful mechanism, this text is a great way to find ways to share and discuss the problem more. I collaborate with Sophie Hope on the project *Manual Labours* and we talk about this struggle a lot.[5] Often working freelance, *Manual Labours* is another part of my work that I don't get paid for, yet Sophie can count it as research and part of her academic job. We tried to address this in the recent funding we received, in which Sophie's research 'payment' was offset with a cash payment to me. While we wanted to address this structurally, it did feel like an uncomfortable solution which relied upon inadequate capitalist valorisation to bring about some equity; because, of course, Sophie works way over the hours she is paid for as well!

3 Both Helena and Jenny's conference fees were supported by the University of Edinburgh, following applications by the session conveners, as Helena's application for funding to Goldsmiths was turned down and Jenny does not work in academia. To offset costs, Helena and Jenny also both stayed with friends in Edinburgh.

4 In the interests of transparency, we initially kept a log of the time that we spent working on this text. This work included hours of preparatory reading, two hours and thirty-three minutes of Skype calls, over 100 emails, and a collective writing session lasting two hours thirty minutes. However, as the subsequent process of editing and revising this text took place over the course of several months, often in brief bursts, the work of maintaining the log proved too demanding.

5 *Manual Labours* is a practice-based research project exploring physical and emotional relationships to work, initiated by Jenny Richards and Sophie Hope in 2012. The project reconsiders current time-based structures of work (when does work start and end?) and reasserts the significance of the physical (manual) aspect of immaterial, affective and emotional labour. For more, see www.manuallabours.co.uk.

HR   Academia has started to resemble the artworld in its reliance on precarious labour. Many academics are employed on sessional contracts, and those with permanent jobs are often, like myself, hired part-time. Even those with permanent posts are encouraged to see themselves as so much dispensable, surplus labour. We are an extension of what Gregory Sholette calls 'dark matter', the ranks of 'unsuccessful' and aspirational artists without whose emotional and financial investments the artworld would collapse.[6] Yet British universities expect academics, including part-timers, to submit all their research as outputs that can be counted towards the REF; that is, apart from those hired as 'Teaching Fellows', whose contracts do not recognise or provide time for them to carry out research, which they have to undertake in their own non-work time if they are to stand a chance of getting a lectureship contract that covers research. Thus they carry out this 'free' research labour anyway. I have even heard anecdotal evidence of instances of Teaching Fellows' research being submitted for REF, despite their research hours not forming part of their contracted labour.[7] In addition to allowing little provision for research time, contracts don't recognise, and implicitly don't value, the emotional (or 'pastoral') labour that academics carry out, and which, in the UK, appears to have increased following university fee increases in 2010, which has led more students to report experiencing anxiety and stress.[8] Unsurprisingly, most socially reproductive work is carried out by women and other feminised subjects who in turn employ other people, generally poor women, women of colour, and those from migrant backgrounds, to perform domestic and caring labour for them.

DC   We are, of course, drawing on our own experiences within academia in the UK as an example of how neoliberal working models encourage and extract surplus labour from intellectual labourers here. Elsewhere, this experience is both divergent from (particularly in terms of wages) and comparable to (on an ideological level) those experienced in the UK. The similarities are perhaps evident in the recent return to thinking about the university as a factory (Gerald Raunig) and the coining of the term 'edu-factory' to affirm these associations.[9]

JR   If we consider that 'loving your work' becomes an underlying mantra for all forms of work, maybe it can help us discuss part of the complexity in terms of the conditions we, and others, find ourselves working under today; what it is we are actually passionate about. *Manual Labours* traces transformations of labour processes through an exploration into physical and emotional relationships to work. It began from our own experiences of neglecting our bodies, leaving them at the door as computer-based working commenced. In 2014, we explored the connections between labour and love with workers across different sectors: artists, educators, call centre workers and complaints administrators. Through workshops, love was exposed as a catch-all term that can hide a diverse array of work processes that are alienating, disenfranchising and motivated by values of status, and by cultural, social and economic obligation. We wanted to see if an argument can be made that if we have a passion for work, we are only fit for exploitation under a capitalist organisation of work that thrives on maximising productivity and minimising costs. Or is there something more complex at play in loving

6 Gregory Sholette, *Dark Matter: Art and Politics in the Age of Enterprise Culture*, Pluto Press, London, 2011

7 I am grateful to Angela Dimitrakaki and Kirsten Lloyd for their insights into the role of Teaching Fellows.

8 A report to the Higher Education Funding Council for England by the Institute for Employment Studies (IES) and Researching Equity, Access and Partnership (REAP), from July 2015, listed 'greater financial and academic pressures on students' as among the factors that have contributed to the increase in student demand for support for mental health problems in English universities, which had risen from c 8,000 to 18,000 in the four years to 2012/2013. http://www.hefce.ac.uk/media/HEFCE,2014/Content/Pubs/Independentresearch/2015/Understanding,provision,for,students,with,mental,health,problems/HEFCE2015_mh.pdf, accessed 27 July 2016.

9 Gerald Raunig, *Factories of Knowledge, Industries of Creativity*, Aileen Derieg, trans, Semiotext(e), Los Angeles and The MIT Press, Cambridge, Massachusetts, 2013

Manual Labours, *The Complaining Body*, 2015, image courtesy: Manual Labours

work? And if so, how might we problematise and strategise collectivity around these issues?[10]

HR   The rise of zero-hour contracts in art and academia as well as throughout the labour market does not help. Although she does not focus on the cultural or academic sector per se, the journalist Dawn Foster writes evocatively of the psychological toll felt by people employed on zero-hour contracts:

> Every colleague is competition. As a result you're constantly on edge, aware that the tiniest slip of the tongue or careless mistake could mean a fall from grace and attendant loss of income. In such circumstances, it's almost impossible to organise collectively. No one employed so precariously dare step out of line first, knowing the inevitable consequences. Such workplaces rarely recognise unions and actively discourage workers from joining or trying to form unions.[11]

JR   This definitely resonates with findings in the current stage of *Manual Labours* called *The Complaining Body* which investigates workplace complaints.[12] While we are familiar with freelance roles and precarious contracts in the art field, our research with those working in salaried positions, including staff at a London borough council, shared the same challenging conditions faced by freelancers. It appears that many of the traits of precarious work – including the shift of responsibility onto the individual so that you effectively become your own boss, flexible work hours, and 'hot desking' – become shared working conditions for all. The common denominator is the breaking down of spaces, both verbal and physical, for collegial relationships and collective workplace complaining. Every colleague is a competitor, as Foster says, and the ideology that bad working conditions are ones you should be able to cope with makes it impossible to discuss challenges at work. Cultures such as 'hot desking' and 'shift work' also reduce any time you have together with colleagues and the chance for workplace solidarity.

HR   This prevalent isolation and atomisation you are describing reminds me of how feminists previously discussed housework. It's so creepy, this culture of self-management and self-monitoring. The feminist economic sociologist Emma Dowling analyses it in terms of financialisation, where

> we count up what we are, what we do and what we achieve in constant ratings and measurable outcomes that can, in turn, be routed through financial markets for the purposes of extracting surplus value.[13]

DC   This is precisely the nature of the neoliberal political project post-Thatcher. The more we compartmentalise ourselves, the less likely we are to collectivise; individuals are less threatening to the dominant order than a collective.

JR   Yet, as we discovered during our research into workplace complaints in *Manual Labours*, complaining nonetheless occurs. Individualised workers' bodies endure, suffer and complain about their working conditions. Unable to be heard within the current system of online forms

10   *Manual Labours* (Sophie Hope and Jenny Richards), 'Loving Work: Drawing Attention to Pleasure and Pain in the Body of the Cultural Worker', *European Journal of Cultural Studies*, vol 18 no 2, April 2015, pp 117–141

11   Dawn Foster, *Lean Out*, Repeater Books, London, 2016, pp 39–40

12   *Manual Labours: The Complaining Body* is the second stage of the practice-based research project *Manual Labours. The Complaining Body* developed from a series of workshops with call centre workers in a London borough council, commuters on a train station platform, and university staff dealing with student complaints. It explores the physical and emotional effects of complaining, receiving complaints and not being able to complain in the context of work. For more, see www.manuallabours. co.uk.

13   Emma Dowling, 'Love's Labour's Cost: The Political Economy of Intimacy', VersoBooks.com, 2016, http://www.versobooks. com/blogs/2499-love-s-labour-s-cost-the-political-economy-of-intimacy, accessed 13 July 2016

Hamish MacPherson, *Breastbeating*, 2016, commissioned by Manual Labours, exhibited within *The Complaining Body* at The Showroom, London, 2016, image courtesy: the artist and Manual Labours

14 For discussions of how some of the artists in exhibitions curated by Harald Szeemann protested his dominance over them and their art see Beatrice von Bismarck, 'Relations in Motion: The Curatorial Condition in Visual Arts – and Its Possibilities for the Neighbouring Disciplines', *Frakcija* 55, 2010, pp 50–57, and Dorothee Richter 'Artists and Curators as Authors – Competitors, Collaborators, or Team-workers?', *On Curating* 19, 2013, pp 43–57. For a more recent critique of curatorial dominance, see Anton Vidokle, 'Art without Artists', *e-flux journal* 16, 2010, www.e-flux.com/journal/art-without-artists, accessed 13 July 2016.

15 See Kate Fowle, 'Who Cares? Understanding the Role of the Curator Today', in Stephen Rand and Heather Kouris, eds, *Cautionary Tales: Critical Curating*, apexart, New York, 2007, pp 10–19. Boris Groys suggests that artworks are sick, and that curators 'cure' them by giving them public vitality and visibility, in 'Politics of Installation', *e-flux journal* 2, 2009, www.e-flux.com/journal/02/68504/politics-of-installation/, accessed 13 July 2016.

16 I unpack some of the implications of curators directing their affective labour towards maintaining relationships with private philanthropists in 'Support Acts: Curating, Caring and Social Reproduction', *Journal of Curatorial Studies*, vol 5, no 1, 2016, pp 6–30.

17 Victoria Horne, Kirsten Lloyd, Jenny Richards, Catherine Spencer, 'Taking Care: Feminist Curatorial Pasts, Presents and Futures', *On Curating* 29, April 2016, 'Curating in Feminist Thought', Dorothee Richter, Elke Krasny and Lara Perry, eds, pp 116–128

and automated phone services, their grievances manifest themselves as bodily complaints – sickness, depression, diarrhoea; physical responses that leak out of the body when the voice is consistently silenced.

HR   To pick up on our discussion about how to build collectivity in a climate that encourages division, the contemporary art field seems to have inherited the assumption that curators work *for* rather than *with* artists. This sets up a hierarchy which privileges artistic labour, and sees curatorial labour in feminised terms as flexible, responsive and supportive. In contrast to the long-standing complaint that curators do not care *enough* about the artists that they work with, and that their curatorial agendas ride roughshod over art and artists,[14] recent curatorial discussions have highlighted practices and ethics of curatorial care, often foregrounding the etymological roots of 'curating' in the Latin word for 'caring' (curare).[15] Yet even when they foreground curatorial care, these accounts generally overlook where much of that care is directed, and how, in today's increasingly privatised non-profit art sector, curators' caring and affective labour goes towards maintaining relationships with wealthy philanthropists, donors, and collectors.[16] Furthermore, scant attention is paid to the need to extend care to those workers who struggle to sustain themselves in the art sector.

JR   I'm not sure if the patriarchal hierarchy of the curator has been unhinged though – I still feel that the assumption that the curator is in the position of power, and the artists serve that position, is prevalent (and reflected in my reluctance to call myself a curator). In terms of 'curare', we used that reference in a recent collaborative text.[17] However, the distinction was in analysing the shift in curating as an idea of caring for the artist, to caring for the context the work is produced within – the community, the audience, the political commitment.

HR   I have evoked 'curare' when writing about curating, too. I don't mean to be unnecessarily critical, and I value your efforts to extend care to the conditions under which curating occurs. Rather than pitting curators and artists against each other, it seems important to think them together in terms of solidarity.

JR   It's a great point – you also mentioned earlier in our conversations – when we say care – who and what are we caring for? Like love, it has become a catch-all term for justifying or ethically motivating dubious practices in some cases!

DC   This idea of the curator working for the artist reminds me of an anecdote I recently read from Pablo Helguera about how the curator was immediately on the phone to the gallery education department demanding children when Rirkrit Tiravanija wanted to create a piece in the gallery with children.[18] This also highlights another overlooked labour within the gallery – that of the museum educators, whose jobs are increasingly precarious when faced with funding cuts to museums. As educators, all three of us know how much surplus that role entails. Notably, when Marx addresses unproductive labour in his analysis of

18 In the spirit of acknowledging hidden labour, I have my doctoral student – Gemma Meek – to thank for drawing my attention to this anecdote. Cited in Helen Reed and Pablo Helguera, 'Bad Education Interview', *The Pedagogical Impulse*, no date, http:// thepedagogicalimpulse. com/a-bad-education-helen-reed-interviews-pablo-helguera/, accessed 27 June 2016.

capitalism, teachers are also included in his categorisation. Another 'labour of love'?

HR   Institutionally, art educators have been treated as if they occupy the lowest ranks of curatorial and programming teams. This hierarchy no doubt stems from educators' primary contact with the 'unschooled' general public, and their association with reproductive, rather than productive, labour, which doesn't leave a tangible – or saleable – trace. That art education has historically been a female-dominated field, and thus devalued, can't be accidental, either!

II Unlearning to Love Your Labour: How to 'Dis-Identify' Rather Than 'Over-Identify' with Working Roles

HR It's clear from our discussion that over-identifying with our work can have damaging consequences. Drawing on anti-work theory developed by feminist scholars like Kathi Weeks, which itself builds on social-reproduction thinkers like Federici and Leopoldina Fortunati, I wonder if dis-identifying with work roles could be a productive alternative tactic?[19]

JR   Yes, exactly. I'm wondering how to begin dis-identification – maybe to start, it is important to confess to ourselves and each other some of the bad institutional behaviours we collectively share, in order to then be able to dis-identify from them? Reflecting on this might also expose how we have learnt and developed some of the reproductive skills for the jobs we carry out.

ALL   Following this, and as part of the collective process of writing this paper, we held a collective brainstorming session to identify some of the bad habits we currently practice:

19 Kathi Weeks, *The Problem with Work: Feminism, Marxism, Antiwork Politics, and Postwork Imaginaries*, Duke University Press, Durham, North Carolina, 2011; Leopoldina Fortunati, *The Arcane of Reproduction – Housework, Prostitution, Labor and Capital* [1981], Autonomedia, Brooklyn, 1995

- Presenting the 'clean gallery' and the 'welcoming smile' and so mystifying the labour within cultural work
- Not distinguishing between work and life
- Constantly checking emails – whether at home or during 'social' events – as if we are constantly on the brink of missing something really important
- The academicisation of how we valorise the work we are doing; that and visitor figures feel like the only forms of value the art world clings on to, but what about space for collectivity/democratic conversation?
- Working seventy per cent over what we get paid for
- Doing projects even if the funding received is fifty per cent less than what we need
- Sacrificing our own maintenance for that of our job: not taking care of ourselves, not listening to when we've had enough, both physically and mentally
- Prioritising attendance at academic and artworld events over those with family members and friends

- Agreeing to things that, realistically, we don't have time for because it is 'good' for our 'career' – never saying 'no'
- Agreeing to do things before we know if we will be paid
- Acting like we can afford things that we can't (maybe this is more a life thing…) but keeping quiet about the distinction between artist income and curatorial income
- Agreeing to let videos of talks that we have taken part in be posted online when permission was not sought in advance, or additional fees offered
- Facilitating unpaid internships at prestigious galleries and institutions (because students want the work experience) without pressurising those organisations to pay
- Doing far more lecture preparation than is allocated for the task
- Feeling guilty for reading something not related to our research
- Allowing colleagues to take on the tedious work of ordering office supplies or co-ordinating recycling, by letting them asume that we don't understand the administrative systems for doing so
- Posting personal images and stories on Facebook, where we contribute our free labour and instrumentalise social relationships for the benefit of social media corporations
- Writing about the importance of acknowledging the collective nature of knowledge production while presenting our work (exhibitions, articles) under our own names alone and not listing all those who have fed into the process
- Organising events or curating exhibitions that deal with artistic and cultural labour but which do not interrogate the conditions under which our, and our collaborators' labour, occurs

JR Where do we learn these bad habits? If I think back to the type of work I was engaged in since school – waitressing – it was highly gendered and flexible. The task of caring for demanding customers, or trying to please closed-mouthed ones; working as a team just to get through the twelve-hour shift, then realising that hierarchies reappear as soon as the intense period is over; and the costuming of myself to appear reliable so that I'd be offered further work. While Brian Holmes describes in his text of the same title 'the flexible personality' which outlines precisely this condition of contemporary labour, his analysis also allows you to see how this figure or 'ideal type' is born right from the word 'go' for many women.[20] In *Manual Labours* we often ask how many people have done unpaid internships and it is rare that men ever say yes to this question while myself and many other women have done. How do we change our expectations about the conditions we build for ourselves to work within? Helena, I remember you discussing your experience of growing up and the effect this had on your skills in reproductive work. How would you describe this and the connection to bad habits?

HR That's a big one! I grew up in a thoroughly neoliberal household. My art school-trained dad was an advertising executive and my mum, who left school at sixteen, ran an employment agency for secretarial staff in the media: classic feminised labour in a prototypical neoliberal industry. Rather than stressing academic achievement, our parents encouraged my sister and me to cultivate our social skills and appear-

20 Brian Holmes, 'The Flexible Personality', in *European Institute for Progressive Cultural Policies*, 2002, available at http://eipcp.net/transversal/1106/holmes/en, accessed 5 May 2016

Claire Fontaine, *Untitled (Open)*, 2012, window mounted sign, argon and neon filled glass, transformer, cables and chains, image: courtesy the artists

'Don't Think You Have Any Rights: The Challenges of Italian Feminisms', featuring (left to right) Francesco Ventrella, Zach Blas, Maria Drakopoulou, Fulvia Carnevale of Claire Fontaine, and Giovanna Zapperi, The Showroom, London, as part of 'Now You Can Go', 12 December 2015, photo courtesy: Helena Reckitt

ances, to be agreeable, popular – and thin! That the importance of agree-ability was ingrained in me from a young age probably explains why I am so drawn to the affective withdrawal strategies that some feminists have developed. For women to refuse to be 'nice', attentive and supportive to their detriment feels radical, necessary – and hard! Shulamith Firestone, in *The Dialectics of Sex*, writes how she tried to train herself to stop smiling. Her proposal for a smile boycott, in which women abandoned their 'pleasing' smiles and only smiled when something genuinely pleased *them*, resonates with how Wages for Housework campaigners withdrew their domestic and affective labour in order to render it visible and demand its payment.[21]

JR   Yes, in 2012 the airline Cathay Pacific threatened a smile strike in a struggle over working conditions too! Have you managed to put any of these forms of affective resistance into practice, Helena?

HR   Resisting the ingrained feeling that it's my responsibility to 'fix' things, practically but especially emotionally, professionally as well as in my intimate relationships, is really tough. A programme that I organised with six feminist colleagues in 2015 called *Now You Can Go* explored feminist tactics of withdrawal and dis-identification.[22] We took our cue from practices within Italian feminism and from the collective 'readymade' artist Claire Fontaine's concept of the human strike, which proposes that strategically withholding affective labour can serve both to reveal and resist stereotypical behaviours, and enable as yet unknown subjectivities to emerge.[23] We looked at how the writer and feminist organiser Carla Lonzi withdrew from several roles throughout her life, in a process she termed 'decultura-tion': first, in the 1960s, as an art critic; then, in the 1970s, from feminist leadership; and eventually from her romantic partnership with the sculptor Pietro Consagra.[24] We took the programme title from *Vai pure* (Now You Can Go),[25] the book Lonzi published recording the conversation between herself and Consagra that documented their separation. Rejecting the idea that women act in complementary and supportive ways to men was central to Lonzi's concept of 'deculturation', which included resisting the presumption that the productive work involved in making art was more important than the reproductive work of maintaining life.

DC   When employed in service work, such as bar work, I fought to reject gender-informed stereotypes; I avoided dressing up for the (male gaze of the) customer and refused to accept or 'play along' with customers' inappropriate or sexist comments. However, I've always been aware of my class identity – having a Yorkshire accent in an (largely middle-class) academic world – and I think my working-class upbringing installed a work ethic in me, which has mutated into its overworked form today. I always treated any work that I got as something I needed to do to get to where I wanted to be. So, for example, when I was on zero-hour contracts teaching as an Associate Lecturer, I knew I was working more hours than I was being paid for, but I told myself that I was doing it for my CV and that I needed to do this to get a permanent job, which I eventually secured.

21 Shulamith Firestone, *The Dialectics of Sex*, Bantam Books, New York, 1970, p 90

22 The *Now You Can Go* planning team was Angelica Bolletinari, Giulia Casalini, Diana Georgiou, Laura Guy, Irene Revell, and Amy Tobin and myself, with the administrative assistance of Dimitra Gkitsa. See http:// nowyoucango.tumblr.com.

23 See Claire Fontaine, *Human Strike Has Already Begun & Other Writings*, Mute, Berlin, 2013.

24 See Claire Fontaine, 'We Are All Clitoridian Women: Notes on Carla Lonzi's Legacy', *e-flux journal* 47, 2013, www.e-flux.com/journal/we-are-all-clitoridianwomen–notes-on-carla-lonziil-legacy/, accessed 13 July 2016.

25 Carla Lonzi, *Vai pure, dialogo con Pietro Consagra*, Scritti di Rivolta Femminile, Milano, 1980

'Our Future Is Elsewhere', Goldsmiths MFA Curating Students, 2016, photo courtesy: Christian Luebbert

I'm not sure if that makes me a really bad role model for young academics?

HR   I don't think we should berate ourselves for trying to survive in tough times. But we must develop new forms of supporting one another and speaking about the insidious demands that we face so that we recognise them as systemic issues and not individual problems.

DC   Yes. I also think we can learn from the younger generation; there's a group of BA Interactive Arts students at Manchester School of Art, where I work, who have instigated a regular 'Slow Lunch'. Everyone in the school is invited to bring their lunch to a designated location to have a 'proper' lunch break with others.

HR   I too am learning – or unlearning! – from younger people. At Goldsmiths this year [2016], rather than organising an exhibition during the MFA degree show, for which the college provides no funds and which does not count towards coursework, curating students are leaving the space empty apart from a poster that reads 'Our Future Is Elsewhere'. Instead of putting their energies into a public outcome, they organised a rural retreat where they explored propositions for collectivity and the politics of mutual and self-care.

JR   What a great response! Within *Manual Labours* we were looking for ways to care for the 'uncomplaining body' and to refuse or start to unlearn the performance of the happy, productive, healthy body which appears to have no need to complain at all. One small gesture we developed was to write collective complaint letters. A letter to the thing or person you can't complain to, about the thing you can't complain about, in order to acknowledge our marginalised complaints, and validate our yet to be articulated challenges and then to share them verbally, physically with other uncomplaining bodies.

HR   That sounds like a terrific collective effort. Perhaps the more widespread adoption of anonymous group authorship would encourage workers to speak out when they experience exploitation and abuse, given that doing so as an individual can feel so risky in today's precarious climate, and in a context in which institutions often make employees sign confidentiality agreements.

JR   Yes, the solidarity created through anonymity is a great tool for starting to speak out about these issues and recognise the bad habits. There are also more public ways. *Manual Labours* has been trying to develop a practice of dis-identification through commitments such as showing the budget during each exhibition or publication, so that the economics of the project aren't concealed from the 'public face' of the work.

HR   In *Be Creative*, her book about employment in the cultural industries, Angela McRobbie discusses how the ideology of 'passionate work' has replaced romantic love for many people, especially women, and how this mindset can lead to dangerous levels of self-precarisation. To counter this tendency McRobbie invokes Richard Sennett's book on craft, which seeks to replace 'art' with 'craft'. Paraphrasing Sennett, she writes:

> If the work is less important the worker can detach and invest less of a sense of self-value in its outcomes. He or she can perhaps 'clock off' at the end of the day and relax with the children at the weekend.[26]

While there are major problems with this idea that childcare is *not* a form of work – and McRobbie herself raises concerns with Sennett's romanticisation of craftwork – nonetheless I find this proposal to demote work and divest it of the mythologies of self-realisation helpful, given the prevalence of the 24/7 work ethic in the cultural sector.

DC   Although I understand McRobbie's point, I find it really problematic to use the term 'craft' to devalue work. I think this is steeped in class- and gender-based prejudices about craft versus high art.[27] My research often considers the overlooked fabricators in artistic practice, whose labour is often hidden, for the sake of maintaining the appearance of a single author and the financial value associated with this mythology. Their 'skills' are associated with craft and valued less than the 'conceptual' labour of the artist. Furthermore, the handicraftsperson is also someone whose labour is considered unproductive by Marx. Even when employed by the artist, it is a service that is being purchased which does not immediately transmute into profit once the labour power is expended; it entails an expenditure of revenue rather than the production of capital. In selling a service, Marx writes, 'what is paid for is the performance of the service as such, and by its very nature the result cannot be guaranteed by those rendering the service'.[28] In this way, we might think of the unknown assistant or craftsperson as akin to those engaged in reproductive labour, whose labour is not acknowledged by the wider capitalist system nor those for whom they work. In using the term 'craft' to devalue work in our own minds, we might as well just consider it a labour of love!

HR   How might dis-identification play out in your work, Dani?

DC   Dis-identification is a really difficult question for me as being an academic is so engrained into my identity. I find it difficult to switch off. In recent years, I have started to do non-work activities in which I cannot be attached to my phone. This is a very small step towards my learning to live without a stream of work-related information. But, it's hard because, as an art historian, I also distinguish between the majority of my employed labour – teaching/admin – and research, which I see as something I would do unpaid (and herein lies the problem). Is going to an art gallery for pleasure/interest not switching off from work?

HR   Not all work is bad! And taking pleasure from your work is something to value, if not to imbue with the mythology of privilege.

26 For discussions of gender and craft, see Rozsika Parker, *The Subversive Stitch: Embroidery and the Making of the Feminine*, I B Tauris, London, 2010; Patricia Mainardi, *The Feminist Art Journal*, vol 2, no 1, 1973, pp 18–23; and Janis Jefferies's writings on gender and textiles.

27 Angela McRobbie, *Be Creative: Making a Living in the New Culture Industries*, Polity Press, Cambridge, 2016, p 150

28 Karl Marx, 'Theories of Surplus Value', in David McLellan, ed, *Karl Marx: Selected Writings*, 2nd edition, Oxford University Press, Oxford, 2007, p 431

III 'Not All Work Is Bad!': Modes of Valuation

JR Federici discusses the double character of work through her analysis of domestic work: that it at once 'reproduces us and valorises us not only in view of our integration in the labour market but also against it'.[29] The feminist position, to seek to struggle for reclaiming work from its alienation and devaluation under capital, feels much more empowering in terms of the potential we have to reclaim and insist that all of our life activities are not reducible to profit and exploitation.

DC One of the problems that Emma Dowling has noted, in her text on affective remuneration (which we read in preparation for this discussion), is that socially reproductive work is increasingly valorised by neoliberalism, but not valued.[30] I find it fascinating that two modes of labour that were historically deemed unproductive (in the Marxian sense) – socially reproductive and artistic labour – are now key working models within Western neoliberal economies.

JR Absolutely, and it becomes more pressing to think about different ways we can value what is marginalised, undervalued work. How can we reorganise the categorisation of labour from within? As Dowling argues,

> gaining control over the means of social reproduction increases the power people have to reproduce their livelihood without having to rely on the sale of their labour to do so.[31]

Dowling makes a distinction between the valorisation of labour and the valuation of labour. Valorisation denotes capital's methods of valuing labour, which we see through the wage; while valuation relates to how we as human beings conceptually struggle to value for ourselves the activity that we engage in. As the financialisation of work intensifies, it is increasingly difficult for people to see and qualify work that is not represented by monetary value.

DC And Dowling also warns us about the danger of adding a monetary value to socially reproductive labour. Once it has a financial value, it is, in effect, put to work for capital.

JR Thus, cultivating methods of valuation built out from the home is central to not only valuing this work for ourselves but for insisting on the valuation as a form of anti-capitalist struggle and as the basis for building solidarity and new social structures in society. As both Federici and Dowling note, key to this transformative process is the means, time and capacity for engaging in social reproductive work: a first hurdle that feels hard to overcome when considering the persistent diminishing of social spaces and free time. This issue was clear when feedback from local council workers, after a series of *Manual Labours'* workshops in 2015, described that the most important result was getting to know who their colleagues were.

DC Yes, I heard somewhere recently that Amazon 'fulfilment centre' workers are kept very separate – different timings for breaks, different

29 Silvia Federici, 'Revolution from Ground Zero: Revolution, Reproduction and Feminist Struggle', in *Revolution at Point Zero: Household, Reproduction, and Feminist Struggle*, PM Press, Oakland, California and Autonomedia, New York, 2012, p 2

30 Emma Dowling, 'Valorised but Not Valued? Affective Remuneration, Social Reproduction and Feminist Politics beyond the Recovery', *British Politics*, vol 11, no 4, December 2016, pp 452–468

31 Ibid

buildings etc – which makes it incredibly difficult for the workers to come together collectively to organise, or, as you say, Jenny, even to complain. I like that Dowling introduces a third meaning of investment, to counter the traditional notion of financial investment and the more recent notion of 'social investment' (which is also becoming increasingly valorised as people calculate the wage equivalent of charity work, for example). This third type is 'affective or emotional investment' which is based on the idea of use value, which is often lost in the analysis of the commodity. As I said earlier, Marx – looking at industrial work – saw work as 'productive' only when it directly created profit. Labour that we might also value – housework, care work, artistic work – now needs to be looked at through a different frame or the terms need to be updated for contemporary capitalism. Maybe it's not about monetary value either – Dowling's argument precipitates the question, how else can we value this work?

IV Art, Feminism and Social Reproduction Labour

DC   The 'Labours of Love, Works of Passion' panel openly called for a reconsideration of labour or, perhaps an insertion, of (socially reproductive) labour to the writing of art history, and especially within accounts focused on earlier periods. I also feel quite strongly about this; I 'grew up' (as an art historian) in a department with a strong lineage of both Marxist and feminist art historical approaches. However, the question of labour within approaches to a feminist art history were largely lost to poststructuralist and psychoanalytic theory, which I know wasn't historically the case (Valerie Mainz and Griselda Pollock's two-volume *Work and the Image* has proven invaluable for an art historian engaged in questions about labour in art, as has Pollock and Fred Orton's *Avant-Gardes and Partisans Reviewed*).[32] So, as a working-class student, I chose to engage with Marxian approaches to the study of art history. Only now am I re-engaging with a Marxist feminism that addresses questions of labour through an economic lens, of which there is still important work to be done. Again, thinking about Helena's earlier comments on culture historically being for the privileged class, I'm wondering if this separation of labour from art is due to class.

HR   The lack of attention paid to class in feminist art history and theory before about 2000 is a key focus of Angela Dimitrakaki's 2013 book *Gender, ArtWork and the Global Imperative*.[33] She argues that the critical and artistic emphasis on semiotics and psychoanalysis led feminists to foreground debates on visuality and subjectivity above those around economics and work. So, for instance, Mary Kelly's *Post-Partum Document*, 1973–1979, was discussed primarily via Lacanian theories about maternal subjectivity and not in materialist terms as an exploration and example of maternal labour.[34] To Dimitrakaki's analysis I would add that when feminist critical and curatorial reflections did highlight women's work, they generally involved reappraising craft and domestic traditions associated with the female realm, where issues of class were often not foregrounded. One aspect of feminised labour that did preoccupy second-wave feminist artists was that of maintaining female

32 Valerie Mainz and Griselda Pollock, eds, *Work and the Image, Volume One, Work Craft and Labour: Visual Representations in Changing Histories*, Ashgate, Aldershot, 2000; Valerie Mainz and Griselda Pollock, eds, *Work and the Image, Volume Two, Work in Modern Times: Visual Mediations and Social Processes*, Ashgate, Aldershot, 2000; Fred Orton and Griselda Pollock, *Avant-Gardes and Partisans Reviewed*, University of Manchester Press, Manchester, 1996

33 Angela Dimitrakaki, *Gender, ArtWork and the Global Imperative: A Materialist Feminist Critique*, Manchester University Press, Manchester, 2013

34 Ibid, p 115

attractiveness. I'm thinking of artists like Eleanor Antin, Hannah Wilke, Martha Wilson, Suzy Lake, Lorraine O'Grady, and Sanja Iveković, and of projects that emerged from *Womanhouse*.[35] In the light of current awareness about the affective labour involved in maintaining the branded self under networked capitalism, these practices feel ripe for re-evaluation.

DC   Maintaining the self-image in the age of the 'selfie' is an interesting approach. I still feel, however, that there are works by women artists, identifying with feminism, that directly address productive and social-reproduction labour that haven't been thoroughly addressed in feminist art history, such as Margaret Harrison, Kay Hunt and Mary Kelly's *Women and Work: A Document on the Division of Labour in Industry 1973–75*, on which I spoke at the AAH conference, and which brings productive and unproductive labour side by side without any demarcation or hierarchical structure in its exhibition. I maintain that this work is atypical for this reason.

JR   It feels like central to the politics and struggle within *Women and Work* was the solidarity it created and speculated on between workers from different fields (women art workers and women factory workers) and the distinction between paid and unpaid labour. Often, academic analysis and activism create research frames that don't allow for cross-field comparison (or solidarity).

HR   Dimitrakaki discusses *Women and Work* as a rare example of feminist art of the era that foregrounds class and labour.

DC   I think, perhaps, the lack of attention to class could be a victim of the 'divorce' (to use Cinzia Arruzza's term) of feminism and Marxism in the 1970s.[36]

HR   Indeed. Arruzza highlights the limitations of feminist theorisations of gender as a class, which deny the material differences between women. Yet the reasons that prompted feminists to seek this divorce in the first place, stemming from the Marxist devaluation of gender and deferring the transformation of the sexual division of labour until 'after the revolution', remain powerful concerns. The need for a politics grounded in an ethics of care and politics of social reproduction has never been clearer.

DC   In Marx's defence… in his analysis of the capitalist system, Marx was largely concerned with economic structures, following the money and the process in which money was created. So, anything that did not produce surplus labour that could be turned into profit was of no interest to his analysis of industrial labour. Hence why labour in the home is excluded (or labelled as 'unproductive'). However, we also have to understand that 'unproductive' relates to the production of surplus value (which then transmutes into profit) and is not necessarily – in my reading, at least – a judgement call on the quality of the work. It is not 'useless work', but in Marx's theory of the commodity, value is not produced from use values alone. Of course, we all know that, in reality, the labour in the home is essential to supporting capitalism, and I think Fed-

35 *Womanhouse* (USA 1972) has been an iconic feminist art project; see http://www.womanhouse.net/, accessed 10 June 2017.

36 Cinzia Arruzza, *Dangerous Liaisons: The Marriages and Divorces of Marxism and Feminism*, Merlin Press, London, 2013

erici made this very clear with the Wages for Housework campaign of the 1970s. I also think that Federici is right in asking for Marxist theory to rethink the question of 'reproduction' from a planetary perspective if it is to speak to the twenty-first century.[37]

JR I also think it's worth remembering that Marx's focus on waged labour was connected to his argument that the technological advancements of capital would fuel the revolution of the working class. Of course, developments in technology not only have produced more work but have found ways to exert further controls – ie the continual surveillance of workers via the iPhone, GDrive and Skype etc. In what we might call his oversight of reproductive work, we can now see a potential that reproductive labour and the home, rather than technology, offer the sites and processes to consider for generating anti-capitalist struggle, something bell hooks picks up on in her essay 'Homeplace (as a Site of Resistance)'.[38]

DC I completely agree that the increase in workplace or connective technologies have exerted a larger control over us as workers. For example, all three of us are now sat, presumably at home or in a non-traditional workplace, connected via the internet, working. I'm not convinced that this technology can be neutralised because of its inherent ties to the capitalist system. In reading Marx's 'Fragment on Machines', the Operaismo (Workerist) thinker Raniero Panzieri has argued that informational techniques tend to 'restore the charm of work' which obfuscates its hold over us.[39] While I disagree with Marx on the idea that social-reproduction labour does not contribute to capitalism, I do wonder if the 'apparent' freedom of this form of labour, like artistic labour, allows for it to more easily work against capitalism.

JR The 'apparent' freedom in artistic labour, I think, is more of a dangerous thought, and a perspective that plays into those precise structures that suppress us. However, an openness, transparency and reflectivity on how we can work from our positions within these relations has informed some compelling practices and radical spaces like CASCO, Utrecht, and Cyklopen, Stockholm.

HR Speaking of CASCO, the question of how to unlearn bad habits informed their 'New Habits' project, undertaken with the artist Annette Krauss, which attempted to make visible the maintenance labour that they carried out at the institution so that they might change their behaviours and priorities.[40]

DC When I talk about the 'apparent' freedom from capitalism, I am doing so cynically. This is precisely why neoliberal labour models – ie affective and immaterial labour – no longer look like 'work': because they adopted the 'artist' as a model worker. This point is, of course, indebted to Luc Boltanski and Eve Chiapello's argument in *The New Spirit of Capitalism* in which they argue that the 'artist critique' post-1968 was adopted by capitalist ideologies, turning workers into apparently free-thinking, flexible employees, while capitalising on their labour.[41] I like Paolo Virno's response to the co-optation of these forms of labour. He argues that the

37 Silvia Federici, 'The Reproduction of Labour Power in the Global Economy and the Unfinished Feminist Revolution' [2008], in *Revolution at Point Zero*, PM Press, Oakland, California, 2012

38 bell hooks, *Yearning: Race, Gender, and Cultural Politics*, Turnaround, London, 1991

39 Raniero Panzieri, 'The Capitalist Use of Machinery: Marx versus the Objectivists', 1964, Libcom.org, http://libcom.org/library/capalist-use-machinery-raniero-panzieri, accessed 27 June 2016

40 See Annette Krauss and Casco Team, 'CASCO Case Study #2: Site for Unlearning (Art Organization)', 2014, CASCO, http://cascoprojects.org/casco-case-study-2-sitefor-unlearning-art-organization-0, accessed 13 July 2016.

41 Luc Boltanski and Eve Chiapello, *The New Spirit of Capitalism*, Gregory Elliott, trans, Verso, London, 2005

intellect gained through work should be used for action rather than work.[42] I think this might be akin to what you're thinking, Jenny? The knowledge produced from work in the home could be put to work for political action.

ORCID

Danielle Child ⬤ http://orcid.org/0000-0001-7426-3338

42 Paolo Virno, *A Grammar of the Multitude*, Isabella Bertoletti, James Cascaito, Andrea Casson, trans, Semiotext(e), Los Angeles, New York, 2004

Third Text, 2017
Vol. 31, No. 1, 169–170, https://doi.org/10.1080/09528822.2017.1366752

Contributors

Larne Abse Gogarty is the Terra Foundation for American Art Postdocoral Teaching Fellow in the Institut für Kunst- und Bildgeschichte at the Humboldt University, Berlin. Previously she was a teaching fellow in History of Art at University College London. She has recently published her work in *Tate Papers* and *Kunst und Politik*.

Elisa Adami is a doctoral candidate at the Royal College of Art London. Her research focuses on the narrativisation and fictionalisation of history in post-war Lebanese art through the use of archival documents and storytelling.

Beth Capper is a doctoral candidate in modern culture and media at Brown University. Her writing has been published in *Art Journal* and *Media Fields*; she is also Assistant Editor of a forthcoming consortium issue of *TDR: The Drama Review* on 'Reproduction and Performance'. Beth also participates in a collaborative effort to build a digital archive of materials from the 1970s Wages for Housework movement.

Danielle Child is Lecturer in Art History at Manchester School of Art. She is currently working on her forthcoming book titled *Working Aesthetics: Labour, Art and Capitalism* (Bloomsbury Academic). Her articles include 'Dematerialisation, Contracted Labour and Art Fabrication: The Deskilling of the Artist in the Age of Late Capitalism', *Sculpture Journal*, vol 24, no 3 (2015).

Angela Dimitrakaki is a writer and Senior Lecturer in Contemporary Art History and Theory at the University of Edinburgh and the author of over fifty articles and book chapters on contemporary art. Her books include *Gender, ArtWork and the Global Imperative* (2013), *Art and Globalisation* (2013, in Greek) and *ECONOMY: Art, Production and the Subject in the Twenty-First Century* (2015, co-edited with Kirsten Lloyd).

Alex Fletcher is a doctoral candidate at the Centre for Research in Modern European Philosophy, Kingston University. His research focuses on the essay form in and as film, and is concerned with providing a deeper critical account of the genre.

Manon Gaudet graduated in 2016 with an MA in Art History from Carleton University, where her thesis on Mary Weekes was awarded a Senate Medal for Outstanding Academic Achievement. She has previously held positions at the J Paul Getty Museum, the Metropolitan Museum of Art and the Smithsonian Institution.

Victoria Horne is Lecturer in Art and Design History at Northumbria University. She is currently preparing a book titled *Against Absence: How Feminism Reshaped Art History*. Recent publications include *Feminism and Art History Now* (2017, co-edited with Lara Perry) and articles in the *Journal of Visual Culture*, *Feminist Review*, *Radical Philosophy*, and *Map*.

Elke Krasny is Professor at the Academy of Fine Arts in Vienna, in 2012 she was a Visiting Scholar at the Canadian Centre for Architecture in Montréal. She is co-editor of *Women's: Museum: Curatorial*

Politics in Feminism, Education, History, and Art (2013). Her curatorial projects include *Suzanne Lacy's International Dinner Party in Feminist Curatorial Thought* and *Hands-On Urbanism 1850–2012: The Right to Green*.

Kirsten Lloyd is Lecturer in Curatorial Theory and Practice at the University of Edinburgh. Her chapter "*If You Lived Here…*': A Case Study on Social Reproduction in Feminist Art History' appears in *Feminism and Art History Now* (2017). Between 2010 and 2015 she curated a series of exhibitions and events titled *Social Documents* in Edinburgh and Glasgow, including ECONOMY with Angela Dimitrakaki.

Lara Perry is Principal Lecturer in the School of Humanities at the University of Brighton and a feminist art historian. Her work primarily concerns nineteenth-century British art and art collections including contemporary museums, historiography and curatorial practice. Her books include *History's Beauties: Women and the National Portrait Gallery, 1856–1900* (2006) and *Politics in a Glass Case* (2013, co-edited with Angela Dimitrakaki). From 2010 to 2012 she led the Leverhulme international network Transnational Perspectives on Women's Art, Feminism and Curating.

Helena Reckitt is Senior Lecturer in Curating at Goldsmiths, University of London. With Jennifer Fisher she edited two issues of the *Journal of Curatorial Studies* (2016) on curating, affect and relationality. Her essay 'Generating Feminisms: Italian Feminisms and the "Now You Can Go" Programme' appears in *Art Journal*'s special issue on Curating Diversity (2017).

Jenny Richards collaborates with Sophie Hope on the practice-based research project *Manual Labours* and is curator of Marabouparken Konsthall, Stockholm. She was previously co-director of Konsthall C, Stockholm where together with Jens Strandberg she developed *Home Works*, an exhibition programme exploring the politics of domestic work and the home.

Marina Vishmidt is a writer and lecturer in Culture Industry at Goldsmiths, University of London and the Dutch Art Institute. Her work has appeared in *South Atlantic Quarterly, Ephemera, After-all, Journal of Cultural Economy, Australian Feminist Studies*, and *Radical Philosophy*, among others, as well as a number of edited volumes. She is the co-author of *Reproducing Autonomy* (2016, with Kerstin Stakemeier) and is currently completing *Speculation as a Mode of Production* (2017).

Third Text, 2017
Vol. 31, No. 1, 171, https://doi.org/10.1080/09528822.2017.1377522

Erratum

Katarzyna Cytlak, '*La rivoluzione siamo noi*: Latin American Artists in Critical Dialogue with Joseph Beuys', *Third Text*, vol 30, nos 5-6, 2016, pp 346-367

http://dx.doi.org/10.1080/09528822.2017.1358019

In the published article detailed above, the image caption for the image on p. 348 was given incorrectly both in the print and online versions. The correct caption for this image is:

Nicolás García Uriburu with Joseph Beuys, *Rhein Coloration*, 1981, colour photography and fibre ink pencil on paper, 52×62 cm. Ed. 1/3. Collection: Private Collection, photo courtesy of ISLAA, Institute for Studies on Latin American Art and Henrique Faria New York & Buenos Aires. Copyright: Azul García Uriburu

Taylor & Francis apologises for this error.

Before preparing your submission, please visit our web site for a complete style guide (contact details are given below) or send an e-mail inquiry to rdyer@thirdtext.org

Papers for consideration should be sent via e-mail to Richard Dyer, Editor in Chief, at rdyer@thirdtext.org

Papers are accepted for consideration on condition that you will accept and warrant the following conditions. In order to ensure both the widest dissemination and protection of material published in our Journal, we ask authors to assign the rights of copyright in the articles they contribute. This enables Taylor & Francis to ensure protection against infringement.

1. In consideration of the publication of your Article, you assign Third Text with full title guarantee all rights of copy right and related rights in your Article. So that there is no doubt, this assignment includes the right to publish the Art in all forms, including electronic and digital forms, for the full legal term of the copyright and any extension or renewals. You shall retain the right to use the substance of the above work in future works, including lectures, press releases and reviews, provided that you acknowledge its prior publication in the Journal.
2. We shall prepare and publish your Article in the Journal. We reserve the right to make such editorial changes as may be necessary to make the Article suitable for publication; and we reserve the right not to proceed with publication for what ever reason. In such an instance, copyright in the Article will revert to you.
3. You hereby assert your moral rights to be identified as the author of the Article according to the UK Copyright Designs & Patents Act 1988.
4. You warrant that you have secured the necessary written permission from the appropriate copyright owner or authorities for the reproduction in the Article and the Journal of any text, illustration, or other material. You warrant that, apart from any such third party copyright material included in the Article, the Article is your original work, and cannot be construed as plagiarising any other published work, and has not been and will not be published elsewhere.
5. In addition, you warrant that the Article contains no statement that is abusive, defamatory, libellous, obscene, fraudulent, nor in any way infringes the rights of others, nor is in any other way unlawful or in violation of applicable laws.
6. You warrant that any patient, client or participant mentioned in the text has given informed consent to the inclusion of material pertaining to themselves, and that they acknowledge that they cannot be identified via the text.
7. If the Article was prepared jointly with other authors, you warrant that you have been authorised by all co-authors to sign this Agreement on their behalf, and to agree on their behalf the order of names in the publication of the Article.

There are no page charges in *Third Text*.

Corresponding authors can receive 50 free reprints, free online access to their article through our website (www.tandfonline.com) and a complimentary copy of the issue containing their article. For enquiries regarding reprints, please contact the Taylor & Francis Author Services team at reprints@tandf.co.uk. Additional copies of the journal can be purchased at the authors' preferential rate of £15.00 per copy.

Editorial Office:
Unit 6, Enclave Studios, 50 Resolution Way, Deptford, London SE8 4AL, UK
e-mail: rdyer@thirdtext.org

Please refer to the following website for the journal style guide:
http://www.tandfonline.com/ctte

For more information on our journals and books publishing, visit our Taylor & Francis website:
http://www.tandfonline.com

If you are unable to access the website please write to: Journals Editorial, Taylor & Francis, 4 Park Square, Milton Park, Abingdon, Oxfordshire OX14 4RN, UK.